Over 50 and *Motivated!*

A Job Search Book for Job Seekers Over 50

Brian E. Howard, JD, CCMC, CJSS, CPRW
Certified Career Management Coach
Certified Job Search Strategist
Certified Professional Resume Writer

Virginia

Published in the United States by WriteLife Publishing
(An imprint of Boutique of Quality Books Publishing Company)
www.writelife.com

Printed in the United States of America

978-1-60808-162-2 (p)
978-1-60808-163-9 (e)

Library of Congress Control Number: 2017930857

Book design by Robin Krauss, www.bookformatters.com
Cover design by Ellis Dixon, www.ellisdixon.com
First editor: Ty Mall
Second editor: Paige Duke

OTHER BOOKS BY BRIAN E. HOWARD

The Motivated Job Search

The Motivated Networker

The Motivated Job Search Workbook

Motivated Resumes & LinkedIn Profiles

This book is dedicated to every job seeker over fifty who felt fear and uncertainty about their future but persevered. It is dedicated to those who faced the unknown and defeated all biases in their path. This book is written to your success.

Message from the Author

If you are over fifty, you know that looking for a job can be more challenging. Though unspoken, stereotypes, biases, and age-related perceptions are very real in today's job market. It's unfair! But they are present, and they *will* lengthen your job search unless you do something about them. This book contains information and proven strategies to help you defeat those stereotypes and biases, compete successfully against other job seekers (of any age), and shorten your job search.

Given who you are as a professional, what you know, and what you have experienced over the course of your career, you are valuable to an employer. Perhaps more than you might believe.

This is not to say that your job search will be easy. There will be disappointments, setbacks, and adjustments to be made. You will adapt. However, if you believe that employers value job seekers over fifty (they do) and you follow the guidance in this book, you will noticeably shorten your job search and find a fulfilling career position.

Good luck, and to your success!

Brian E. Howard

Table of Contents

Introduction   1
  What You're Up Against   2
  The Advantages of Your Age   6

Part I
Getting Your Mind Right before Starting Your Search   9
  Resentment and Bitterness   9
  Keeping a Positive Attitude   11
  Your Career . . . Your Responsibility   14

Part II
Strategy Is Everything: The Self-Motivated Approach   19
  The Advantages of a Self-Motivated Job Search   19
  The Psychology of Persuasion and Your Job Search   22

Part III
Things to Know about Your Job Search   29
  Job Search Assessment   29
  Getting off to a Successful Start   32
  More about Job Alerts   34
  How Long Will Your Job Search Take?   35
  Answering Questions about Your Unemployment: Your Exit Statement   37
  Searching for a Job While Employed—The Confidential Job Search   39
  The Age Discrimination in Employment Act   40

Part IV
Profiling Your Next Career Opportunity—The Target Opportunity Profile 43
  A Passions Inventory   45
  Creating Your Target Opportunity Profile   47
  Step One—Consider Your Career Wish List   47

Step Two—Identify and Evaluate the Factors 48
Step Three—Complete Your Profile 53
Questions to Ask in Interviews 54

Part V
Essential Job-Search Topics and Tools 57
Understanding the Employer's Mindset 57
Knowing What an Employer Wants in an Open Position 58
Matching Experience and "Word Clouds" 59
Transferable Job Skills and Professional Qualities 60
The Sum Total 64
Success Stories 65
Branding 67
Word Choice 70
Branding Is Important 70
Elevator Speech 71
Business Cards 75
Impactful Resumes 80
    Do Job Seekers Need a Resume AND a LinkedIn Profile? 80
    What a Resume is NOT 81
    Time is of the Essence 82
    Your Resume is Your Marketing Brochure 82
    Use of Keywords 83
    Resume Formats 84
    The Dateless (Ageless) Resume 85
    Parts of a Resume 85
    Use of Recommendations on a Resume 97
    Information NOT to be Included on a Resume 98
    Testing the Impact of Your Resume 99
    QR Codes 99
    Attaching Your Resume to your Online Profile 99
    Dealing with Employment Gaps on a Resume 100
    Creating Your Own Resume 102
LinkedIn 104
    Use of Keywords 106

Your LinkedIn Profile-Sections 107
Keep your Profile Current 114
Customize your LinkedIn URL 114
Introducing LinkedIn Optimization 115
How does it work . . . How does an HR Recruiter use
LinkedIn to find candidates? 115
The Goal of Optimization 116
Keyword Location 117
Keyword Stuffing 122
Completeness 122
Connections 125
Compelling 126
Put it to the Test 127
Strategies for your LinkedIn Profile when you are unemployed 128
Which Strategy would be best for you? 131
Job Alerts 131
The Open Candidates feature on LinkedIn 134
Consider Upgrading your LinkedIn Account 137
Measuring the Effectiveness of Your LinkedIn Profile 138
What do you do with your LinkedIn profile after you get a new job? 138

Part VI
Cover Letters and Other Written Communications **139**
Types of Cover Letters 140
The Cover Letter Success Formula 140
Cover Letters and Career Transition SEALs 145
Cover Letters and Recruiters 146
Thank-You Letters 146

Part VII
Professional Networking **153**
Hidden Job Market 153
Networking 154
Fear of Networking 155
Why Networking Is So Effective 156

Types of Networks   156
Evaluating the Strength and Quality of Your Network   157
Who to Connect and Network With   158
LinkedIn   159
Create Your Professional "Cabinet"   160
Create Your Sales Company   161
The Peripheral and Pruning   162
Spreading the Word—Asking for Help   163
Networking in a Local Market for a Local Position   164
Get Busy! (And Keep Momentum in Networking)   165
Maintaining Your Network   165
Professional Associations   165
Association/Industry Conferences   166
Icebreaker Questions for Conferences and Events   169
Goals of the Networking Conversation   170
Face-to-Face Networking as an Introvert   171

Part VIII
Social Media and Networking: Twitter and Facebook   **175**
Twitter   175
Facebook   179
A Caution about Online Networking/Posting   180
What Employers Find on Social Media   180

Part IX
Working with Recruiters   **183**
What Recruiters Can and Cannot Do for You   183
Retainer and Contingency Search Firms   185
Contract or Project Firms   186
How to Find Recruiters   186
Calling Hiring Executives   186
Calling Your Colleagues in the Industry   188
Researching LinkedIn and the Internet   188
Contacting a Recruiter   189
Finding a Recruiter Who Can Help You   189
Some Final Advice Regarding Recruiters   190

Part X
Proactively Marketing Your Professional Credentials   **193**
    The Work   195
    Determine Your Target Employers   195
    Identify the Hiring Executive   196
    Research the Hiring Executive's Email Address   196
    Using the Telephone   197
    The Positive Impact of Using the Phone   197
    Excuses for Not Using the Phone in a Job Search   198
    Getting Started: Making Calls   200
    Phone Zone   200
    Phone Phear: The Pre-Game Jitters   201
    The Marketing Call Script   201
    Objections   204
    Ask One Question after the Objections   205
    Rejection   205
    Screening   205
    Voicemail   206
    Email Marketing Your Professional Credentials   206
    Sending Your Marketing Emails   207
    Email Marketing through LinkedIn   208
    Follow-Up Calls   208
    Drip-Email Marketing   208
    The Research Interview   210
    Using Videos or YouTube in Your Job Search   211
    When All Else Fails . . .   212
    Where to Spend Your Time and Effort   214

Part XI
Interviewing   **215**
    How Much Are Interviews Worth?   215
    How an Employer Views an Interview   217
    Can You Do the Job?   217
    Will You Do the Job?   218
    Will Your Performance Have a Positive Impact on Company Goals?   218
    Do You Fit In?   219

Are You Affordable?   219
Strategy for a Successful Interview   219
Strategy for Opening the Interview   220
First Impressions   221
Interviews: Progression   222
Interview Preparation   223
Interview Formats   225
Practice Interviews   226
Answering Traditional Interview Questions: The UPAC Method   227
Telephone Interview   228
The Unannounced Telephone Interview   230
Webcam or Skype Interviews   230
Screening Interview Conducted by a Human Resources Representative   231
Meal Interview   233
Behavioral Interview   235
Preparing for and Answering Behavioral Interview Questions   236
Common Competencies Covered by Behavioral Interview Questions   238
Your Interview Wardrobe   239
Interviews with Potential Peers or Subordinates   239
Explaining a Job Termination in an Interview   240
Explaining Employment Gaps or Long-Term Unemployment   241
Explaining Job Hops in an Interview   242
Tough Questions Made Easy   243
Handling the Money Question   245
Closing the Interview   246
General Interview Tips   246
Debrief Yourself   248
Write a Thank-You Letter   249
Second and Home-Office Interview Strategies   249
Common Interview Mistakes   250
Game-Day Tactics   251
Strategy for a Successful Interview   251
Not Getting the Job: Handling the Rejection   254
Hiring Timeline: A Longer Process   255

Part XII

Unique Tactics That Create Differentiation   **259**

Brag Book   259

When to Present the Brag Book   261

Career Summary Sheet   262

Testimonial Sheet   265

Action Plan   270

Advanced Techniques to Create Differentiation   271

    Personal Website   271

    A Blog   273

    Infographic Resume   274

Part XIII

References   **277**

Choose Your References Wisely   278

References and a Secret Job Search   278

Unsolicited Third-Party Affirmation   279

Part XIV

Evaluating and Negotiating a Job Offer   **281**

Never Play Hardball   282

Ten Steps for Evaluating and Negotiating an Offer: The WITS Approach   282

Negotiations Fail   289

Declining an Offer of Employment   289

Negotiation Mistakes   290

Final Thoughts on Successful Negotiation   291

Part XV

Resignation and Counter offers   **293**

Resignation   293

Counter offers   297

    Financial   297

    Promotional   298

    Emotional   298

    Preemptive   298

Career Hazards of Accepting a Counter offer   298
Detachment: A Technique to Defuse the Emotions of Resignation   300

Part XVI
Covenants-Not-To-Compete and Non-Solicitation Agreements   **301**
Definitions of a Covenant-Not-To-Compete and a Non-Solicitation Agreement   302
Where They Appear   302
Determining Which Kind of Agreement You Have   302
Enforceability   303
Reasonable in Scope, Space, and Time   303
Employer's Reactions to Breaches of Agreement   304
Right-to-Work States   305
Practical Application—Effects of These Agreements on Your Job Search   305

Part XVII
Working Successfully for a Younger Boss   **307**

Part XVIII
How to Relaunch a Stagnant Job Search   **311**

Part XIX
Hire Yourself—Becoming a Consultant or Opening a Franchise   **315**
Opening a Consulting Practice   316
Job-Search Strategy: Offering Yourself as a Consultant   317
Opening a Franchise   318

Part XX
A Personal Letter to You about Career Management   **321**

Appendix A: Success Story Worksheet and Samples   **329**
Appendix B: Sample Resumes   **331**
Appendix C: Sample Letters   **345**
Bibliography   **355**

Introduction

Don't bunt. Aim out of the ballpark. Aim for the company of immortals.

David Ogilvy[1]

This job-search book is written for professionals over fifty years of age who desire to take control of their job search and commit to the work necessary to succeed. Tenured professionals over fifty face unique job-search challenges. Stereotypes, biases, and age-related perceptions make finding a fulfilling career position more difficult. This book tackles those issues head-on and provides a proven methodology to get you a job (the job you want) in the shortest amount of time possible.

There are several advantages of your age, more of which will be discussed later in this book. For now, keep in mind that if you are like most over-fifty job seekers, you are:

Stable—emotionally balanced and even-keeled.

Experienced—you have done and seen things that only time and living can bring.

Accomplished—you have achieved and brought ROI (Return On Investment) and value to previous employers.

---

1 "David Ogilvy Quotable Quote," Goodreads, http://www.goodreads.com/quotes/262108-don-t-bunt-aim-out-of-the-ballpark-aim-for-the (accessed March 28, 2016).

Loyal—you know what it means to stick around. Job seekers over fifty stay in positions up to three times longer than their younger counterparts.[2] This is valued by employers because it saves time and money.

This makes you a *SEAL*—stable, experienced, accomplished, and loyal. We will use the acronym SEAL throughout this book when referring to job seekers over the age of fifty.

By loose correlation, the US Navy SEALs—a premier special forces unit—also have these qualities of being stable, experienced, accomplished, and loyal. Consider adopting the attitude of being a premier job seeker—a SEAL!

As you read this book, have a highlighter and a pen available. Highlight concepts you want to remember. Write in the margins. Dog-ear or electronically bookmark pages. Use a notepad to write down thoughts and to-do's as they occur to you. Then, after your job search is underway, review this book to stay motivated and on track. Be careful! It is easy during a job search to cross the line from being productive to just doing busywork disguised as being productive. Ask yourself: Am I being productive with my time and effort, or am I just doing busywork, thinking that I am being productive? You'll know the answer.

Pay particular attention to the **SEAL Icon throughout this book.** These useful insights, powerful job-search concepts, and techniques are specifically designed for you, as a SEAL, to combat the stereotypes and age biases you may face in your job search.

Above all, remember that a successful job search is all about presenting yourself in a professional manner, engaging in conversations with those who can help and hire you, and providing real-life examples of your skills and accomplishments.

What You're Up Against

Well…here you are. You're over fifty and engaged in a job search. You might be unemployed, anticipating a company change that could affect your job, or needing to make a career move. Either intellectually or intuitively, you know that finding new employment as a SEAL (job seeker over fifty) poses new job-search challenges. And you would be right. There are stereotypes, biases, and age-related perceptions that could be held against you. Ageism is real in today's job market.

According to US government studies, job seekers over fifty are penalized for their age

---

2 Dugan, Dawn. "10 Tips for Job Hunters Over 50: How Older Workers Can Better Overcome Obstacles to Getting Hired," Salary.com, http://www.salary.com/10-tips-for-job-hunters-over-50/ (accessed March 28, 2016).

when looking for new employment. A SEAL "is likely to be unemployed for 5.8 weeks longer than someone between the ages of 30 and 49, and 10.6 weeks longer than people between the ages of 20 and 29."[3] And here's something more disheartening: "the odds of being re-employed decrease by 2.6 percent for each one-year increase in age."[4] What are the underlying causes of these statistics? Here is a list of the ten major biases that SEALs most commonly come up against during a job search:

A bad attitude—No hiring executive on the planet wants to hire "an attitude problem." Poor attitudes can spread like a cancer in a department or company and destroy productivity and company culture.

The perception is many job seekers over fifty are bitter, resentful, and have a chip on their shoulder as a result of their current employment situation. They hold a grudge, are cynical, and don't trust management or the ownership group.

Not only will a bad attitude make your job search more difficult, it can seriously damage your employment tenure when you do get a job. According to research reported in Forbes, of twenty thousand new hires, 46 percent failed within eighteen months. Of those who failed, 89 percent were not terminated because of skills, but rather their poor attitude.[5]

Inflexible—This is the perception that you are stuck in your ways, stubborn, intellectually closed-minded to new ways of thinking, not innovative, and resistant to doing things differently—because of what worked for you previously, or another reason.[6] This can be especially true if you were in your last position for a long time or with the same company for a long time.

Tired—The perception here is after twenty-five-plus years in your career, you have low energy, have been beaten down, and lack the enthusiasm to do the job.

On cruise control to retirement—Closely related to low energy is the bias that you are only willing to work long or hard enough until retirement arrives. The perception here is you are not fully committed to succeeding in a position, won't give it your all, and will just draw a paycheck and do only the minimum (or a little more) to keep your job while you pass the time.

---

3 Brenoff, Ann. "Older Workers Stay Unemployed Much Longer Than Younger Ones, Study Says," Huffington Post, June 17, 2015, http://www.huffingtonpost.com/2015/06/17/finding-a-job-after-50-study_n_7603590.html (accessed March 28, 2016); See also, US Department of Labor, Bureau of Labor Statistics, "Displaced Workers Summary," news release, August 26, 2014, http://www.bls.gov/news.release/disp.nr0.htm (accessed March 28, 2016).

4 Brenoff, ibid; See also, US Department of Labor, "Displaced Workers."

5 Murphy, Mark. Interview by Dan Schawbel, "Hire for Attitude," Forbes, January 23, 2012, http://www.forbes.com/sites/danschawbel/2012/01/23/89-of-new-hires-fail-because-of-their-attitude/#425a5f366742 (accessed March 28, 2016).

6 See also, Dugan, "10 Tips."

Poor technology skills—Depending upon your circumstances, this bias could be accurate. For some SEALs, staying current or learning new technology was not required. You had assistants or others help you or do it for you. If you are unemployed, now would be a good time to get up to speed on the new (or necessary) technology for your industry. Evening classes or online classes should not greatly interfere with your daytime job search.

Entitlement mentality—This is the feeling that your experience and knowledge entitles you to treatment above what "lesser" employees receive, whatever what you "deserve" may be. The perception here is that you will not roll up your sleeves and do the job yourself but would rather direct others regarding what to do, or delegate duties to them.

Poor cultural fit—This bias is based on the fear that you will not get along with younger employees. Employers want to avoid disruptions and interpersonal relationship problems in the employee ranks. Too often they homogenize their employees in the hopes that everyone will get along because they are all similar (younger).

Difficulty reporting to a younger boss—This perception is that your ego will get in the way of succeeding in the position, and that you will resent reporting to or being judged or evaluated by someone notably younger. This in turn feeds the fear that productivity and good company culture will suffer as a result.

Lacking communication skills—This bias is that SEALs are long-winded, repetitive, and that they constantly compare the present to the past and only perceive things in light of "the way things used to be" and "the good old days."

Out-of-date appearance—This bias has two components—physical body and clothing. Some of us SEALs have let ourselves become . . . uh, less than physically fit, feeding the perception that all SEALs are lazy, listless, and will need more sick days. And for some of us, it's time for some conservative yet stylish new clothes. Presenting yourself in old, worn clothes is unimpressive regardless of age.

Requires higher compensation and benefits—SEALs are viewed as expensive hires. Many have received promotions over the course of their careers with increases in compensation and benefits. As a result, their lifestyles—as well as the expenses to maintain them—increased. The bias is because these job seekers are exceedingly more expensive to hire (than younger professionals), it might be better to pass them up for somebody else.

These biased perceptions can be an obstacle in your job search. And, yes, they are unfair.

Some SEALs (not all) inflict upon themselves other biases and obstacles—in addition to physical appearance, or being unaware of and therefore unable to anticipate and defeat the age bias—that make their job search more difficult. Many of these topics will be covered later in this book. They are:

Bad attitude—this was mentioned as a bias previously, but it's worth mentioning again because it plagues so many SEALs. Leaving a bad attitude behind is very important.

Lack of understanding and commitment to their job search—including being unaware of changes in job-search methods or lacking the desire to succeed.

Over-reliance on online job postings—which are often viewed as one of the most ineffective ways to find a new job. A self-motivated and proactive approach, mentioned later, will lead to success much faster.

Underuse of LinkedIn—most SEALs have weak or nonexistent profiles.

Poor resume—using an out-of-date or poorly formatted document.

Resisting networking—being hesitant to reach out to others.

Unwilling to proactively market their professional credentials—nervous about proactively contacting companies that could hire them.

Weak interview skills—rusty, outdated, or ineffective approaches to interviewing.

Unprofessional appearance and attire—being out of shape and/or wearing outdated clothing.

Ignoring the age bias—failing to appreciate that "age bias" (ageism) is real and not knowing how to defeat it.

As you read these lists and consider the statistics and other obstacles, you might feel the cards are stacked against you. They're not. Some of the biases you can easily defeat—for example, you're energetic and passionate about work (now you just have to convince the hiring executive). Some biases are not an issue and don't even enter the mind of the hiring executive. So don't worry about the list and the statistics! They are presented to educate you. In the chapters that follow, you will learn other unique and innovative techniques to meet these biases head-on and defeat them.

Besides, there's great news to come! There are massive, real-life advantages to your age where your job search is concerned.

The Advantages of Your Age

Now for the good news. There are far more advantages than biases related to your age and experience—not only in number, but also in the depth of their value to an employer (despite negative statistics). In fact, according to one study conducted by Adecco, an international firm specializing in employment consulting and research, if an employer was given a choice between hiring a millennial (someone born between 1981 and 2000) or a job seeker over fifty, 60 percent would hire the SEAL.[7] Below is a non-exhaustive list of advantages your tenure provides you that far outweigh any age biases:

Judgment—One of the advantages of tenure is the ability to judge and evaluate situations. You keep your cool during a crisis (perceived or real). You have insight based on experience. Employers value a cool head during stressful times.

Reliability—Job seekers over fifty tend to be more reliable than younger employees. You are more punctual and have less absenteeism. Employers value someone they can count on.[8]

Work Ethic—A growing number of employers are discovering that SEALs demonstrate a "stronger work ethic" than their younger counterparts.[9] This trend flies in the face of the previously accepted bias that SEALs are tired and on cruise control to retirement. You don't need someone looking over your shoulder, because you require less supervision and know what's expected—results. Many SEALs (especially those who went through challenging job searches) have also learned to be appreciative when they have a job and don't want to risk losing it.

Critical Thinking—Hiring executives often experience that SEALs are good at problem solving.[10] This is closely aligned with having good judgment. Having frequently "been there, done that," you know how to take apart problems, analyze options and solutions,

7 Adams, Susan. "Older Workers, There's Hope: Study Finds Employers Like You Better Than Millennials," Forbes, September 24, 2012, http://www.forbes.com/sites/susanadams/2012/09/24/older-workers-theres-hope-study-finds-employers-like-you-better-than-millennials/#658b87014aa6 (accessed February 4, 2016).

8 Ibid., and Society for Human Resource Management, "Executive Summary: Preparing for an Aging Workforce," https://www.shrm.org/hr-today/trends-and-forecasting/research-and-surveys/Documents/14-0765%20Executive%20Briefing%20Aging%20Workforce%20v4.pdf p. 6, (accessed February 4, 2016).

9 Society for Human Resource Management, "Executive Summary," p. 6.

10 Ibid., and Adams, "Older Workers, There's Hope."

and implement a plan of attack. This gets problems solved quicker and more cost effectively. SEALs are confident in the decisions they make and don't need unnecessary guidance. They focus and execute to move projects forward.

Reading People—During the course of your twenty-five-plus-year career, you have probably encountered thousands of people. You know that people's attitudes and behaviors are motivated by something. Your experience often tells you what that "something" is, and you use that insight to make business decisions.

Networking—If you have been active in your industry and kept up with your network, this can be a big advantage. You can reach out, likely to other tenured professionals, and get information far more quickly and effectively than others, including younger job seekers whose network may not be as broad, deep, or knowledgeable.

Market Knowledge—Hiring executives often come to realize SEALs have superior knowledge and skill compared to younger workers.[11] This comes in two forms. If you remain in the same industry, you understand the products, services, processes, and competitors within that industry. You have market insight that only experience can give. The other form of market knowledge is business acumen. You know how business works. You understand that you must provide value to your employer[12] or you risk losing your job.

Commitment to Quality—Most SEALs want to do the job right; they want to achieve quality results the right way. This is highly valued by employers.

Professionalism—Due to your experience and tenure, you know how to conduct yourself as a professional more so than younger workers.[13] This includes the use of your knowledge, integrity, image, and more. It is the totality of all things in your career used and presented in a visible, professional way.

Wisdom—Setting aside the dictionary definition, SEALs have a unique combination of knowledge and experience. Knowledge without experience is just facts (book learning). Experience without knowledge is just time. But together, that's wisdom. Enlightened employers value that in the workplace.

Stable—Being over fifty often means your personal life is more settled. You tend to

---

11 Society for Human Resource Management, "Executive Summary," p. 6.

12 Whitcomb, Susan Britton. *Job Search Magic: Insider Secrets from America's Career and Life Coach.* (Indianapolis, IN: JIST Works, 2006), p. 274, 289.

13 Society for Human Resource Management, "Executive Summary," p. 6.

have fewer life crises, family distractions, and so on, which allows you to focus and be a more productive employee.

Experienced—You often understand why things have developed over time, and you have been through more situations.

Accomplished—You have brought ROI (Return On Investment) and value to previous employers.

Loyal—You know the value of sticking around. On average, SEALs stay in their jobs longer than their younger counterparts.[14] This is a tremendous cost savings to employers in hiring and training.

There are many more advantages to your age, some of which may be unique to you and may occur to you as your job search progresses. Write down these advantages, think about how they can positively impact your job search, and use them. You will find out these advantages are real and have true value (they will make or save a company money).[15] The age biases, in many cases, are just perceptions that you can overcome by educating hiring executives about your background and accomplishments, and by properly using the techniques in this book.

When you think about it, you should feel reasonably optimistic about the prospects of your job search and what you can offer an employer!

---

14 Dugan, "10 Tips."

15 Whitcomb, *Job Search Magic*, Chapter 11, "Tap the Hidden Job Market with a Targeted Search," p. 274–275.

Part I

Getting Your Mind Right before Starting Your Search

Resentment and Bitterness

It takes a lot of courage to release the familiar and seemingly secure, to embrace the new. But there is no real security in what is no longer meaningful.

—Alan Cohen[16]

We need to talk about emotions, because having the right frame of mind is crucial to a successful job search. If you lost your job unexpectedly, you know it means more than just losing your paycheck. It can mean possible embarrassment, having feelings of emptiness or of no longer being productive, a huge change in your daily routine, and loss of identity, self-esteem, and sense of purpose. It can mean losing friendships with those at work and feeling that your situation has become too much to handle. It's a jolt, and there's a lot to process, especially emotions. It's okay to cry . . . more than once if you have the feelings to do so. Let the emotions out—don't bottle them up.

Harboring negative feelings (including holding grudges) about your employment situation will negatively impact your job search. A poor attitude or an unintended slip of the tongue in an interview will generally dissuade many employers from hiring you. Employers will not knowingly hire someone who can poison company culture with an attitude problem.

---

16 "Alan Cohen Quotable Quote," Goodreads, http://www.goodreads.com/quotes/46591-it-takes-a-lot-of-courage-to-release-the-familiar (accessed April 12, 2016).

Setting aside clinical psychology, holding a grudge harms you mentally and physically as well. As difficult as it is, you must take steps to "let it go." Here is some layman's advice to get you thinking and moving in the right direction:

Releasing your feelings of resentment and bitterness is a process, not an event. But you must begin by intellectually and emotionally moving on from the pain that has been inflicted into the future of a fulfilling new career position. The longer you wallow in self-pity, the longer you will obsess and continue to have intense, negative feelings. It's fine to take time to vent; in fact, it's healthy to do so. But don't get stuck and dwell on the past. At some point you must take steps to move forward.

One helpful technique is to write about your feelings. Don't hold back. Write how you feel. Write what you wish you would have said to your former boss and others. Write about anything that bothers you. Do this repeatedly if you feel you need to—it's okay. Getting it down on paper releases the mental pressure inside you, helps relieve the bad, obsessive thoughts in your head, and prevents you from repeating those thoughts.

You are a mature adult, and you know that holding on and obsessing only continues to force out good feelings, joys of life, and family. Obsessing also clouds your thinking about your future career fulfillment. When you're thinking "bad," you can't be thinking "good." Open your mind and your heart to the value of releasing the resentment and bitterness. Ask yourself, "What will I gain by letting go of these bad feelings?" (The answer is "plenty!") Once you do, you will begin to feel lighter, energized, and more optimistic about the tasks of your job search.

Actively choose a new way of thinking, a fresh outlook, and a better attitude. Do what you can to think differently. Try to fill your mind with positive thoughts (more on that later).

Take active steps in your job search using the techniques in this book. This will help lessen the feelings of resentment about the past and move you to optimism about your future. "Act your way into right thinking,"[17] as the saying goes.

Stop viewing yourself as a victim. That is a defeatist attitude. Instead, see your situation as a blessing . . . an opportunity to write the next chapter in your life! What's the story going to be? You can control much of what happens, but you will diminish your career fulfillment (your story) if you cling to resentment and bitterness.

Besides the mental torture resentment and bitterness can bring, "Feeling bitter interferes with the body's hormonal and immune systems, according to Carsten Wrosch, an associate

---

17 "Bill Wilson Quotable Quote," Goodreads, http://www.goodreads.com/quotes/805288-you-can-t-think-your-way-into-right-action-but-you (accessed February 5, 2016).

professor of psychology at Concordia University in Montreal . . ."[18] Not only that, but "studies have shown that bitter, angry people have higher blood pressure and heart rate and are more likely to die of heart disease and other illnesses."[19] You're already over fifty. Why invite more physical ailments into your life?

Here's the best way to put it: "Resentment is like taking poison and waiting for the other person [such as a former employer] to die."[20]

If you believe you have significant feelings that are holding you back from beginning your search and a professional therapist would be helpful, by all means seek help. There's no shame in that. Getting over these emotional hurdles is important, and the sooner you can clear them, the sooner you can meaningfully pursue your job search.

Keeping a Positive Attitude

Always bear in mind that your own resolution to succeed is more important than any other one thing.
—Abraham Lincoln[21]

Looking for a job is work . . . at times, very hard work, both physically and emotionally.

Despite the best job-search strategies, it's disheartening not to receive a job offer after making networking contacts, sending resumes, and going on interviews. The process can take a toll on your self-image and self-worth. And, of course, if you are unemployed, the financial hardship of little or no income with bills to pay can be difficult as well.

We've talked about how to get bad feelings out of your life so you can move forward with your job search. Now let's talk a little more about how to put good feelings in. Stacey A. Thompson is a certified career coach and marketing professional with more than twenty years of experience in marketing communications, public relations, and business writing. She is also the founder of Virtues for Life, a website designed to inspire and coach people

---

18 Cohen, Elizabeth. "Blaming Others Can Ruin Your Health," *CNN.com*, August 18, 2011, http://www.cnn.com/2011/HEALTH/08/17/bitter.resentful.ep/ (accessed February 5, 2016).

19 Ibid.

20 "Malachy McCourt Quotes," Goodreads, http://www.goodreads.com/author/quotes/3373.Malachy_McCourt (accessed February 5, 2016).

21 "Lincoln's Advice to Lawyers," Abraham Lincoln's letter to Isham Reavis, November 5, 1855, Abraham Lincoln Online, http://www.abrahamlincolnonline.org/lincoln/speeches/law.htm (accessed May 27, 2015).

in the daily practice of virtues. She has written about insightful virtues to practice during a job search.

These tips can be found on her website:

1. **Faith.** Having faith that you will find a job and really believing this in your heart—even when there is no evidence that this is true—is an enlightened way of thinking. Part of such faith is the understanding that whatever happens, there is a good reason for it, even if you don't know it at the time. As the saying goes, "Everything happens for a reason." Who would have thought that when you got laid off from your last job it would lead to a more fulfilling and joyful career? It can happen. Or it can catapult you into your own business. That happens more often than you might think. No matter how much you may dislike something that happened to you, having faith in the journey of life and what it may hold will help you to free yourself from worry and fear.

2. **Perseverance.** As weeks or even months pass, job searching may take a toll on your willpower. You also may feel that you can't look at one more job posting, make one more phone call, type one more cover letter, or attend one more networking event. But the mindset it takes for a runner to finish a marathon—uphill in the rain—is what it takes to land a job. Keeping your eye on the goal and becoming unstoppable in the quest for professionally satisfying employment can mean the difference between success and failure. No matter how many times you get rejected, how much you are suffering financially, or how fed up you become, persevering *will* get you a job.

3. **Courage.** It takes great courage to keep trying and sticking your neck out there to find a job even when the results seem futile. But practicing courage helps you to press on as you market yourself, write cover letters, attend networking functions (where you know no one), and face interview after interview to eventually achieve your career goals.

4. **Confidence.** While the job search continues and more rejection follows, your confidence can suffer even more. But understanding that rejection is part of the process and is not personal can make you stronger and more resilient. It's easy to lose sight of your talents, strengths, and experiences when you receive little validation or acknowledgment. Focusing on your abilities and the value you will add to potential employers will boost and maintain your confidence. Posting daily reminders or repeating affirmations to yourself relating to your abilities and your

value as a person, or visualizing yourself happy and fulfilled in your next job can help you stay motivated and confident.

5. **Gratitude.** The practice of gratitude can have a significant impact on a person's well-being. There is always something to be grateful for in life. It isn't always easy to see this, especially during hard times, but being thankful for the many blessings and simple pleasures of life will make you happier. Grateful people—according to scientific research—experience higher levels of positive emotions, cope better with stress, recover more quickly from illness, and benefit from greater physical health. Having an attitude of gratitude shifts our mental focus from negative to positive. Positive thinking, as we well know, has transformative powers. Practicing gratitude in life and during the job search is a powerful tool we can use to help prevent negative emotions, focus our thoughts on what is working in life, and make positive change. There may come a time or a day when you feel all is lost in regard to your job search. Before this happens, write a gratitude list of all the things that you have, including all the experiences, all the people, and everything in your life that you are grateful for. Write this list, review it, and continue adding to it. You will be surprised how it will lift your spirits and actually motivate you to persevere. Remember, "This too shall pass."

6. **Hope.** Without hope, finding a job would be next to impossible. Hope is the fuel to keep you going in the darkest of times, the feeling that your next job is right around the corner and it's just a matter of time until you find the right position. Remain hopeful by thinking about what's possible for you and your career, and not on what's not happening for you. Every part of the job search has value, even if it doesn't feel that way. Through the practice of hope, our journey becomes lighter as we shift our focus from hardships to wishes.[22]

Being mindful of these virtues will help you stay emotionally centered during the ups and downs of your job search. They can inspire and motivate you. However, a job search always requires action. It has been written, "faith without action is dead."[23]

Throughout your job search, there are ultimately three things in your control: effort, attitude, and beliefs. This includes how many hours/days per week you devote to your search, how many times you will network per day or week (whether calling or emailing), and more. Be productive with your effort, stay positive, and believe in yourself!

---

22 Thompson, Stacey A. "6 Virtues to Practice for Job Search Success," *Virtues for Life*, http://www.virtuesforlife.com/6-virtues-to-practice-for-job-search-success/ (accessed June 1, 2015).

23 "In the same way, faith by itself, if it is not accompanied by action, is dead" (James 2:17, NIV).

Your Career . . . Your Responsibility

What is a career? Really, it's a series of experiences in your professional working life. It is your responsibility to make your career as fulfilling as possible, whether you intend to work five more years or twenty more years.

As you move forward as a SEAL, here are some career perspectives to consider adopting. They should add clarity, understanding, and perception to your view of your career. These perspectives are:

1. **I am solely responsible for my career success.** You took the initiative and put in years of hard work to get where you are. Own your career by guiding and directing your job-search pursuits.[24] Conducting a professional and effective job search (from opportunity profiling and your resume, to the interview process, negotiating an offer, and more) is part of your success and responsibility as well.

2. **It is my responsibility to enhance my value proposition.** As a SEAL, you can't fall out of touch or fall behind. Your experience tells you that all industries and all functions within industries evolve, advance, and change. It is your responsibility to your career to stay current and enhance your skills. This can be especially true with technology-focused careers.

3. **I must deliver an ROI (Return on Investment).** It is your responsibility to bring value to your employer. As a SEAL, you know that not delivering value to your employer can negatively impact your job security.[25]

4. **I am responsible for my work-life balance.** Work and career are important, but so are family, friends, and living a fulfilling life outside work. You control where you place your priorities.[26]

5. **It is my responsibility to stay informed about the financial health and well-being of my employer and the industry in which I work.** For some SEALs, being uninformed had significant and negative career ramifications. Always be informed and aware of how your employer is doing. Look around. Is your employer investing in the company, technology, people, and/or other resources? Are people leaving?

---

24 "Proactive Career Planning at Any Age," Aequus Wealth Management Resources, http://www.aequuswealth.com/newsletter/article/proactive_career_planning_at_any_age (accessed July 10, 2015).

25 See also, Whitcomb, *Job Search Magic*, p. 12–13.

26 See also, Yate, Martin John. *Knock 'em Dead Social Networking for Job Search and Professional Success*. (Avon, MA: Adams Media, 2014), p. 246.

Is there expansion and hiring? Is the industry contracting or expanding? Are there new competitors (a possible sign of a healthy industry)? How are other competitors doing? Read about your company (for publicly traded companies, take a look at the annual report). Ask a stockbroker to assess your company or industry. As you know, SEALs are more vulnerable to organizational changes. Job searches usually take longer. Do your best to stay informed and stay ahead of possible negative career events. Make changes as needed.

6. **Change is inevitable in my career.** How I respond to change is completely within my control. Despite your best knowledge and foresight, unforeseen things will happen in your career. Merger. Acquisition. Reorganization. Layoffs. Downsizing. Promotions! Change often creates opportunities you can capitalize upon if you have perspective, knowledge, a positive attitude, and focused effort. All SEALs know that change often comes with a natural level of discomfort, uncertainty, and a dose of anxiety. But all SEALs also know that change frequently accompanies growth, which is the gift of change.

A STORY OF INSPIRATION

It was an emotional time. I was sixty and out of work. Internal questions bombarded me. *Who am I? What do I want to do? When should I start?*

My initial thought was to take a few weeks off, that I deserved it because it had been a rough year. It didn't take long before I recognized that I could easily become my own worst enemy when it came to looking for a job. Luckily I came to my senses and saw the "time off" ploy for exactly what it was—procrastination, the evil to all things.

Once I overcame the inclination to procrastinate, I knew I needed to get organized and get a plan. I started thinking about defining myself, what I wanted to do, how to present myself, where to present myself, and how diligent I was going to be in my pursuit of a job.

I'm classically trained in French cooking so I went to my training basics and acknowledged that I needed to do my Mis en Place (culinary term for "putting in place" or "everything in its place").

I started a list of what I needed to "put in place" before beginning my job search:

- **Resume**

  - It needed rewriting, but in what style?

  - What updates did it need to get ready for the company(ies) I wanted to target?

  - Did it represent well for the employers (field) that I was targeting?

- **Cover Letter**

  - Did I have a killer cover letter that I could tweak for each company I was going to apply to?

- **What else did I need before putting myself out there?**

  - I wasn't sure so I started looking for resources that could help me. I found *The Motivated Job Search* by Brian E. Howard and it became my blueprint for getting organized and in the right mind set. [Editor's note: *The Motivated Job Search* is the first book in the Motivated Series and a forerunner to this book].

Once I was in the right mindset, had a strong resource, and became organized, the last step for me was to understand that I now had a full-time job to find a job that I desired. So, I set up office hours to work at that goal, and it all paid off. I am once again happily and gainfully employed.

My advice is to recognize procrastination or fear and face them head on. Don't concentrate on your age but on your experience and skill set. Get your mind around what you want to do going forward and what it will take to make that happen. Find good resources to guide you on the task, get organized, and then set up shop and make getting a job your full-time job until you too are once again happily and gainfully employed.

G.L.
Age 60

Part II

Strategy Is Everything: The Self-Motivated Approach

Plans are only good intentions unless they immediately degenerate into hard work.

—Peter F. Drucker[27]

The Advantages of a Self-Motivated Job Search

There are two ways to conduct a job search: self-motivated or passive. Being passive in a job search is similar to using a saw to do a hammer's work—it's ineffective, makes the job (your search) longer, and may result in failure. The passive search bases all sense of direction on jobs posted on the Internet. In contrast, the self-motivated method is both effective and efficient, making it the best way to conduct a job search. Why? This method is proactive—the job seeker actively engages the job market to discover opportunities where their skills and competencies bring the greatest value to an employer. There are several distinct advantages of conducting a self-motivated job search that help you get a job more effectively.[28] These advantages can also help you get the job offer you want. These advantages include:

Hidden Job Market

A self-motivated job search will tap the Hidden Job Market, uncovering unadvertised positions.[29] Statistically speaking, 75 to 80 percent of all open jobs are not advertised.[30] Instead of searching passively, you'll proactively engage the job market by networking and

---

27 "Peter F. Drucker Quotable Quote," Goodreads, http://www.goodreads.com/quotes/65135-plans-are-only-good-intentions-un-less-they-immediately-degenerate-into (accessed April 12, 2016).

28 Joyce, Susan P. "Job Search Success Strategy: PROactive vs. REactive Job Search," Job-Hunt.org, http://www.job-hunt.org/article_proactive_job_search.shtml (accessed July 14, 2015).

29 Whitcomb, *Job Search Magic*, p. 274–275.

30 Kaufman, Wendy. "A Successful Job Search: It's All About Networking," *National Public Radio*, February 3, 2011, http://www.npr.org/2011/02/08/133474431/a-successful-job-search-its-all-about-networking (accessed June 2, 2015); "Developing Job Search Strategies," *University of Wisconsin*, https://www.uwgb.edu/careers/PDF-Files/Job-Search-Strategies.pdf (accessed June 3, 2015).

contacting target companies to create your own pipeline of opportunities with as many leads as your well-planned efforts can produce.[31]

Solution/Value Proposition

Your professional value proposition is the totality of your education, experience, and other intangible factors that an employer views as valuable to the company. When you present yourself as a solution to a hiring need, this professional picture of you sparks the employer's interest and motivates them to evaluate the benefits and costs of making you an employee of the company. You will discover how to transform information about the company, products, services, executives, industry, company news releases, and so on into messages to the hiring executive of how you can prevent, solve, or divert a business problem.[32]

In the end, your value proposition must make or save the company money beyond the costs of hiring you and keeping you as an employee (leading to positive return on investment, or ROI).[33]

Attitude/Confidence

A self-motivated job search puts you in control. Rather than being at the whim of posted job openings, you make things happen. This will keep your attitude about your job search positive, helping build confidence and self-image. Believe it—maintaining a positive attitude and showing confidence is a big deal, and being proactive will keep things moving forward.[34] It's likely you won't fall victim to the negative emotions a stale job search may bring if you're feeling good about how your search is progressing.

Direct Contact with Hiring Executives

One of the keys to landing job offers is getting hiring executive(s) inspired about your background and the benefits you can bring to the company. Enlisting a champion for your cause will significantly increase your odds of securing more interviews and job offers.[35]

---

31 Whitcomb, *Job Search Magic*, p. 274.

32 Ibid., p. 289.

33 Ibid., p. 274.

34 Kanfer, Ruth, and Charles L. Hulin. "Individual Differences in Successful Job Searches Following Lay-off." Abstract. *Personnel Psychology* 38, no. 4 (December 1985): 835–847, http://www.researchgate.net/publication/227749499_INDIVIDUAL_DIFFERENCES_IN_SUCCESSFUL_JOB_SEARCHES_FOLLOWING_LAYOFF (accessed July 9, 2015); Moynihan, Lisa M., Mark V. Roehling, Marcie A. LePine, and Wendy R. Boswell. "A Longitudinal Study of the Relationships Among Job Search Self-Efficacy, Job Interviews, and Employment Outcomes." Abstract. *Journal of Business and Psychology* 18, no. 2 (2003): 201–233, http://link.springer.com/article/10.1023%-2FA%3A1027349115277 (accessed July 3, 2015).

35 Kurtzberg, Terri R., and Charles E. Naquin. *The Essentials of Job Negotiations: Proven Strategies for Getting What You Want.* (Santa Barbara, CA: Praeger, 2011), p. 18.

Networking

Networking is proactively reaching out to others in your professional and personal database, both online and face-to-face, offering yourself as a resource to help others, knowing that they will do what they can to help you in return. Networking keeps you engaged with others and with the events, news, and emerging trends in your industry. Networking will include reaching out to your contacts in a variety of settings, including LinkedIn, your local Chamber of Commerce, professional associations, and civic and philanthropic organizations, among others. Networking creates relationships. Your next job will likely be as a result of "people, talking to people, about people." It's estimated that from 60–80 percent of jobs are filled by networking.[36]

Referrals

As your networking expands and your relationships mature, you will receive a steady flow of referrals and recommendations from colleagues, insider-employees, former bosses, and others. Your reputation and sphere of influence will grow, and you will gain the inside track regarding open positions.

Competition

It's no secret that in today's market, job positions teem with competing candidates, all with the same goal: to be hired. However, in a self-motivated search, you could precede the stampede and become one of just a handful of referred or recommended candidates, or in some cases the only job seeker under consideration, minimizing competition.

Direct Insider Information

You will quickly learn what the hiring executive wants from the person filling a position. This invaluable information allows you to focus your background and achievements to fulfill those expectations.

Rapport

A self-motivated job search encourages building rapport. If you are introduced to a hiring executive by a referral from your network, you may be able to speak with others who know the individual. They can give you valuable insight on personality, hot buttons, and

---

36 "Using LinkedIn to Find a Job or Internship," LinkedIn, https://university.linkedin.com/content/dam/university/global/en_US/site/pdf/TipSheet_FindingaJoborInternship.pdf (accessed June 7, 2015); Kimberly Beatty, "The Math Behind the Networking Claim," *Jobfully Blog*, July 1, 2010, http://blog.jobfully.com/2010/07/the-math-behind-the-networking-claim/ (accessed June 11, 2015); Steven Rothberg, "80% of Job Openings are Unadvertised," *College Recruiter* (blog), March 28, 2013, https://www.collegerecruiter.com/blog/2013/03/28/80-of-job-openings-are-unadvertised/ (accessed June 11, 2015).

so on. And if the executive is the decision maker for hiring, you avoid Human Resources, sometimes until after you're hired.

⬧ A self-motivated job search is a great approach for a SEAL. This approach gets you moving, thinking, reaching out to others, and working toward your future. It puts you in control and boosts your attitude and job-search confidence. This approach also helps defeat age-related biases and obstacles that some SEALs may put in their own way to make things difficult. It's generally accepted that hiring executives view the self-motivated approach favorably because they see you taking action.

The Psychology of Persuasion and Your Job Search

Before we dive into the steps and techniques for conducting a job search, it's beneficial to talk briefly about the psychology of persuasion and how it will affect your job search.

What follows are some very important concepts woven throughout the rest of this book. Knowing them will help you maximize your job-search success because they combine so effectively with the self-motivated approach.

According to Robert Cialdini, a leader in the field of psychology and persuasion, there are six principles that persuade others to think and act as they do. They are:

1. Scarcity
2. Authority
3. Liking
4. Social Proof
5. Consistency and Commitment
6. Reciprocity/Reciprocation[37]

We will briefly discuss these principles and how they relate to your job search.

Scarcity

If a job seeker is seen as unique or special, he or she is seen as valuable.[38] How do you capitalize upon the persuasion principle of scarcity? Answer: Differentiation.

Creating differentiation (separation) between yourself and other job seekers is important when you look for a job. During the course of the interview process, seemingly small and isolated thoughts of differentiation—such as he/she dresses well, is knowledgeable on

---

37 Cialdini, Robert B. *Influence: Science and Practice*, 4th ed. (Needham Heights, MA: Allyn & Bacon, 2001), p. x, quoted in Kurtzberg and Naquin, *Essentials*, Chapter 5, p. 94–101.

38 Cialdini, *Influence*, p. 204–205, and Chapter 7, "Scarcity: The Rule of the Few," quoted in Kurtzberg and Naquin, *Essentials*, p. 94–101.

industry trends, has a professional designation, and so on—compound upon themselves in the mind of the hiring executive. All of this affects your perceived value and motivates the hiring executive to continue the interview process with you, hopefully ending in an employment offer.

The more uniquely you can justifiably portray yourself, the more you are using the persuasion principle of scarcity.

Authority

Most people respond to and respect authority, whether it is a title, position, professional designation, experience, or station in life.[39] A good example of creating intangible authority is through appropriate interview attire: A starched white shirt or stylish blouse, pressed suit, polished hard-soled shoes, the pen you use, or even the watch you wear can all convey authority that others may react to favorably.

Any job-search technique or information that triggers professional respect (or elevation) with the hiring executive is using the persuasion principle of authority.

Liking (and Personal Chemistry)

Sixty percent of most hires are based on personal chemistry.[40] In other words, hiring executives are persuaded to hire job seekers they personally like. Getting others to like you is often based on identifying similarities or common interests. We tend to like other people similar to ourselves.[41]

There are several ways to lay the foundation for similarity and personal chemistry. Here are a few ideas:

1. Mentioning common industry associations or groups
2. Discussing common personal interests
3. Acknowledging common former employers
4. Giving the hiring executive a sincere compliment
5. Name dropping (identifying common friends or professional colleagues the hiring executive feels good about)
6. Being employed (perhaps formerly employed) by an industry-leading or innovative company

---

39 Cialdini, *Influence*, p. 180–185, and Chapter 6, "Authority: Directed Deference," quoted in Kurtzberg and Naquin, *Essentials*, p. 94–101.

40 DiResta, Diane, interview by Christina Canters, "Episode 29—How to Blitz Your Job Interview—Secrets of Executive Speech Coach Diane DiResta," *DesignDrawSpeak*, podcast audio, June 12, 2014, http://designdrawspeak.com/029/ (accessed June 19, 2015).

41 Byrne, Donn Erwin. *The Attraction Paradigm*. (New York: Academic Press, 1971), quoted in Kurtzberg and Naquin, *Essentials*, p. 35.

Any job-search technique that creates a positive impression on the hiring executive based on association or personal chemistry relies on the persuasion principle of liking (and personal chemistry).

Social Proof

Others mentioning good things about you is more persuasive than you promoting yourself.[42] That's the power of social proof.

Psychologically, social proof is most influential and persuasive when decisions are shrouded in uncertainty. A hiring executive may be thinking: Which candidate is better qualified? Who would fit in best? What about compensation? (And so on.) This is why recommendations, references, or any form of affirmation from a trusted source can impact the hiring decision.

Any job-search technique that contains or references a recommendation or positive affirmation of you as a job seeker is using the persuasion principle of social proof.

Consistency and Commitment

People desire a reputation of upholding their own commitments and generally do not like to go back on their word.[43] It's that simple.

An example of this principle in action is when you close an interview by asking if you will be proceeding in the hiring process. If the hiring executive indicates that you will, it will be more difficult for them to retreat from that answer due to the persuasion principle of consistency and commitment.

Any job-search technique that creates a self-imposed course of action (from the hiring executive's perspective) is using the persuasion principle of consistency and commitment.

Reciprocity

There is a strong psychological motivation to return favors and not to feel indebted to others. People feel compelled to repay others. This can be especially true if the item (of whatever nature) was given for free.[44]

An example of using this persuasion technique in a job search would be providing the hiring executive a free sales lead, nonproprietary industry information, or information regarding the whereabouts of a colleague. To be most effective, the gesture should be

---

42 Matt. "How to Use a Brag Book to Differentiate Yourself From the Competition," Career Enlightenment, April 19, 2013, https://careerenlightenment.com/how-to-use-a-brag-book-to-differentiate-yourself-from-the-competition (accessed November 4, 2015).

43 Cialdini, *Influence*, p. 53, and Chapter 3, "Commitment and Consistency: Hobgoblins of the Mind," quoted in Kurtzberg and Naquin, *Essentials*, p. 94–101.

44 Cialdini, *Influence*, p. 144, 161, and Chapter 5, "Liking: The Friendly Thief," quoted in Kurtzberg and Naquin, *Essentials*, p. 94–101.

made with the expectation of receiving nothing in return, but with the awareness that the psychology of reciprocity is present.

Any job-search technique that endears you to a hiring executive by doing something for him or her (especially for free) is using the persuasion principle of reciprocity.

By raising your awareness of these persuasion principles, you will be on the alert for opportunities, and you will be able to capitalize upon them when they present themselves. You can use these psychology and persuasion principles to advance your candidacy.

Now that you have a basic understanding of the principles of persuasion, you understand the reasons for (and persuasive power of) the job-search techniques presented throughout this book—the same techniques used successfully by many others. As you go along, try to identify the persuasion principle (there could be more than one) that makes a technique useful. Occasional reference is made to these persuasion principles to help your job search be more effective.

A STORY OF INSPIRATION

For nearly forty years I have worked in the employee benefits industry in various capacities. It has been a wonderful and fulfilling career. For the past five years I was in sales with a company which ironically was the most stressful position that I have ever had. So much has changed in business today and I'm not referring to advancements in technology. There is simply a lack of business-honor, unlike the past.

In March I turned sixty and was having another good year in sales. Then, in July I was unexpectedly fired. It came from out of the blue! My employer's justification was weak since my sales numbers were good. It was tough going home that night telling my wife that I had been fired. There were some tears.

Now who is going to hire a sixty-year-old man? That was the question swirling around in my mind. I was referred to a book, *The Motivated Job Search* [Editor's note: *The Motivated Job Search* is the first book in the Motivated Series and a forerunner to this book]. Two take aways that changed everything for me:

1. Don't waste time brooding! Clear your head, put all bitterness aside, and get on with your life and a new search for employment. "Don't be bitter, be better" became my mantra!

2. Think about reinventing yourself. Think outside the box. Find a new angle.

With these concepts in mind, I started making calls to my close colleagues and contacts in the industry. I sought their advice on ideas of what I might be suited for in their view. Ideas started to flow as I considered everything that they said. I opened myself up to anything and everything.

After one week, I made a decision to explore a certain service sector of the employee benefits industry. I identified several companies in this new sector based on company name I gathered during my networking calls and simple Internet research.

I decided to contact these companies directly by phone. I created a simple presentation about myself so I had something to say, and started calling the companies. I spoke with anyone who would listen and got transferred around several times. Eventually, I spoke with those who could make or influence a hiring decision. In this new industry sector, it was common to hire independent contractors, which was what I wanted.

The plan worked! Two weeks and a day after being fired, I was offered a job! And, my first work assignment was just a few weeks out. Mission accomplished!

While not at the same pay or potential income annually, I was free of corporate shenanigans and all that goes with it. I am so excited that I have a new career direction still in the employee benefit space with companies that actually love my experience! That to me is worth its weight in gold!. . .to be appreciated.

I know it's a challenge for those of us over fifty to conduct a job search, especially when we find ourselves suddenly unemployed. The emotions of doubt, fear, and uncertainty can easily get to you quickly. It's hard. I know because I lived it! But you can't let this new reality beat you down and in particular, stress you to the point of causing illness or death.

My advice . . . Take heart! Get up and dust yourself off! Seek guidance in the counsel of others and in reading. Plot a course of action and get on with it! Just like me, you CAN write a new chapter in your career. You CAN continue your career until you want it to end. . .not the other way around.

A.R.
Age 60

Part III

Things to Know about Your Job Search

In the end, what we regret most are the chances we never took.
—Frasier Crane[45]

Job Search Assessment

Whether you are beginning a job search, actively engaged in a search, or relaunching a search, it is important to understand and assess your job search. Your job search can be more effective if you are properly prepared and have a clear-cut plan. The checklist that follows is a very worthwhile tool to use and review during a job search to help you measure your effort regardless of where you are in the search process. As you use the assessment, be thoughtful and honest with yourself. Each item on the checklist has a corresponding topic in the book to guide you and is a major point of reference to examine about your job search. You must be strong in all of these areas. Failing to do so in one or more areas can add up to a less effective and longer job search. Major items for you to consider include:

Emotions

These emotions concern your job search itself, not emotions about your life situation. Be prepared for ups and downs. There are moments of energy and depletion, excitement and rejection. There may be a few times of confusion and chaos.

Profile

You must have a Target Opportunity Profile. Do you know what kind of opportunity you are looking for?

---

45 Frasier. "Goodnight, Seattle: Part 2," first broadcast 13 May 2004 by NBC. Directed by David Lee and written by Christopher Lloyd and Joe Keenan.

Job Search Tools:

1. **Keywords.** These are the special words that describe you, your skills, and your achievements—"What do you want to be known for?"[46] Or found for? Keywords are the DNA of your job search.

2. **Accomplishments.** These are your professional achievements, documentation that you added value to your employer, and so on.

3. **Exit statement.** This also includes explanations for extended unemployment.

4. **Branding.** Having a personal brand succinctly announces to the market who you are and what your value proposition is.

5. **Elevator speech.** A thirty- to sixty-second speech incorporating your branding into a verbal commercial about yourself.

6. **LinkedIn profile.** Evaluate your LinkedIn profile:

    A. Photo

    B. Complete

    C. Optimized (and tested)

    D. Compelling

7. **Resume.** Evaluate your resume:

    A. Consistent and synced with your LinkedIn profile

    B. Format, content, and appearance

8. **Cover letter.** Templates as a starting point for written communications

Engaging the Market—Spreading the Word

There are four ways to spread the word in your job search that can result in networking opportunities, job leads, interviews, and eventually job offers. They are:

1. **Networking**

2. **Contacting recruiters**

3. **Proactively marketing your professional credentials**

4. **Submitting online applications**

---

46   Whitcomb, *Job Search Magic*, p. 68.

Interviews

Preparation and evaluating performance

1. **Preparation**

   A. Research

   B. Pre-scripted answers to known questions

2. **Self-Praise for good interviews and results**

3. **Adjustments for poor interview performances and results**

Measuring your progress

If you want to improve your job-search results, start counting!

1. **How many LinkedIn views are you getting each week?** Minimum of twenty. This will be influenced by your outbound communication activity.

2. **Outbound communications.** Minimum twenty, both for outbound emails/InMails and outbound calls, per day.

3. **First-stage interviews.** This is where things really begin. Set an appropriate goal for yourself regarding the amount of first-time interviews, and strive to exceed it. At minimum, work to have at least one first-time interview a week (preferably more!).

4. **Second-stage interviews.** Not all first-time interviews will turn into second-time interviews, but it is important to measure how often you advance in the interview process.

Job offers

The ultimate goal.

1. **Evaluated against your Target Opportunity Profile.** Does the job offer match (closely enough) your profile of your target opportunity? How do you feel emotionally about the overall fit and opportunity?

2. **Professionally negotiated.** Set a tone of professional cooperation. Justify requests when possible. Be open to give in order to get something in return.

As you work through the assessment, critically evaluate how you are doing and make necessary adjustments. There may be moments of discomfort as your critical assessment reveals areas requiring improvement. Review this book for guidance and advice.

Here's a harsh truth: All of the instruction and guidance of this book or any other source will not advance your search if you lack the motivation and effort to put what you learn into action. You will succeed! Simply get into action, persevere, and don't stop!

Getting off to a Successful Start

Too many SEALs believe that if you can do a job, you can get a job. This is simply not true. They are entirely different skillsets. And the skills necessary to find employment today are drastically different than they were just a few years ago. Advances and changes in the use of technology have changed how job seekers look for employment and how employers find qualified job seekers.

Beyond "I need to update my resume," many SEALs have no idea what to do, or the order things need to be done, especially if they are starting the job search from scratch. It can easily be overwhelming, especially if you didn't expect to become unemployed, haven't looked for a job in a long time, or need to find a new job. Relax and take a deep breath. In this section we will list, then briefly discuss, the A-1 priorities to successfully launch your job search and reduce any feelings of anxiety. They are:

1. **Get (and keep) your emotions in check.** We have already discussed emotions, and it's possible that they could flare up every once in a while—that's normal. Just remember, the more real steps you take moving your search forward, the sooner those emotions fade in intensity and frequency. Not dwelling on the past moves you forward to your future and your next job!

2. **Identify your keywords.** What words apply to you? Start simple. What titles have you held? What industries have you worked in? What knowledge do you have? These concepts and others will form the messaging behind who you are and how you present yourself to the job market.

3. **Get organized.** You will need to make lists—of companies, people, and "to-do's." Relying on your memory or sticky notes in a shotgun fashion is a recipe for disaster. In the thick of your job search, you won't be able to keep track of what you're doing without a system. Keep the information collected as a result of your research organized on an Excel spreadsheet using this or a similar format:

Company Name / Website / Industry / Contact Name / Title / Email Address / Phone / Notes

The Notes column will help you keep track of dates of contact, what you have sent, and more. Don't get carried away by recording non-useful information.

There are two services you can explore that will help you stay organized during your job search: JibberJobber (www.jibberjobber.com/login.php) and CareerShift (www.careershift.com). You can also use Microsoft Outlook's calendar feature to record tasks to be done, timing of follow-up calls, and so on.

4. **Create a short list of target employers you would be interested in working for.** It may be only three, five, or ten companies. Add to the list as you discover new companies. But the point here is to start the list and get you thinking. Now, look up the companies on LinkedIn. Follow them by setting up alerts to receive news, press releases, and job postings. You may also use Google Alerts. If you have Twitter, follow the companies (check out Twellow at www.twellow.com) to receive information/ tweets. This starts the flow of information from these companies (and others you'll add), including jobs, industry trends, and other benefits to your job search. Use the ideas on Excel spreadsheets in the previous section to create a complete picture of each company before moving ahead, to eliminate needless backtracking for additional research.

5. **Create a short list of networking contacts.** This one is like the list of companies from the last step. Make a list of close professional colleagues you feel very comfortable speaking to about your circumstances and job search. As you think of more, add to the list. This list likely will not exceed twenty to twenty-five names to begin with (although it could be more). After you make out the list, do not contact them! You are not ready (even though you may think you are!). Regardless of your business or personal relationships here, don't "blow it" by not being properly prepared. Be patient. Read the Professional Networking section, and do things right the first time. Just like with your target companies, be sure to include all relevant information before moving on.

6. **Update your resume.** Read the Impactful Resumes section, and either prepare one yourself, or seek professional services (which will free your time for other job-search activities). If you have an out-of-date resume, having your resume professionally updated could be a good investment.

7. **Update your LinkedIn profile and expand your network.** Your former employers and dates of employment on LinkedIn and your resume must match exactly. After you look at the Networking sections, expand your network by adding new

connections. These have to be the right kind of high-value connections (explained later) who will significantly advance your job search.

8. **Create job alerts.** Use websites like Indeed.com and SimplyHired.com that have features to alert you about titles, locations, specific companies (your short list), and so on. Set up alerts on LinkedIn too. Companies (and recruiters) post jobs on LinkedIn, and you can receive notifications when they do. Are there any industry-specific or niche job boards you could search? Check out http://airsdirectory.com to research them, as well as recruiters, and then set up alerts. Get a sense of the job market and start the flow of opportunities you are looking for. If a position pops up and you're interested, do not apply for it through the website! Research the likely hiring executive(s) and contact them directly. This is a much more effective way to pursue the position than applying for it online. (More on this technique later.)

More about Job Alerts

The number of job openings you receive from your job alerts can be an indication of the market demand for someone with your skillset or whether your target market is broad enough. There are a host of factors that can influence the number of jobs that pop up from your job alerts. As you evaluate the number of jobs that fit your job-alert parameters, here are some general guidelines:

Eight or fewer job openings per month. If the trend indicates that you are getting eight or fewer job openings per month (two or fewer per week), it could be an indication that the demand for your specific skillset may not be strong enough to drive your job search, or your target market is too limited. In the latter case, you should broaden the parameters of your job alerts to capture more openings.

Nine to thirty-six job openings per month. This range is likely healthy—you are being alerted to three to eight openings a week. There is demand for your skillset, and your target market is large enough. As you screen the openings, the number you choose to pursue is manageable.

Thirty-seven or more openings per month. In this case, you may want to consider tightening the parameters of your job alerts. You are being alerted to eight or more openings a week. Depending upon the quality of the openings, the number of openings could become unmanageable to effectively evaluate and pursue.

How Long Will Your Job Search Take?

Over the years, an easy formula has evolved regarding the length of time it takes to successfully conduct a job search: one month for every $10,000 of income.[47] If you were earning $80,000, your search will take eight months.

To the best we can determine, this formula is not supported by much (or any) credible empirical data. It may have been developed by job seekers as an easy measure to track their search efforts against the calendar—which in the end is fine; the formula can create a level of urgency because it is time relevant.

For this book's objectives, your challenge and goal is to beat the formula—by a wide margin! For example, if you make $80,000, your goal is to land a professionally satisfying job in less than an eight-month time frame.

Factors unique to your personal situation will influence the amount of time it takes to find a new job. Here are some common factors that tend to influence a SEAL's job-search timeline:

Factor 1: Your Skillset and Track Record

Do you have the skills—those professional value propositions—or something of value in your background and experience to benefit an employer? Transferable job skills? Do your skills and experience make or save an employer money?[48] For sales professionals, product knowledge and distribution channels would factor in here. How many other job seekers have similar skills? Supply and demand can have a huge impact on the length of your search. Do you have a track record of success utilizing your skillset that demonstrates Return on Investment (ROI)? This would help to differentiate you from other job seekers.[49]

Factor 2: Relocation and Travel

How do you feel about moving? Would relocating to a new location for the right job lead to a better future with better compensation? Remember that cost of living differs across the country. How about the effect on immediate family? Would extended family be affected? Some positions require frequent travel. Your search will probably be longer if you can't or won't travel as the position demands.

---

47 Elaine Varelas, "How Long Will My Job Search Take?" *The Job Doc* (blog), *The Boston Globe*, June 12, 2013, http://www.boston.com/jobs/news/jobdoc/2013/06/how_long_will_my_job_search_ta.html (accessed June 4, 2015).

48 See also, Whitcomb, *Job Search Magic*, p. 274.

49 Ibid., and p. 35 and Chapter 2, "Getting Your Job Search Plan Together."

Factor 3: Sales, Account Management, or Other Customer-Facing Roles

- Relationships—Do you have the right kinds of business relationships? The right distribution channel?

- Location—Are you located in or near an open territory?

- Product Knowledge—Are you familiar with the requisite product knowledge of the employer (i.e., less training, quicker ROI for you)?

Factor 4: Compensation

For SEALs, this may or may not be an issue depending upon your personal situation. Does your compensation match market conditions and the prevailing wage for the position? It has been cited that some SEALs may need to take as much as 20 percent less in compensation.[50] This is not a pleasant thought, but for some SEALs it could be necessary to gain employment and shorten their search. Besides, is it better to take less or continue to be unemployed?[51] There is more on compensation and negotiation later in this book.

Factor 5: The Strength of Your Network and Online Visibility

Networking is the most effective mechanism to land your next position. Most estimate that 60 to 80 percent of jobs are found by networking.[52] The size, depth, and effective use of your professional and social network(s) will affect your job search's duration. This is also why you need a robust profile on LinkedIn for your job search; without it, recruiters will pass you over as invisible—especially if information about your qualifications is weak or missing.

As a SEAL, will you put in the effort to network? It's easier for some than others, but it's still necessary to shorten your job search. Failing to effectively reach out and network with others means you are missing 60 to 80 percent of your opportunities to find a new job.[53]

Factor 6: Job-Search Strategy and Your Effort

Have you profiled your desired position, industry, and target companies? Will you conduct a passive or self-motivated job search? Developing a sound strategy will positively

---

50 "Think Over 50 Is Over the Hill? Think Again: Job Search Tips for People Over 50," Career-Intelligence.com, http://career-intelligence.com/job-seekers-over-fifty/ (accessed February 8, 2016); See also, Eisenberg, Richard. "Older Job Seekers: You're Hired (For Less)," *Forbes.com*, March 30, 2015, http://www.forbes.com/sites/nextavenue/2015/03/30/older-job-seekers-youre-hired-for-less/#66c814595d60 (accessed February 8, 2016).

51 Career-Intelligence, "Think Over 50."

52 LinkedIn, "Using LinkedIn to Find a Job"; Beatty, "The Math Behind the Networking Claim"; Rothberg, "80% of Job Openings."

53 Ibid.

affect the job-search timeline. Taking a casual, shotgun approach will significantly lengthen your job search. Work hard and work smart—even if that means thirty to forty hours per week if you're unemployed, or six to eight if employed—to get a new job. Your effort can yield success with companies on and under the radar if you focus, show courage, and persist.

Factor 7: Your Economic Environment and Personal Life

External economic factors can adversely affect a job search. Hiring does occur, even in an economic downturn. Stick to your plan, put in the effort with a positive attitude, and you will succeed. Remember: The economy is not standing in your way . . . you are. Life does have seasons, which tend to bring new joys, challenges, and distractions (some are simply annoying while others can be debilitating). As a SEAL, you could have a personal issue that is distracting you from a self-motivated job search (a sick or aging parent, adult children's issues, or something else). Is the issue you are facing honestly preventing you from pursuing your job search? Or is it an excuse to put off your search? Your heart will know the answer.

Answering Questions about Your Unemployment: Your Exit Statement

If you are unemployed, it is inevitable that you will be asked questions like: "What happened? Why are you looking for a job? Why are you unemployed?" Or perhaps when speaking with another SEAL, "You too?" Outside the odd humor of the last situation, these kinds of questions can create an awkward moment unless you are prepared with a professional, honest response. That response needs to be fit for social acquaintances, colleagues, and potential employers, and it should be fair to your former employer. Write your explanation and commit it to memory. Remember these concepts to help you formulate your response about your unemployment:

1. **Keep it aligned.** Make sure your statement reflects what happened and what your former employer may say.

2. **Keep it positive.** Do not make any negative statements about your former company, boss, or colleagues.

3. **Keep it factual.** Do not unload emotions into your explanation.

4. **Keep it short.** Do not get into an extended explanation. Make your statement and be done.

Some poor explanations would be:

> "Those jerks over at XYZ can't find their butts with both hands! Yet they fired *me*!"

> "I gave XYZ twenty-five years of my life, and what did it get me? A ticket in the unemployment line, that's what!"

Here are some good, brief explanations:

- "The company went through a reorganization."
- "The company was purchased."
- "The company had to make budget cuts, and there were departmental layoffs. I was a casualty."
- "Based on company direction, we mutually agreed to part ways."

If you follow this advice, you will be less likely to receive additional probing questions regarding your circumstances.

There will be times, though, when a short one- or two-sentence response simply does not fit the circumstances, such as in an interview with a senior executive. For those situations, you must be able to provide additional information while still adhering to the general rules (aligned, positive, factual, and short). Below is an example of one such exit statement.

> *I was hired four years ago to build the sales structure and process to put Up-and-Comer, Inc. on a solid growth trajectory. I was responsible for driving the strategies that generated over 40 percent additional software revenue and a robust client base increase from ninety-two to over 650 clients, including an increase from two to nine Fortune 50 clients. In 20XX, we achieved 101 percent client-revenue retention.*
>
> *Our current CEO is the founder of the company. He is a brilliant man with a passionate vision for Up-and-Comer's position in the market and society. It has been a delight and a privilege to be his partner in achieving the company's status as a proven, transformative solution for employers.*
>
> *I am still invested in Up-and-Comer's success; however, over the course of the last [a time frame] the CEO and I reached a conclusion that we had different visions regarding the direction of the company. Together we agreed that it was time I move on. So the CEO and I amicably agreed to a severance arrangement from the company.*

Note that the first paragraph of the exit statement showcases accomplishments. You want to emphasize achievements upfront. The statement is positive in tone and is written in a factual way. The length is about 175 words and should be delivered in a little over one minute (given a normal rate of speech of 150 words per minute).[54] That is short, given the level of content.

Once you have written your exit statement, memorize it. Read it over and over. Then create "talking points" for the statement. These are the major points you'll make in your statement. Use those as guides as you rehearse your speech. This will help you deliver your statement in a conversational tone.

Searching for a Job While Employed—The Confidential Job Search

Initiating and conducting a job search while employed poses notable challenges.[55] You've concluded that it is time to find a new opportunity. To ensure that your confidential job search does not raise red flags with your current employer, follow the suggestions below: Be aware of your behavior. You may have intellectually and emotionally "turned the corner" at your current employer. But do things just like before and go out of your way to defuse suspicion. Keep your current job a priority (you owe that to your employer) and finish strong. Resist the urge to tell coworkers of your intentions (which may not be easy), and do not use your employer's computer equipment or email for your job search (use your personal email, even if you have to create one). When you network (as you will and should), let your contacts know about the confidential nature of your search—they'll understand, but they must be made aware first. You should arrange similar confidentiality with recruiters at search firms; they can be great eyes and ears for new opportunities, and they are trained to keep dealings confidential.

Update your LinkedIn profile. Depending on the changes you make to your LinkedIn profile, they could be broadcast to your network connections and raise suspicion. To hide your changes on LinkedIn, go to your Profile page and turn off your network notifications. After your job search is complete, you can restore your notifications if you want.

Be careful about asking for employment documents. Requesting copies of past performance reviews, covenants-not-to-compete, and the like are unusual requests. Some larger employers have policies to keep requests confidential when Human Resources' proper channels and protocols are used. Hopefully you kept copies of these documents and you do not need to ask for them.

Be aware of telephone communications. Avoid having job-search telephone (or cell

---

54 Walters, Lillet. *Secrets of Successful Speakers: How You Can Motivate, Captivate, and Persuade.* (New York: McGraw-Hill, 1993), p. 59.

55 See also, Beshara, Tony. *The Job Search Solution: The Ultimate System for Finding a Great Job Now!* 2nd ed. (New York: AMACOM, 2012), Chapter 13, "Looking for a Job When You Have a Job."

phone) conversations in the office, especially in open spaces. Go to a conference room and close the door (keep your voice down), go out into the hallway, outside, or to your car. And keep conversations brief. The wrong set of words overheard by the wrong person will blow your cover.

Inform employers that your search is confidential. In your first conversation with a potential employer (HR or the actual hiring executive), state that you are currently employed and your search is confidential. This puts the topic on the table, and every employer will understand. Do what you can to schedule interviews (of whatever nature) early in the day, during lunchtime, or after working hours. If you happen to be a remote employee, you have more flexibility, but don't take advantage of your flexibility to conduct a job search on company time (and dime). As your search progresses, you will likely need to take a day off (PTO or paid vacation) for longer, more involved interviews. Try not to take too many PTO days too close together. Your sudden disappearances from the office may create suspicion.

Be aware of your attire. If your office dress code leans more toward business casual, showing up in "interview attire" is a sure tip-off. This may require you to change clothes before returning to the office after an interview.

Anticipate that your confidential job search will eventually become known. Plan on your confidential job-search efforts being discovered by your coworkers, boss, or others, despite your efforts. Think about what you will say if a coworker or boss confronts you. Be honest. Get a short answer together and memorize it. Getting caught by surprise and stumbling through an explanation is the embarrassing alternative. You could say: "Yes. I have been approached with another opportunity, and I thought I needed to explore it, just as you would if the circumstances were reversed." The phrase "if the circumstances were reversed" often squelches a detailed conversation on the topic.

Searching for a job while employed is similar to having a second job. Stay organized and understand the time commitment necessary to succeed.

The Age Discrimination in Employment Act

Disclaimer: The contents of this section are not legal advice. They are for educational purposes only. None of the information provided should be construed, interpreted, or acted upon in any way in determining a course of action. If you have or believe you may have been discriminated against due to your age or other protected characteristic(s), seek legal counsel. Do not rely on the information contained in this topic, chapter, or book.

There is little doubt that age plays a role in discrimination in today's job market. However, pursuing legal action for age discrimination is difficult and could make finding a job even more difficult.

This discussion on the legalities of age discrimination will be a brief, generalized overview only. If you believe you have been discriminated against based on your age, seek legal counsel.

The Age Discrimination in Employment Act applies to all workers over the age of forty.[56] It forbids employment practices affecting job seekers or employees due to their age.

Proving age discrimination is difficult. In 2009, the US Supreme Court changed the standard of proof required to prove age discrimination.[57] As a result of that case, a person must now prove that age was *the* determining factor (not just a contributing factor) for not being hired. That level of proof is not easy to gather to make a case.

If you do pursue action, make sure you do so with the advice and counsel of an attorney. Know that if other employers and hiring executives learn that you are pursuing legal action, they may be dissuaded from pursuing you as a candidate. In their view, it's simple: They don't want to hire a future source of legal trouble.

---

56 US Equal Employment Opportunity Commission. The Age Discrimination in Employment Act of 1967, 29 U.S.C. § 621, http://www.eeoc.gov/laws/statutes/adea.cfm (accessed February 8, 2016).

57 Gross v. FBL Financial Services, Inc., 557 U.S. 167 (2009), http://www.supremecourt.gov/opinions/08pdf/08-441.pdf (accessed February 8, 2016).

Part IV

Profiling Your Next Career Opportunity—
The Target Opportunity Profile

You've got to be very careful if you don't know where you are going because you might not get there.

—Yogi Berra[58]

The most important part of a successful search is figuring out what you really want. Your journey to your next career position is about to begin. How will you know you have arrived if you have no idea or sense of direction? You will need to create a Target Opportunity Profile.

For most SEALs, there are five options for their career path. These choices are really quite logical. They are:

- Keep your job and industry the same
- Change jobs, but stay in your industry
- Keep your job and move to another industry

58 "Yogi Berra Quotes," *Baseball Almanac*, http://www.baseball-almanac.com/quotes/quoberra.shtml (accessed February 19, 2016).

- Change both your job and industry[59]
- Start your own business[60]

We'll briefly discuss the considerations for each choice.

The first option is to pursue the same job in the same industry. Factors in pursuing this path include:

- Liking what you do because it fulfills your career passions and goals.
- Being willing to relocate or work remotely, depending upon the local market.
- Identifying new employers is easier due to your familiarity with the industry.
- Networking is easier, too, for the same reason.

The second option is a different job in the same industry. Considerations for this one are:

- Your industry appeals to you, and there are available opportunities.
- You think it is time to repurpose your experience in a new role.
- Your interest in your job function has changed. Perhaps you're bored.
- You feel a need to grow and expand your horizons.

The third option is the same job in a different industry. You may be thinking the following:

- The position and its function fulfill your passion and career goals.
- It may be time for a change due to events and market trends in your previous industry.
- Your interests have changed.

The fourth option is a different job in a different industry. Things you'll need to consider are:

- This is a complete career transition.
- Making this a successful transition will require research into new industries and an evaluation and assessment of career interests.

The fifth option is starting your own business (including consulting and franchises).

---

59 Whitcomb, *Job Search Magic*, p. 34.

60 Claycomb, Heather, and Karl Dinse. *Career Pathways—Interactive Workbook.* (1995), Part 1, "Career Assessment"; Whitcomb, *Job Search Magic*, p. 478.

As a SEAL, you'll encounter these opportunities. Keep in mind:

- Starting a business can be an intriguing idea filled with excitement and rewards for those with an entrepreneurial spirit and a very strong work ethic.

- Getting a business off the ground can carry challenges, obstacles, and formidable financial risk. Avoid the idea of buying yourself a job (especially when it comes to a franchise).

- It is crucial to research everything fully before investing a lot of time and energy (especially for SEALs, who usually have unique risks and other factors involved— e.g., timing in your life, timing in your career, family issues and concerns, financial resources to pay your bills during the start-up period, the consumer market for your business venture, and so many others).[61]

- Having a strong interest or passion for your intended venture is very important. There's nothing worse than buying into a business you end up disliking. It can create havoc in many areas of your personal and professional life.

- For additional advice, seek the counsel of an attorney, accountant, or business advisor(s), and refer to Part XIX of this book: Hire Yourself—Becoming a Consultant or Opening a Franchise.

A Passions Inventory

For SEALs wanting to explore an entirely new career path, those wanting to launch a second career, or those curious about the positions that would be a good match, there is an insightful exercise that can help identify possible career paths by capitalizing upon passions, interests, and/or skills. This exercise can lead to entrepreneurial ventures and exciting new career directions.

In concept, a passions inventory is a reasonably simple exercise, though it could require some deep thought. Take all practicality out of the equation, including an amount of money or education level needed. Let's start: List what you enjoy doing. What captures and holds your attention? What do you find fulfilling or interesting? Ponder what you read, listen to, or watch. Hobbies can be a great source of insight for your list. What are you particularly good at? Make this list before moving to the next step.

---

61 See also, Whitcomb, *Job Search Magic*, p. 478, and Appendix A, "Magic Job Search Tips"; and Patel, Neil. "90% of Startups Fail: Here's What You Need to Know About the 10%," *Forbes*, January 16, 2015, http://www.forbes.com/sites/neilpatel/2015/01/16/90-of-start-ups-will-fail-heres-what-you-need-to-know-about-the-10/#157870a455e1 (accessed February 17, 2016).

Once you have your list compiled, look it over and see if there are any closely related items that could be grouped together. There may be some items that stand alone. That's okay too. From this "grouping" step, you may see one or two interests that stand out, with many closely related items. Take note of these groups—the things that interest you the most.

Now, let's shift gears a bit. What skills have you used in the past that you enjoy using? Perhaps these are the ones you are good at and you know it. These include both your technical skills (your expertise) as well as your soft skills. Sales, listening, and writing are examples.[62] This list could include any number of skills. Write them down.

Now cross-reference the two lists. This is where the fun (but also the work) begins as you make discoveries. Are there any interests, passions, or skills that, in combination or standing alone, you can "commercialize?" In other words, can you use your interests or proven skills and have someone pay you for it, either as an independent consultant, contractor, or employee? Do research about what you discover about yourself, your skills, and your passions. Are they marketable? Don't be too quick to dismiss any possibilities. You could be surprised and have your mind opened to new career avenues.

For example, let's assume you have an interest in writing. You've always seemed to have a knack for it, and over the course of time others have commented that you write well. Further, let's say you have an inherent interest in employment, the unemployment rate, the labor participation rate, and the news commentaries on employment. You read about job hunting, resumes, LinkedIn, and so on. Pulling these passions and skills together equates to becoming an author of job-search books. (By the way, now you know how this author used his passions inventory to open a new career direction in addition to being an executive recruiter!) There could be (and likely is) more than one avenue to pursue as a result of this exercise.

Once you have completed the exercise and have a sense of your passions and applicable skills, you might consider contacting people who may help you evaluate the practicality of your intended pursuit(s). This could take the form of a research interview (more on that later in this book). Set up appointments ("interviews") with professionals who are doing what you think you would like to do. Ask them about what it is like to be in that role or do what they do. Can you see yourself being happy doing their job? And is it financially viable for you?

In addition to the passions inventory, there are several proven tools available that, combined with the inventory, can provide you with an empirical read on your options. These online career-assessment tools include:

---

62 See also, Yate, Martin John. *Knock 'em Dead—The Ultimate Job Search Guide.* (Avon, MA: Adams Media, 2014), p. 23–25.

Myers-Briggs	www.mbticomplete.com/en/index.aspx
Keirsey Campbell	www.keirsey.com/advisorteam/KTS-CISS_bundle.aspx
Career Liftoff	www.careerliftoff.com
Golden Personality	www.goldenllc.com
Structure of Intellect	www.soisystems.com
Strong Interest Inventory	www.cpp.com/products/strong/index.aspx

This discovery process can bring up fascinating things to think about, but be cautious about getting too dreamy. The pursuit of these options may need to be prioritized against more pressing and urgent needs (e.g., income to pay the mortgage). But they should not be dismissed either. It might come down to a matter of timing.

Creating Your Target Opportunity Profile

Using a Target Opportunity Profile to find your next opportunity will help eliminate that "go with your gut feeling" approach to a job search that could lead you astray. Replace that potential derailer with a clearer understanding of what you require from your next opportunity.

A Target Opportunity Profile will:

• Clarify what you are looking for.

• Target opportunities that meet your needs and criteria.

• Allow you to evaluate opportunities by measuring them against it.

• Assist you in preparing various job-search materials such as your brand, elevator speech, resume, cover letters, and LinkedIn profile.

The following brainstorming exercise will identify, prioritize, and profile the important elements of your next career opportunity. The results will affect your career satisfaction, employment longevity, and personal happiness in your next position. Your Target Opportunity Profile will also encourage rational decisions about your career based on a thorough, factual self-evaluation.

Step One—Consider Your Career Wish List

As you begin formulating your Target Opportunity Profile, reflect on your current and past positions. A technique to add tremendous clarity and spark your thinking is a Career Wish List.

On a piece of paper list everything you like about your current and past jobs. This can be anything from the kind of work, environment, and people, to the company's product(s), service(s), company culture, and so on.

Once you have listed the likes, consider the flipside. List those things you dislike about your current and past jobs. And if you have poor feelings about your current or former employer, writing down the negatives may have some added psychological benefits.

For every dislike you list, contrast it with the opposite. In other words, turn that dislike into a like.

Finally, toward the bottom of the page (or on a separate piece of paper), list what you want in your next career position.

The point of this brainstorming exercise is to articulate your likes, dislikes, and desires so you can keep your likes, remove your dislikes, and move toward what you want in your next career opportunity.

Many SEALs find this to be an eye-opening exercise. Many have not taken the time over the course of their careers to deeply consider their likes, dislikes, and desires. They've been busy doing their jobs and concentrating on what's familiar, which is perfectly understandable. But now could be the time for introspection. The conclusion might be to continue on the same path, or maybe change course. Either way, you'll know how to move forward.

Step Two—Identify and Evaluate the Factors

Step Two of creating your Target Opportunity Profile includes considering significant categories. For each category, make notes on anything—don't prioritize your thoughts by order of importance right now. This exercise will stimulate your thinking about the various considerations affecting your profile. Some—though not necessarily all—of the items you listed in your Career Wish List from Step One could appear here.

Equally important, as you think through these considerations, are the knock-out factors for each consideration. These could be: the skills, duties, and responsibilities that you dislike or don't want to use; an industry you don't want to be in; functions you don't want to do; categories of companies you'd rather not work for; and so on. As you profile your next career opportunity, knowing what you don't want is equally as important as what you do want. Based on these knock-out factors, you can eliminate opportunities and better focus your efforts on those opportunities that better fit what you are looking for.

Skills/Strengths

What skills (or strengths) of yours give you energy and fulfillment, or make you feel intellectually alive? Think about the results of your Passions Inventory. You may lose track of time when using these skills. Psychologists refer to this as "flow."[63]

There are a handful of online tools that can help you explore and identify your strengths. They include:

StrengthsFinder 2.0   www.gallupstrengthscenter.com

Dependable Strengths   dependablestrengths.org

Weaknesses/Disinterest

This part of the profiling process is the opposite of the first and has two parts: identifying weaknesses you want to improve and recognizing those weaknesses you're disinterested in.

Part of profiling your next opportunity is being aware of the weaknesses that you want to improve upon and pursuing opportunities for improvement.

On the other hand, areas of weakness you're not interested in are the skills or job functions that are pure drudgery—the ones that make your skin crawl and you would just as soon walk barefoot for a mile over broken glass than do them. With this information in hand, you can filter and avoid opportunities that require you to use a skill you are not interested in using. The point here is that you need to know everything about what you will or won't do.

Industry

What industry do you want to work in? For many SEALs, it is the same industry in which they have the most experience. The key issue is the future viability or health of the industry of interest. A few things to consider: Is there growth? Are there new companies entering the market? What are the legislative/legal considerations, both positive and negative? Are there new innovations or products/services to propel those companies ahead of the competition?

Normally there is a host of disciplines that comprise any industry. As an example, the insurance industry has a plethora of distinct disciplines: property and casualty, life and health, group or individual, and workers' compensation. Inside that, there are carriers, health plans, brokers, consultants, third-party administrators, cost containment, networks, wellness, care management, stop loss, and more.

---

63 Cherry, Kendra. "What Is Flow? Understanding the Psychology of Flow," *Verywell.com*, last updated May 6, 2016, https://www.verywell.com/what-is-flow-2794768 (accessed May 10, 2016).

The point? Feel good about your selected industry's future. Just as you want to grow and prosper, you want that industry to grow and prosper.

Function

What do you want to do in your chosen industry? Your function or role ties into what your unique set of qualifications and overall skillset are.

Based on your qualifications, identify positions that interest you. Does your experience transfer to different positions you have had before? For example, if insurance is your target industry, could your proven skills move you to consider account management, auditing, call center, finance, human resources, management, marketing, public relations, risk management, operations, network development, sales, underwriting, and so on?

Feel comfortable—if not downright passionate—about your function or career position.

Company

What does your next employer look like? There are many considerations that may or may not be of any consequence to you, such as:

- Publicly held
- Privately held
- Large
- Small
- Start-up
- Venture-capital backed
- Aggressive growth strategy
- Standing in the industry
- Products—innovative or commoditized

⚓ As a SEAL, consider companies whose customers and clients more closely match your age. There are a lot of companies whose products and services target consumers over age forty, fifty, sixty, and beyond.

⚓ Some companies have signed a pledge with AARP to be age friendly. The AARP site identifies companies that have signed the pledge.[64] You should review the list for potential companies to target in your job search.

⚓ If your career has been with larger, more prominent employers, consider smaller businesses or even nonprofits. There are likely executives from smaller employers who

---

64 Employer Pledge Program. http://www.aarp.org/work/job-search/employer-pledge-companies/ (accessed November 14, 2016)

would value the experience from "one of the big guys." These positions can be very enjoyable because you can have a significant impact on the business.

🔱 There is a very informative website you can use to identify growing companies and companies potentially gearing up to hire. CrunchBase (www.crunchbase.com) tracks companies that have received venture capital and other investment capital. It's generally accepted that when a company receives funding, there is often a correlation to hiring.

🔱 There are job boards that are designed for the fifty-plus crowd. They include: www.boomerplaces.com/jobs/, www.workforce50.com, and jobsover50.com, among others. These sites identify companies that are age friendly.

Location

Where do you want to work? List the cities, states, or countries where you could go. If you don't want to move, write down the town or city you're in now. If you are willing to move, consider these factors:

- What areas of the country would interest you?
- Are there particular cities you would like to live in?
- Are there family motivations to stay or move?
- What areas of the country would you not relocate to?
- Are international locations a possibility?
- Do you have limitations on commuting time?

Title

How important is a title to you? For some SEALs, it has limited importance. For others, it matters more. Here are some things to consider:

- What titles would be acceptable to you now that you are a SEAL?
- Is there a minimum title level you want?
- Is there a titling concept you prefer (e.g., business development versus sales)?
- What about a titling "prefix" (Senior Account Manager, Executive Vice President)?

Work Setting

What type of work environment is best for you? List the characteristics of the environment you would like. For example:

- Do you want an office environment?
- Would you like a home-based office?

- Are you willing to travel? If so, how much?
- Do you prefer a larger corporate environment?
- Do you like smaller, more entrepreneurial companies and their setting?

Compensation and Employee Benefits

For some SEALs, this topic will require serious thought. What would you (realistically) like to be paid? What benefits are important to you? Some issues to consider include:

- What is your minimum salary requirement? How flexible can you be?
- If variable compensation is a component to your overall compensation package, at what level or potential additional earnings?
- Will variable compensation affect your minimum salary requirement? Can you accept a lower salary but be open to more incentive-based pay?
- Employee benefits: Will your family be added to your benefits? Or, as a SEAL, can you be put on your spouse's insurance plan and thereby not need benefits from a new employer? If so, this can lower your cost of hire to a new employer.
- Do you need specific benefits based on a loved one's needs?
- Vacation: How many weeks would you prefer?
- Retirement programs: 401(k), pension, or another type?
- Are perks such as a company car, health- or country-club membership(s), paid parking, and so on, a realistic expectation for your desired position?
- What is your overall threshold? Are you willing to be reasonable?

Reward System

How do you want to be rewarded for positive performance? What kind of reward system would be motivating to you? Compensation immediately comes to mind, but there are other considerations that could apply to you, including:

- Increases in salary
- Bonuses
- Stock options or equity
- Private recognition from management, peers, vendors, customers
- Public recognition—awards banquets
- Increases in vacation and PTO in lieu of compensation increases

- Flexibility to work remotely—not having to be in the office

- Any other motivational factors that could be woven into a professional setting

Career Purpose

What role will this next position play in your overall career? Contemplate what you want this position to accomplish. Here are some other suggestions:

- What is the career goal for this position?

- What skills do you want to continue to utilize?

- What skills do you want to improve or learn?

- Is stability a factor for you (which may be affected by how big or small the company is)?

Other Considerations

These previous categories are by no means exhaustive. In fact, you have likely thought of a few considerations unique to your situation. Add them to your list, including aspirations as well as other factors that truly matter to you.

Step Three—Complete Your Profile

Now, compile your completed profile. Prioritize your responses in terms of importance. The list will likely contain points from both Steps One and Two. For example, your top priority might be to work for a smaller company (from the *Company* section). Your second priority may be to earn a minimum salary of $80,000 (*Compensation/Benefits* section). And your final goal may be to move to Charlotte (from the *Location* section) where your daughter lives so you can be closer to grandkids (*Other Considerations* section).

Pull it all together. Create your Target Opportunity Profile by listing what's most important in the order that matters to you.

Another technique to help you prioritize is a point system. Start with one hundred points and assign a value to each item on your priority list, which will help clarify the importance of each item.

As your job search progresses, your Target Opportunity Profile will likely undergo revisions—take the time to do that when necessary.

Use your Target Opportunity Profile to check out possible career positions. Next, you'll figure out how to use your Profile to formulate questions for potential employers, based on your career priorities.

Questions to Ask in Interviews

Once you have created your Target Opportunity Profile, use it to formulate questions to ask employers to ensure the position aligns with your criteria, needs, and priorities. For example, if you determine that you prefer to work remotely, you may ask an employer, "Does this position require me to be in the office, or can I work from a home office?"

For some SEALs, setting up a Target Opportunity Profile can involve serious reflection and can take a while. That's fine—but be careful not to get stuck. For others, the process is relatively quick.

The true purpose of your Target Opportunity Profile is to help you know what you are looking for. You will make more rational career- and job-related decisions by consciously comparing opportunities to your Target Opportunity Profile.

A STORY OF INSPIRATION

Getting Started

For thirty-eight years, I worked for one company. It was a monumentally emotional challenge coming to grips with leaving the only company I had ever worked for. I was fifty-five years-old, youthful minded, in great shape, with plenty of gas left in the tank. I was high on the organizational chart with a multi-national corporation but swept aside from the succession plan due to tenure/age. So, with my wife and faith by my side, I resigned, moved back to my hometown, and started a job search.

I started talking with people about the challenges of getting a job while being in my mid fifties. I had zero experience in finding a job and never had a resume in my life! It was recommended I get a career coach. After my first meeting, I was amazed with his depth of knowledge and how much I didn't know.

The initial hurdle in my search was I did not know what I wanted to do. The only thing I did know was what I didn't want to do. I used this reverse engineering to profile my "target employer" in a small to medium sized business community.

Trust the Experts

I originally thought I could put a resume together and easily find work based on the nameplate of my previous employer. I found this simply not true!

Finding a career coach was a very smart move for me. He connected me to others, especially a resume writer who helped tremendously. This team took me through the rigors of understanding my accomplishments, who I was professionally at this point in my career, and where I could possibly go.

If you are not absolutely positive you know what you're doing in a job search, get expert guidance. Find them, trust them, and allow them to be critical.

Network

I spoke with many people who exited a company after long careers who expected doors to fly open, which will not happen! You must network, network, network!

Having worked in a very closed corporate culture, I had to re-learn how to meet people who could help open doors and learn how the real business world worked in contrast to the closed culture of a big multi-national corporation.

I spent a tremendous amount of time attending networking and social events of all kinds to meet as many people as possible while being astute to protocols, social mores, and sharpening my communication skills.

Some Final Advice

Embrace the change that is happening or you will not survive. Sharpen your technology skills. Read as many books and local business publications as possible to understand what's going on in the business world. Even humbly change your swagger to align with local business culture.

Battling the emotional highs and lows, dealing with self-doubt as an over fifty year old are all part of the process and part of the journey. You'll be okay.

When you do find work, whether in consulting or a job, it is very easy to expect entitlements because of your vast experience, past level of authority and degree of age/maturity. This is quite the contrary. You are the low person on the totem pole with zero tenure or experience with the company. They might have hired you for your experience, but once you are in the door, you must sweat to prove your worthiness.

For me, I secured a senior sales and operations position with a mid-sized company. I am extremely happy with this position. If I can make this transition, so can you!

R.D.
Age 55

Part V

Essential Job-Search Topics and Tools

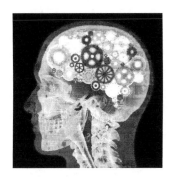

There isn't a ruler, a yard stick or a measuring tape in the entire world long enough to compute the STRENGTH and capabilities inside you.

—Paul Meyer[65]

Understanding the Employer's Mindset

There are a variety of motivations that prompt an employer in the commercial market to hire. However, the true essence underlying each motivation comes down to two reasons: to make or save the company money.[66]

Your career experience as a SEAL tells you that the sole reason a job exists in a company is to contribute to the profitability of the company.[67] The level of your performance in your job must add value. Depending upon the job, you can help an employer's bottom line by:

1. **Making the company money (generating new revenue)**—This can be achieved through sales, client retention, product development, and so on. You make money for the company by generating new revenue and keeping the revenue the company has.

65 "Unleashing Your Genius," *Quotes from the Masters*, http://finsecurity.com/finsecurity/quotes/qm121.html (accessed May 27, 2015).

66 Whitcomb, *Job Search Magic*, p. 274.

67 See also, Yate, *Knock 'em Dead*, p. 17.

2. **Saving the company money (productivity improvements)**—This is achieved by increasing productivity, increasing or creating operational efficiency, saving time, making others' jobs easier (more efficient or effective), and so on.

There are many ways to generate revenue or save money for a company. Revealing them to an employer establishes or increases your value (ROI). Here is a short list to get you thinking:

- Think about your duties and responsibilities from previous positions and how they translate to this position's ROI.
- Implement an improvement that saves time, improves efficiency, and/or streamlines workflow.
- Improve company image and branding.
- Open new sales-distribution channels.
- Improve a current product, or develop a new one.
- Expand business/sales through existing accounts.
- Enhance competitiveness through best practices, innovation, and so on.
- Improve client retention.
- Improve company culture, morale, and/or employee retention.

Whatever value you bring to the table will be directly related to your professional brand, skillset, and value proposition (which we'll discuss in detail later).

Knowing What an Employer Wants in an Open Position

Since an employer's purpose when hiring is to make or save money, how can you get inside an employer's mind and determine what he or she is looking for in the position (or position types) you want? The answer is simple, but you'll need to do a little research:

1. **Gather Job Postings.** Go online and collect some well-written job postings for a job you are qualified for and would enjoy. Websites such as www.indeed.com and www.SimplyHired.com are rich resources.

2. **Create Your Own Master Job Description.** Call the document your "Master Job Description" (or anything else creative you want, i.e., "My Dream Job").

   A. **Title.** What words do employers use? These titles will likely reflect jobs you target when you search. The key is to use these same or very similar words on your resume, business cards, LinkedIn profile, cover letters, elevator speech, and so on.

B. **Skills, Duties, and Responsibilities.** Examine the job postings for skills, duties, and responsibilities that are common or frequently mentioned and note how often they are used.

C. **Match.** Tie these skills to your experience. The more you use the keywords from the skills and titles in your written and verbal communications (including your resume), the higher your chances are of getting noticed because you make yourself directly relevant to an open job position.[68]

Once it's done, familiarize yourself with your Master Job Description. What would you look for to fill this position if you were the hiring executive? Congratulations—you are now thinking like an employer!

Now that you're thinking like an employer, *relate* or *match* how you have generated or saved money with former employers while keeping your Master Job Description in mind. This is a crucial step because you'll be tying an executive's hiring needs to your own experience and accomplishments. Use the insights you discover in your resume, LinkedIn profile, cover letters, emails, and so on.

Matching Experience and "Word Clouds"

There is a very clever way to match your experience with what an employer is looking for in a position(s). "Word clouds" are images made out of large words interspersed with smaller ones (you may have seen them). Some websites that create word clouds include www.wordle.net, www.tagcrowd.com, and www.worditout.com. Here's how you use this concept to your advantage:

Copy the description electronically, go to one of these sites, and put the description into the space provided. Give it a second and *voila*, you have a word cloud. Pay particular attention to the larger words. Those are the words that are mentioned most frequently or deemed more important by the website's programming. Write down these larger words, and make sure they appear on your resume, LinkedIn profile, and other communications. For example, let's say you see terms like "customer experience" or "client success" in the word cloud. You reread the full job description you used to make the cloud and conclude

---

68 Ibid., p. 32.

that these terms mean account management (to you). Therefore, you need to change your terminology to match the language employers are using (at least for that employer).

This technique works especially well when you have an actual job description on a position you are pursuing (and will also be referenced as the "word cloud technique" later on).

Transferable Job Skills and Professional Qualities

Start by doing what's necessary; then do what's possible, and suddenly you are doing the impossible.

—St. Francis of Assisi[69]

Transferable job skills come in two forms. First are the technical skills (expertise or ability) of your profession.[70] If you are an engineer, you know engineering things. An accountant has skills related to accounting, and so on. We will refer to these skills as your "hard" skills.[71]

Hard skills can be transferable by convincing an employer that your skills can be easily repurposed and still be valuable to the employer.[72] An oversimplified example is an accountant using math skills in a new role.

The second type of transferable job skills used in most professional-level positions are "soft." They are in addition to your technical expertise. It is an arena where many SEALs, based on experience, can edge out younger job seekers.[73]

---

69 "Doing What's Necessary, What's Possible, and What Seems to be Impossible," *The Recovery Ranch*, October 29, 2011, http://www.recoveryranch.com/articles/necessary-possible-impossible/ (accessed May 27, 2015).

70 Yate, *Knock 'em Dead*, p. 19.

71 Ibid., p. 32.

72 Leanne, Shelly. *How to Interview Like a Top MBA: Job-Winning Strategies from Headhunters, Fortune 100 Recruiters, and Career Counselors.* (New York: McGraw-Hill, 2004), p. 104.

73 Adams, "Older Workers, There's Hope"; Society for Human Resource Management, "Executive Summary," p. 6.

Here is a list of some sought-after soft, transferable job skills (not listed in any order of preference):

- **Communication Skills (writing, listening, and speaking)**—This is the most frequently mentioned skill employers desire.[74] Many younger job seekers are deficient when it comes to writing skills in particular, and if written communication is important in a position, a SEAL can gain the upper hand.[75]

- **Analytical Ability (problem solving)**—This is your ability to view a situation, identify issues, evaluate relevant information, and implement a plan.[76] A SEAL can gain an advantage here because SEALs know what facts and circumstances to look for to solve a problem. Too many younger people have become reliant on Googling for an answer rather than using critical thinking.[77]

- **Time Management (prioritizing)**—This is your ability to devote the appropriate amount of time to a task.[78]

- **Innovation (out-of-the-box thinking)**—This involves harnessing creativity, reasoning skill, and what you've learned in life to solve problems.

- **Collaboration (teamwork)**—This means working with others toward a shared goal.[79]

- **Management (people leadership)**—This is your ability to gain buy-in or respect from a team, lead by defining goals and methods, and manage and guide a group toward shared goals or production targets.

- **Customer Focus (customer service)**—This is your understanding that your employer must please and serve customers to be successful.

- **Business Understanding (business acumen)**—This is your ability to understand the business realities and influences in the market and how they affect your employer.

Closely aligned with the concept of transferrable job skills are Professional Qualities. Here is a list of professional qualities sought after by employers:

---

74 Hansen, Randall S., PhD, and Katharine Hansen, PhD. "What Do Employers *Really* Want? Top Skills and Values Employers Seek from Job-Seekers," *Quintessential Careers*, http://www.quintcareers.com/job_skills_values.html (accessed May 27, 2015).

75 Adams, "Older Workers, There's Hope"; Wilson, CJ. "Why Millennials Are Often Poor Writers," *LinkedIn Pulse*, December 29, 2014, https://www.linkedin.com/pulse/millennials-cant-write-because-texting-writing-cj-wilson (accessed February 9, 2016).

76 Yate, *Knock 'em Dead*, p. 23–24.

77 Hamodia, "Why the Texting Generation Can't Get a Job," February 2, 2014, http://hamodia.com/2014/02/02/texting-generation-cant-get-job/ (accessed February 9, 2016).

78 Yate, *Knock 'em Dead*, p. 25.

79 Ibid., and Hansen and Hansen, "What Do Employers *Really* Want?"

- **Honesty**—This is the foundation of every employment relationship. An employer must be able to trust you and respect you as a professional for the employment relationship to last and flourish.[80]

- **Positive Attitude**—Make no mistake, this is a big deal, especially for SEALs. Employers gravitate to people who show enthusiasm, energy, and a positive outlook.[81] Displaying a positive attitude gives you a competitive advantage and is a career management strategy. A positive attitude is *that* important.

- **Interpersonal Relationships**—Employers want employees who can get along with other potential coworkers. They avoid those who "rock the boat" and do not fit the culture.

- **Work Ethic**—Employers seek employees who put forth their best effort at all times. They seek out employees who are motivated and internally driven. They want employees who are persistent and passionate about their jobs.[82]

- **Dependable**—Employers seek out employees who will show up on time. They want to rest assured you will "be there" for the company. If you are a remote employee, they want to know you are working even though you are out of sight. According to one survey, this is where a SEAL could have an advantage.[83]

- **Willingness to Learn**—This is your intellectual flexibility, curiosity, and your ability to not get stuck in your own ways (thinking that you're "stuck" could be an age bias for some hiring executives). As a SEAL, you must be willing to learn about new technology and improve your skills (and discover new ones). As you well know, markets change. Business changes. Your industry changes. You must be open and pursue opportunities to learn and change.[84]

These skills are the "bigger" ones. Other transferrable skills and professional qualities include: accuracy, ambition, assertiveness, competitiveness, initiative, motivation, organizational skills, presentation skills, quality management/improvement, tact, and the ability to work under pressure, among many others.

🦭 Some SEALs have difficulty identifying transferrable skills and professional qualities

---

80 Hansen and Hansen, "What Do Employers *Really* Want?"

81 Victoria Andrew, "The Power of a Positive Attitude," *Kavaliro Blog,* Kavaliro Employment Agency, May 23, 2013, http://www.ka-valiro.com/the-power-of-a-positive-attitude (accessed June 8, 2015).

82 Hansen and Hansen, "What Do Employers *Really* Want?"

83 Adams, "Older Workers, There's Hope."

84 Hansen and Hansen, "What Do Employers *Really* Want?"

because they have not had to think about them for a long time. They've been doing their jobs, not thinking about the skills they've been using to succeed. That's normal. There are a couple of ideas that can help you expand upon your transferable skills (and perhaps your professional qualities). Think about your last position or two. What skills did you use? Now, think how you can break down those skills into smaller elements. For example, let's say you were in sales. What does that skill really entail? What's really going on there? Plenty!

- Research on target industries
- Persuasive verbal skills
- Closing
- Identifying decision makers
- Articulation of value proposition
- Negotiating

- Cold Calling
- Presentation skills
- Follow up
- Email marketing
- Overcoming objections
- And so much more . . .

By identifying these skills, you can open yourself to other opportunities and employers who are searching for job seekers with these skills.

Once you have identified your transferable job skills and professional qualities, there are several things you can do with this valuable information. Your skills and qualities could be:

- A component of your branding message.
- Woven into the summary section of your resume and LinkedIn profile.
- Mentioned in a Core Skills, Experience, or Accomplishments section of your resume.
- Used to write success stories.
- Used in cover letters and emails.
- Used as a part of your elevator speech.
- Used in networking conversations.
- Used in interviews.[85]

The key to using these skills in your job search is to interpret those skills and your unique professional qualities as valuable and match them to solve an employer's need. For the most impact, use your accomplishments as evidence of your transferable skills and professional qualities. Provide success stories of the skills and qualities in action. (More on

---

85 Yate, *Knock 'em Dead*, p. 30.

that in a moment.) Providing this connection is especially crucial when you are changing career paths.

Transferable soft skills and professional qualities cut across industry lines. For example, an employer will always value an employee with a strong work ethic whether they are an accountant or a zookeeper.

The Sum Total

Here is the magic formula for becoming a sought-after SEAL:

Your Technical Skills (your ability)

+ Your Transferable Job Skills/Professional Qualities

+ Your Track Record of Success

= A Qualified Candidate!

Once you are a qualified candidate, you must then differentiate yourself from other qualified candidates.

Success Stories

There is no passion to be found playing small—in settling for a life that is less than the one you are capable of living.
—Nelson Mandela[86]

A success story is a description of a career-related event that provides evidence to the hiring executive regarding your skills, abilities, competencies, and motivation to succeed at the job for which you are interviewing. In a business context, success stories are your case studies supporting your professional value proposition.

Writing success stories is often a walk down your professional memory lane. Think about projects, challenges, and problems you have dealt with over your career, or even during a normal workweek. Think in terms of identifying, preventing, or solving a problem.[87] How did you do it? What was the positive result of your success story?[88]

It's highly recommended to compose several success stories. By writing them down and reviewing them, you will be able to more easily remember them, use them in written communication, refer to them in networking conversations, and have responses to interview questions (especially for behavior-based or performance-based interviews).[89] These success stories will support your brand and qualifications.

86 Nsehe, Mfonobong. "19 Inspirational Quotes From Nelson Mandela," *Forbes.com*, December 6, 2013, http://www.forbes.com/sites/mfonobongnsehe/2013/12/06/20-inspirational-quotes-from-nelson-mandela/ (accessed May 27, 2015).

87 Whitcomb, *Job Search Magic*, p. 289.

88 Ibid., p. 119.

89 Ibid., p. 391–402, Chapter 15, "Score Points in Behavioral Interviews."

Writing success stories is an easy and fun exercise in self-discovery. Here is a simple formula that seems to work well:

C. Challenge (Situation, Task)

A. Action

R. Result[90]

Describe the challenge you faced or task you were assigned. Describe the plan of action you took and the positive result. Try to quantify the results with numbers or percentages whenever possible. A positive recommendation from your boss will work, too.

When you write your success stories, do so with different skills and competencies in mind (transferable job skills and professional qualities). For example, stories that reflect true technical ability, analytical thinking, communication skills, leadership, and so on, including complementary combinations of skills and competencies within a single story.

When preparing for interviews, read the job description (if you have one) and think about what the employer is looking for (in terms of hard skills, soft skills, and professional qualities). Then create some success stories that align with what you believe will be asked of you in the interview.

🔥 As you write your success stories, include some that attack age biases. For example, stories that reflect that you had to learn new things, or stories that show commitment, enthusiasm, and energy because you routinely came in early to work to meet a project deadline.

🔥 As you think about and write your success stories, keep them as recent as possible, and never time stamp your stories ("Back in the late 1990s . . ."). You want to illustrate that you have the skills the hiring executive needs and you will use them to get the job done.

Having success stories prewritten, rehearsed, and at your disposal will help differentiate you from other job seekers regardless of age (using the persuasion principle of scarcity) and give you a competitive advantage. You will stand out as being prepared, as opposed to those who choose to wing it.[91]

See Appendix for a Success Story Worksheet and samples of success stories.

---

90 Safani, Barbara. "Tell a Story Interviewers Can't Forget," *TheLadders*, http://www.theladders.com/career-advice/tell-story-interviewers-cant-forget (accessed May 29, 2015).

91 Whitcomb, *Job Search Magic*, p. 119.

Branding

Always remember: a brand is the most valuable piece of real estate in the world; a corner of someone's mind.

—John Hegarty[92]

It is imperative that you craft a professional brand that announces to the marketplace your distinct talents and what you represent. The process of branding is discovering who you are, what you are, your unique abilities, and communicating them through various mediums to your network or target market. To help you in crafting a brand, this section and the following one on the elevator speech work in tandem.

There are numerous benefits of creating an impactful brand, including:

1. You will differentiate yourself from other job seekers and gain a huge advantage.

2. You create the initial impression employers have of you.

3. You can more quickly convey your value.

4. You can more easily match your skills and value proposition to the employer's needs.

5. You can better determine which opportunities to pursue.

🔥 The drawback of not having a professional brand is simple: You become a commodity. There is no perceived differentiation from other job seekers. You cannot command a premium and have reduced leverage when it comes to compensation. Perhaps worse, employers will determine for themselves what they want to see in you. They will cast

92 Design Aglow contributor Jamie VanEaton, "10 Ways You're Building a Fantastic Brand," *Design Aglow* (blog), February 3, 2015, http://designaglow.com/blogs/design-aglow/16728432-10-ways-youre-building-a-fantastic-brand (accessed May 28, 2015).

you in a light based on their own conclusions, which may not be the message you want to communicate,[93] (especially regarding age-related biases). For a SEAL, this situation can be hazardous during a job search. Having a succinct brand immediately redirects the hiring executive's thinking away from biases and toward what you can do for them.

Perhaps the biggest benefit of creating a professional brand as a SEAL is the self-awareness of your unique skills and experience, and recognition of how they work together to create an impact. You will project the value of your abilities more clearly, resulting in a job that's a good match for your skillset. Branding can also help you set your sights on what you want your future career to be.

Additionally, when your networking contacts know your brand, they are much more likely to advance it for you through referrals, recommendations, and so on. When the right opportunities come along, you become top of mind (because of your brand).

The professional-branding process requires introspection and thoughtful reflection. In some cases, thinking through your branding can be both an emotional and a professionally enlightening event.

Think of it this way: As a SEAL, your goal is to connect with employers both intellectually (you can do the job) and emotionally (you're a good fit). Having a well-crafted, professional brand helps on both levels. You must be perceived as the right candidate; and through branding, you are better able to align yourself to an open job position.

Keep in mind that the effectiveness of your brand is determined by the connection that exists between what the brand claims and what it can actually deliver. In other words, you must be able to prove and quantify your professional brand (through experience and accomplishments). Failing to do so will have disastrous results. Don't oversell your brand and capabilities.

Create a succinct brand. Think of it, in analogous terms, as a tagline or a theme that will be the foundation of your job search.

To help determine your brand, ask yourself some questions:

1. What am I good at or an expert in?
2. What have I been recognized for?
3. What is my reputation with others (subordinates, peers, senior management)?
4. What have been my strong points in past job reviews, including notable and consistent comments (if applicable)?
5. What differentiates me from others with the same job?

---

93 Ibid.

6. What professional qualities do I have that make me good at my job?

7. What are the professional achievements I am most proud of?[94]

The answers to these questions and the thoughts they provoke are essential to forming your brand. Now, synthesize the answers and thoughts into single words or short phrases that capture the concept of your responses. Here are some examples:

Sales
Consistently exceeding sales goals. Award-winning sales professional.

Operations Management
Dedicated to improved operational efficiency through effective leadership.

Account Management
Client-minded problem solver focused on client satisfaction and retention.

ERISA[95] Lawyer
Protecting ERISA fiduciaries from the Department of Labor.
A branding statement could also be a few separate descriptive words or phrases:

Process Improvement • Lean Six Sigma[96] • Turnaround Specialist

Marketing • Advertising • Public Relations

When you come to this book's Resume and LinkedIn sections, you will see a few examples of branding in action.

---

94 Ibid., Chapter 5, "Communicate Your Value Via a Career Brand."

95 "Employee Retirement Income Security Act"; see "Frequently Asked Questions About Retirement Plans and ERISA," US Department of Labor, http://www.dol.gov/ebsa/faqs/faq_consumer_pension.html (accessed July 8, 2015).

96 A process that resolves problems while reducing costs; see "What is Lean Six Sigma?" Go Lean Six Sigma, https://goleansixsigma.com/what-is-lean-six-sigma/ (accessed July 8, 2015).

Word Choice

As you consider your branding, be sensitive of the words you use. Some words are age relevant, such as:

Tenured   Mature
Veteran (Vet)   Extensive
Battle-tested   Seasoned
Senior   Considerable
Hardened   Grizzled
And so on . . .

Naturally you will need to use these words as you present yourself, e.g., *Senior* Vice President. But as you create your brand, resume, LinkedIn profile, and other written communications, substitute other words whenever the terms above aren't strictly needed.

Branding Is Important

As a SEAL, creating and deciding on a brand is extremely important. Take the necessary time to reflect on this (which will vary from person to person). What you decide your brand is will form the foundation for much of what will follow in your job search.

You may discover several skills and abilities to showcase in your brand. But for the purposes of your job search and networking, focus on promoting your top one or two choices only. Mention other skills, which will happen naturally during interviews. The purpose of branding is to get you known for your value (and not for preconceived age biases), get you in the door, and differentiate you from other job seekers.

Elevator Speech

The only people who don't need elevator pitches are elevator salesmen.

—Jarod Kintz[97]

The elevator speech is a critical component of your job search. By definition, an elevator speech is "the 30-second speech that summarizes who you are, what you do and why you'd be a perfect candidate."[98] In essence, it is your personal commercial.

The purpose of your elevator speech is to grab the listener's attention, quickly provide relevant information, and initiate conversation. A crisply delivered elevator speech is a differentiator. While others may struggle and stumble, you will be able to concisely inform the listener about your professional value proposition (brand).

Develop a handful of variations, depending upon the situation, including all forms of networking, interviews, association and industry conferences, and strictly social gatherings. Here are some tips on crafting your elevator speech (some examples can be found at the end of this section):

1. Know your target audience. This single factor will give your speech the most impact. For example, if you're targeting a CEO position and you will be speaking to members of the board of directors, you want your elevator speech to include statements of vision, direction, strategy, profitability, and shareholder value (especially for publicly traded companies).

---

97 "Jarod Kintz Quotable Quote," Goodreads, http://www.goodreads.com/quotes/1234580-the-only-people-who-don-t-need-elevator-pitches-are-elevator (accessed May 28, 2015).

98 Collamer, Nancy. "The Perfect Elevator Pitch To Land A Job," Forbes, February 4, 2013, http://www.forbes.com/sites/nextavenue/2013/02/04/the-perfect-elevator-pitch-to-land-a-job/ (accessed May 28, 2015).

If your target position is in operations, and the hiring executive is the COO, you want your elevator speech to contain concepts such as efficiency and operational savings.

Finally, if your target position is in sales, and the hiring executive is the director or vice president of sales, you want your elevator speech to contain information about new business sales and sales-goal attainment.

2. Know what your value proposition is. This is where your branding comes into full play. Identify as precisely as possible what you offer, what problems you can solve, and what benefits you bring to an employer.

As you think of your value proposition, also think of achievements and statements that could attack an age bias, such as instituting a piece of new technology or taking on a project that required extra effort or extra hours at work. Weave these tidbits into your speech.

3. Outline your speech. Give yourself some time to ponder the ideas and concepts you may include—it isn't necessary to start drafting the speech immediately, but begin with notes reminding you of your bottom-line message. Don't worry about proper grammar or complete sentences yet. The objective is to gather concepts and ideas first, so make sure you don't edit yourself. Refer back to the concepts you used to form your brand.

4. Write your speech. Now that you have ideas and concepts about yourself to promote, begin drafting your speech's initial version. Here is a formula to help you:

A. Identify yourself by function.

B. Include a statement regarding your value proposition as a professional (what problems you solve).

C. Mention accomplishments or proof statements that support your value proposition as a professional.

D. End with a call to action in the form of a subtle invitation to have a conversation.

5. Tailor the speech to them, not you. As a rule, people are tuned into WIIFM (What's In It For Me?). So, refer to what you have written to ensure your message addresses their potential needs.

Instead of: "I am a talent-acquisition professional with ten years of experience working for financial services companies," you could say: "I am a talent-acquisition professional with a demonstrable history of identifying and recruiting top-level sales talent." Hear how much more impactful that is—and how much more effective the branding would be?

Using terminology that focuses on the benefits you bring will get the listener's attention.

Benefit-focused terminology persuades the listener that you have the skills and track record of success necessary for the job.

6. Practice, practice, practice—and solicit feedback. Read your speech aloud. Then tinker with the words (the goal is to have a speech that sounds authentic and confident). Now, memorize the speech and rehearse it. Consider practicing in front of a mirror and record it on your smartphone. This could feel odd, but with practice, your delivery will be conversational (one of the keys to making it effective). Smiling while saying the words will increase the impact of the speech. Project your voice so those listening will clearly hear and understand.

When you are ready, try the speech out on some of your friends. Make eye contact, smile, and deliver your message with confidence. Afterward, ask them what they think. If their response doesn't line up with what you want from your speech, the speech still needs work.

7. Prepare a few variations. You'll want to have a different speech for a colleague than for a personal friend at a social gathering. Sometimes you'll have just fifteen seconds for your speech, and in other situations you might have a full minute.

With your key points in mind, create different forms of your speech, depending on the situation. Much of this will happen naturally as you speak with people (as long as you remember your talking points).

Set up shorter and longer versions with your computer's word-count function. It's generally accepted that you can comfortably say about 150 words in sixty seconds.[99]

Remember, the purpose of an elevator speech is to quickly inform the listener of your value proposition as a professional and begin a conversation. Putting these tips into action is the real trick. Check out these websites that contain scores of elevator speeches (not all are designed for job seekers) for a variety of industries: www.improvandy.com and www. yourelevatorpitch.net.

Examples

Note that the last two examples include statements and achievements that attack age-related biases.

Employee Benefits Account Management Professional
    "I am an employee benefits account management professional who helps businesses

---

99 Walters, *Secrets of Successful Speakers*, p. 59.

control their health care and insurance costs. My expertise is in medical self-funding and population health management. I have a documented track record of retaining existing clients; in fact, over the last five years I have a 96 percent retention rate with my client base. I want to make a career move to an organization looking to expand its market share and retain business in the self-funded arena."

Sales Management Executive: Focus on mentorship

"I am a sales management executive, and my forte is training and mentoring sales professionals to achieve higher sales production. During my twenty-year career, I have turned around underperforming sales professionals and trained and mentored several award-winning sales reps. On average, over the course of my career, my sales teams have met or exceeded their group production goals more than 85 percent of the time. I'm looking to make a career move to an organization that needs sales leadership to grow sales and market share."

Operations Professional: Focus on customer satisfaction, commitment, and work ethic

"I am an operations professional, and I specialize in improving efficiencies and expense reduction. In fact, during my last position I was asked to create protocols to decrease customer response time. My team and I put in seventy-hour weeks for six weeks, and the program decreased customer response time by more than 65 percent. Our customer experience scores soared! I am looking to make a career move to an organization that desires to save money by making the client experience better and operations more efficient."

Accounting: Focus on cost savings and technology

"I am a CPA who specializes in identifying cost-saving opportunities in manufacturing. With my former employer, I partially designed and implemented new technology and saved more than $750,000 over five years. The technology increased cash flow through accounts receivable and decreased collections. I want to make a job change to a manufacturing organization that can benefit from my abilities to use technology and identify cost-saving opportunities."

Elevator speeches can emphasize different value propositions. If you discover a particular skill is in demand with a prospective employer and you have it, change your speech to focus on that skill.

🦶 Having a well-rehearsed and impactful elevator speech is important for a SEAL. It portrays you as someone who thinks things through, focuses the listener on your brand and accomplishments, and creates a positive first impression that helps to diminish age-related biases a hiring executive might initially have.

Business Cards

High expectations are the key to everything.

—Sam Walton[100]

Having a business card during a job search is a necessity. Circumstances will present themselves where providing a resume is awkward or inappropriate.[101] Getting a business card should be toward the top of your to-do list, in order to make your job search a success.

There are four different approaches to the standard three-and-a-half-inch by two-inch business card for a job search: traditional business cards, networking business cards, resume business cards, and infographic business cards.

To determine the best business-card approach for your needs, consider this key factor: Which would be best received by a networking contact or the hiring executive for your level of position?

It's easy to get sidetracked when creating business cards, especially the networking, resume, and infographic versions. Resist that urge. Don't overanalyze. Once you choose one of these types, just remember: the messaging behind your brand and elevator speech and the information on your card must match.

A solid case can be made for getting two sets of cards to use in different settings: traditional for truly social events, and a networking or resume card for job networking events.

100 Bergdahl, Michael. *What I Learned From Sam Walton: How to Compete and Thrive in a Wal-Mart World.* (Hoboken, New Jersey: John Wiley & Sons, 2004), p. 39.

101 Leslie Ayres, "Why You Need a Resume Business Card," *Notes from the Job Search Guru: A Career Advice Blog*, March 16, 2009, http:// www.thejobsearchguru.com/notesfrom/why-you-need-a-resume-business-card/ (accessed November 4, 2015).

Here are examples for each kind of job-search business card:

Traditional Business Cards

This business card is simple in design. It contains only your name, city of residence, (street address is optional), telephone number(s), email address, and LinkedIn profile address. It is used for information-exchange purposes only.

Bob Johnson, CSFS®

1340 Main Street   (816) 987-6543 (C)
Blue Springs, MO 64015   Bob.johnson1340@gmail.com
(816) 123-4567 (H)   www.linkedin.com/in/bobjohnson

Networking Business Cards

Networking business cards contain the same key contact information as a traditional card, except this variety also has a title and a concise statement regarding your career focus and unique value proposition or brand.[102] Remember to keep the messaging consistent among your networking card, elevator speech, LinkedIn profile, resume, and so on. There is some room for variation, but the theme of these job-seeking tools must align.

Award-Winning, Population Health Management
Sales Professional

Bob Johnson, CSFS®

National Sales Executive

1340 Main Street   (816) 987-6543 (C)
Blue Springs, MO 64015   Bob.johnson1340@gmail.com
(816) 123-4567 (H)   www.linkedin.com/in/bobjohnson

---

102 Hansen, Randall S., PhD. "Networking Business Cards: An Essential Job-Search Tool for Job-Seekers, Career Changers, and College Students When a Resume Just Won't Do." *Quintessential Careers*, http://www.quintcareers.com/networking-business-cards/ (accessed November 4, 2015).

presentations, and so on. And this can heighten the interest of a hiring executive or HR recruiter, if they should take the time to check them out. This is all good. But the purpose is to get you noticed and create interest; the resume, on the other hand, has a different function.

The Tactical Uses of a Resume. A resume is a completely customizable document. It can, and should be, tailored to specific positions and for particular companies. It allows you to present yourself in a creative way apart from the format limitations of a LinkedIn profile. You can format your resume to showcase your achievements, skills, knowledge, and competencies in a way that appeals to one hiring executive offering one position. When done properly, a customized resume can more easily be used by the hiring executive as a guide for the interview. This is a tactical advantage. Your customized resume plays to your strengths because you designed the format and strategically placed the information to differentiate you from other job seekers. You should feel comfortable about how it represents you, as well.

Resumes Still Required. Most employers, either by direct request of the hiring executive or through the HR department, still require job seekers to submit resumes, via online applications or by email, as an accepted and necessary business practice. If resumes are so passé, why are they still a requirement in the application and interview process? The truth is they are *not* passé. This is not to say that there could be some pockets in some industries that are moving away from using resumes. However, for the vast majority of industries, and for most positions within those industries, the need for a well-written resume lives on.

What a Resume Is Not

🦭 You are not writing an autobiography![107] Too many SEALs put too much historical information on a resume. It's easy to have that happen. You start writing and remembering, and all of a sudden, you have a resume that is a blizzard of words. Hiring executives most often refuse to read resumes like that. It's too much work. A resume must be an informative marketing piece—easy on the eyes with plenty of white space. As a SEAL, you already have forces that could be working against you; don't add to the list of possible negatives with a poorly formatted, poorly written resume.

🦭 Occasionally, SEALs will use personal pronouns ("I" or "we") on their resumes. Don't do this. When you write your resume, the rules of proper sentence structure and

---

107 Claycomb and Dinse, *Career Pathways*, Part 3.

punctuation are relaxed. However, you must convey complete thoughts with good use of action verbs, which will remove the need for personal pronouns.

◢ Time Is of the Essence

Most hiring executives generally spend between five and twenty seconds when first looking at a resume. So, assume your resume will not have much time to make an impact. If you're perceived as valuable to the company, you're in! If not, you're out! An employer must be able to quickly determine your potential value.

How can you make the most of those precious seconds? Showcase your most impactful qualifications and accomplishments on page one of the resume, upper half. The title of your resume, branding words/phrases/statement, the first sentence of your summary, and the first bullet point or two of your first showcase section create the biggest impact. By then, time's up! (More on showcase sections in a moment.) If these grab the interest of the employer, you get the next few seconds and perhaps more. This is another reason to use the word cloud technique—key words and phrases will appear on your resume and "speak" to the hiring executive. Use this technique to capture any buzzwords that employer uses. Titling, branding, and a showcase resume have become important and popular for their ability to keep your resume in the executive's hands even longer. Once you have created initial interest, then the hiring executive will generally look at your current/previous employer, your position/function, length of employment, and successes.

Your Resume Is Your Marketing Brochure

Your elevator speech is your commercial. Your success stories are your case studies. Your resume is your marketing brochure.

Your resume is frequently the first formal presentation of your professional credentials to a hiring executive. Take the time to write an impactful resume. In order for your resume to provide that positive first impression, make sure that it:

- Has a clean, professional appearance. Develop a document with plain, simple language. Also be sure that the use of font size, bold print, lines, headings, spacing, bullet points, and so on, is consistent throughout. Any graphics and shading must be readable. Your resume must have a "wow" factor.

- Has a title. This will announce the professional qualifications to follow in the resume's body.

- Has branding words or a branding statement. Either of these will help present your value proposition.

- Contains accurate contact information. Be sure your contact information is up-to-date.

- Features a concise, professional summary. This should highlight your background and give information to support your professional value proposition.

- Lists core competencies or qualifications. Showcase your strongest skills, abilities, experience, education, and special knowledge.

- Lists achievements. State what separates you from the pack.

- Honestly represents your background. It is estimated that "more than 80 percent of resumes contain some stretch of the truth."[108] Be honest about your background and achievements. If an embellishment is discovered, you lose your integrity and credibility, and it will be extremely difficult to regain it. Your employer (whether current or prospective) won't trust you. And if others find out you embellished your information, that will make it harder still on your reputation.

It is perfectly acceptable, and encouraged, to write a generic form of your resume. You can modify this generic form for specific opportunities that you pursue. Just remember what form of your resume you use with specific employers!

Use of Keywords

Keywords are specific words or phrases that reflect your experiences and abilities; they are frequently buzzwords or terms-of-art. As a SEAL, you are undoubtedly familiar with the keywords of your industry (terms-of-art) and your abilities. Make sure they appear prominently on your resume. Examples include "P and L" and "ROI" for commerce. Others include "pull-through strategies" for sales and marketing or are specific to a particular industry (like a professional designation). Your resume must contain certain keywords to get the employer's attention and communicate that you are qualified for a particular position. The importance of keywords on your resume cannot be overstated.

Keywords can include the following:

- Position title
- Professional designation

---

108 Bucknell Career Development Center, "Creating an Effective Resume," Bucknell University, http://www.bucknell.edu/documents/ CDC/Creating_An_Effective_Resume.pdf (accessed February 19, 2016).

- Skills, knowledge, core competencies
- Industry terms-of-art (and abbreviations)
- Employer names (past or present)
- Licenses, certifications
- Location (city and/or state)
- Software and technologies you're familiar with
- Education (school names and degrees)

It can be impactful to connect a keyword to an accomplishment, whenever possible. For example, *Client Retention—maintained a client retention rate of 94 percent for the last four years.*

Resume Formats

The three fundamental variations are: Chronological, Functional, and Showcase.

- The **Chronological** format is the most traditionally used resume format. A job seeker's experience in the work world is listed in reverse chronological order. This format emphasizes duties and responsibilities with accomplishments listed under each employer. Jobs, as well as managerial and other responsibilities are grouped by title and company, with dates of employment. This is a common format frequently used by tenured professionals with consistent work experience in one field or position type.[109]

- The **Functional** format emphasizes skills and qualifications to strategically sell experience that may align to the needs of the employer. A job seeker's experience is divided into a skill-based section that demonstrates qualifications, training, education, and specific accomplishments, and a reverse chronological listing of employment including company name, title, and dates (toward the end of the resume). This format works well for those with gaps in employment and those whose career has involved several employers.[110] Most job seekers should be careful when considering the Functional format since employers strongly favor a Chronological or Showcase resume.

- The **Showcase** resume is a growing trend that has developed over the last several years and combines the best features of the Chronological and Functional formats.

---

109 Yate, *Knock 'em Dead*, p. 45–46.

110 Ibid., p. 46.

For most experienced professionals and executives (whether they have a more diverse employment background or not), this format is worth serious consideration. The concept is to showcase your best professional selling points—qualifications, industry knowledge, and achievements—immediately in the top half or top two-thirds of the resume's first page. Work and education is then listed in reverse chronological order just like a traditional chronological resume. Using this format, you are allowed to be selectively repetitive. Some of your showcase items can appear again in the chronological section of your resume. This way, the hiring executive knows where and when you learned or achieved your showcase qualifications.

The Dateless (Ageless) Resume

A dateless resume can be any of the resume formats just mentioned, and is void of any dates . . . employment, education, volunteer work, everything. Doing things this way is not recommended because a hiring executive will immediately notice and probably think "Oh my goodness, he [or she] must be ancient!" Raising red flags or emphasizing age biases is not the first impression you want to make. However, there is one viable alternative.

Provide dates going back only fifteen to twenty years, and leave off other dates. This concept can be used with any resume format. You can also group employment beyond your chosen time frame as a subsection to your experience section without using dates. There's a risk the hiring executive may still conclude you are a "tenured" professional. But it is a middle ground if you want to omit some dates from your resume.

Parts of a Resume

No matter what form of resume you choose, each has certain parts in common that appear in the same places or serve the same function. These are:

Identification/Contact Information

This section appears at the top of your resume and includes your name (with notable professional designations), address (providing actual residential address is optional), telephone (home and/or cell), as well as an email where you can be reached. Including your LinkedIn profile address is optional. Omitting your residence address is a new trend. This is acceptable, but still include city and state.

No photos should appear on your resume (unless it is required in your industry). If an executive or interviewer wants to know what you look like, they can check out your LinkedIn profile.

Email Address

Your email address must be professional. Some advocate that you create an email account tailored for your job search and the email address should be supportive of your branding (e.g., engineeringexpert@xyz.net). Avoid this. Many hiring executives view this "technique" with chagrin.

🐦 Make sure your email address does not contain any reference to your age or year of birth, (e.g., Johnsmith1961, or sheila57).

There are several professional formats you can use instead:

- jsmith@xyz.com
- john.smith@xyz.com
- smithj@xyz.com
- john@xyz.com
- johns@xyz.com
- johnsmith@xyz.com

If you need to, add your lucky number, area code, ZIP code, or other number prior to the @ symbol.

Title

By titling your resume, it announces what the resume is going to describe so the reader doesn't have to scan the entire resume to determine your professional background. Be reasonably specific with your title. For example, "Senior Health-Care Sales Representative," "Casualty Field Claims Professional," "Vice President of Operations."

The title of your resume should be nearly identical to the titles in your Master Job Description. The title should also align with your LinkedIn profile, business card type(s) you choose to use, and at least share a theme similar to your elevator speech.

Branding Statement

Your branding statement should appear under your resume's title. This could be either a statement or a few descriptive words that relate to or support your brand. Some examples include:

Dedicated to improving sales through effective leadership.

Process Improvement • Manufacturing Efficiency • Strategy

Objective Statement

The objective statement has fallen out of favor for seasoned professionals and should not be used except for special circumstances (a significant change in career path, industry sabbaticals, and so on).

When using the objective statement, ensure it clearly states your purpose for pursuing a position with the employer. The resume material following the objective should support, as much as possible, that you are able to perform the objective.

Using an objective statement properly means keeping it short. Avoid such nebulous phrases as:

- "Opportunity for advancement" or "Advance my career"
- "Challenging opportunity"
- "Utilizing my experience"
- "Professional growth"
- "Increase in compensation"

State the benefits you can *bring* to the employer—not the benefits you *want* from the employer.

Summary

The summary brings together the experiences of your career into the present. It is a recommended section for seasoned professionals and should be a short paragraph with an overview of your most important job experience, technical or professional proficiencies, traits, and accomplishments.[111]

🐦 There is a fine line to walk when writing your summary. You want to communicate your experience without coming across as old. Here you have some judgment calls to make. Let's say you have over twenty-five years of experience. You could summarize that as "over fifteen years of experience." It is a true statement that communicates experience without emphasizing your age. Or perhaps you have thirty-five years of experience; you could represent that you have "over twenty years of experience." The choice is ultimately yours. The concept is this: it is permissible to generalize your tenure in the summary section of your resume.

A summary section can have several different names, including:

- Career Description

---

111 Ibid., p. 47.

- Career Summary

- Professional Qualifications

- Profile

- Qualifications

- Summary of Qualifications

The summary could contain some of the following information: level of responsibility, skills and responsibilities, potential contributions (as seen from the employer's perspective), and highlights of top strengths and accomplishments. It emphasizes key information detailed later in the resume. Be sure to mention languages, special degrees, and other noteworthy skills. The summary acts much like an executive summary section of a long document or white paper. A simple three-part formula to help you create an impactful summary is:

1. A statement regarding your function or title, possibly including a reference to tenure.

2. A statement identifying your technical abilities and qualifications. Accomplishments can be included here as well.

3. A statement regarding your transferable job skills and/or professional traits.

For example:

Position: Senior Accountant
Statement regarding function or title: A detail-oriented CPA with over fifteen years of experience.

Statement regarding technical ability or qualifications:
Proven ability in financial forecasting and analysis, audit, reconciliation, tax law, and evaluating and consulting with clients regarding business investments and opportunities.
Statement regarding transferable job skills/professional qualities: Conscientious, self-motivated, and service-oriented professional who enjoys client interaction.

Complete Summary:
A detailed-oriented CPA with over fifteen years of experience. Proven ability in financial forecasting and analysis, audit, reconciliation, tax law, and evaluating and consulting with clients regarding business investments and opportunities. Conscientious, self-motivated, and service-oriented professional who enjoys client interaction.

After you have this foundation in place, you can add to it as your discretion dictates. An effective summary section should be concise and to the point. Many professionals make the mistake of making a summary too long. By using this three-part formula you will be crafting a solid, impactful summary.

⅃ Consider adding a short second paragraph that attacks a potential age bias.

For example:

Avid racquetball player. Competes in weekly league and occasional weekend tournaments.

This example attacks the biases of poor physical appearance, and being tired and out of shape. This kind of information can appeal to a younger hiring executive because it lends insight into you as the person, not just the professional. Younger executives tend to want to know this type of information, and it can also establish your cultural fit.

Core Competencies

Almost all resumes for experienced professionals and executives should have a Core Competencies section. Although there are likely hundreds of competencies and skills that could be listed, as a rule keep it to no more than three columns of five, totaling fifteen.

Your competencies should fall into one of the following major areas: technical ability (what you are good at), communication skills, leadership, analytical thinking, teamwork, and time management. These tend to be the broad skills most employers seek.[112]

This section can have other titles, such as:

- Abilities
- Core Strengths and Expertise
- Key Skills
- Skills
- Signature Strengths

Showcase Section(s)

If you elect to use a showcase-style resume, the next section (or two, depending on your circumstances) can be your showcase section. Although you have a lot of discretion on titling and content, the key is to make this section substantive and succinctly impactful. Use lists and bullet points to make the information easier to read.

---

112 Ibid., p. 48.

Possible titles for showcase section(s) include:

- Achievement Summaries
- High-Impact Contributions
- Notable Performance Highlights
- Distribution or Vendor Partners
- Expertise
- Languages (Foreign or IT)
- Marquee Clients
- Product Knowledge
- Recommendations
- Sales Awards

🐦 If any of the items listed in a Showcase section are date- or time-sensitive, consider whether to include that item. If you do decide to, don't time-stamp it.

Employment History

🐦 The employment history section covers work experience for the last ten to fifteen years. List employers in reverse chronological order. Work experience beyond fifteen years can be listed at the end with single sentences or as a grouping of employer names. Don't include dates in either case.

Begin with details on the most important items: current company/employer's name, your title(s), and dates (in years). List what the company's official name is now, even if it was purchased or merged after you began work there, e.g., "GlobalOutlook (formerly Global SpyGlass)." Many company names or initials could make it hard to figure out what the company is or does. Therefore, use a sentence that encapsulates the company's position, earnings, products, and/or other unique qualifiers. As an example: NAME OF COMPANY: *"A worldwide manufacturer of high-end personal-care products with $134M in annual sales."*

Most times, be sure to list the company name first, and only once. This reduces the likelihood employers will think you have job-hopped when you have not.

Next, follow the company name with your title. If this title is in-house and hard to understand, include a translation or generic job title. For example, you can substitute "Purchasing Agent" with "Product Specialist/Purchasing Representative" if that makes things easier for those who aren't a part of your industry or company. Providing a functional title educates the hiring executive about your actual function and role. If you held multiple titles with the same employer, mention a date next to each to show promotions or advancement within an organization.

🔸 The use of certain titles from your work history can date you. For example, Human Resources used to more generally be known as "Personnel." Adjust your titling to currently used terms.

Job Scope Description

For each position, write a four- to six-sentence description of your duties and responsibilities (what you did). This could include information regarding the dimension and scope of the position, function, staff size, geographical reach, budget, reporting relationships, departments, and so on. Here's an example:

Professional Experience
GlobalOutlook (formerly Global SpyGlass), Anytown, Anywhere 20XX–Present

Regional Sales Executive
Promoted to revitalize underperforming Northeast sales territory. Developed new business channels on a regional and national basis. Reestablished relationships with client base. Products included enrollment technology, analytics, and predictive modeling, among others.

This section can have other titles, such as:

- Career Experience
- Employment Background
- Experience
- Professional Experience
- Relevant Experience
- Work Experience
- Career Narrative

Accomplishments

An accomplishment is a detailed account of success regarding the duties and responsibilities of your job. Make sure your *specific* successes are crystal clear to the hiring executive if you use this technique (as you should).

🔸 As a SEAL, accomplishments are vitally important to your job search. It has been said that qualifications often get you an interview, but rapport is what gets you the job[113] (as well as accomplishments). Identify and quantify your accomplishments, and use bullet points for easy reading.

Accomplishments:

- Clearly demonstrate ability to improve a company's efficiency or bottom line.

- Emphasize positive work outcomes with dates, percentages, numbers, and so on.

- Display why an organization will find you effective.

- Translate your value by showing your performance in similar circumstances.

Accomplishments focus on quantities, improvements, and results from an organization's perspective. How did you make or save the employer money?[114] Or how did your actions lead to a beneficial result?[115] Highlight accomplishments with $, %, or # as applicable to enhance credibility (as long as it's true!).

Accomplishments can be a separate "showcase" section on your resume. Or, especially for chronological resumes, they can be a subsection to each position you have held.

What Accomplishments Get Employers' Attention?

Remember that employers generally hire with two main goals: to make or save money.[116] The more obvious your accomplishments appear to achieve either goal, the more powerful the accomplishment is. The following list of accomplishments can help spark ideas as you contemplate your own (refer back to Understanding the Employer's Mindset):

Accomplishments

1. Increased revenue
2. Awards, rankings against your peers, production numbers
3. Process improvement that saves money or time, increases efficiency, makes work easier
4. Improved company image, branding
5. New distribution channels opened for sales
6. Product improvements, product development

---

113 Guest Author (Bob Bozorgi), "Qualifications Will Get You an Interview, but They Won't Get You Hired," The Undercover Recruiter (blog), http://theundercoverrecruiter.com/qualifications-will-get-interview-wont-get-hired/ (accessed February 19, 2016).

114 Whitcomb, *Job Search Magic*, p. 274.

115 See also, Safani, "Tell a Story."

116 Whitcomb, *Job Search Magic*, p. 274.

7. Business/sales expanded through existing accounts

8. Anything that enhances competitiveness

9. Improved client retention

10. Improved company culture, morale, employee retention

The following is a very short list of positions. Under each are ideas from which accomplishment statements can be created. Although a particular position type may not apply to you, adopt this mindset when considering your accomplishments.

ACCOUNTING

- Design and implementation of cost controls and quantifiable results
- Optimization of business output through software or other technology
- Application of tax laws

ACCOUNT MANAGEMENT

- Client retention
- Contribution to sales growth (upselling)
- Key account responsibilities

ENGINEERING

- Financial outcomes from new designs or products
- Patents awarded or pending
- Projects managed and financial results

EXECUTIVE-LEVEL MANAGEMENT

- Measurable increases in revenue, profits, EBITDA,[117] and/or ROI
- Leadership regarding strategic planning, long-term business development
- Mergers, acquisitions, joint ventures

HEALTH CARE

- Increase in quality of patient care, with detailed results

---

117 "Earnings before interest, taxes, depreciation, and amortization"; see Arline, Katherine. "What is EBITDA?" *Business News Daily*, February 25, 2015, http://www.businessnewsdaily.com/4461-ebitda-formula-definition.html (accessed February 19, 2016).

- Increased impact of outreach services, with their results
- Attainment and maintenance of stringent regulatory requirements
- Reduction in re-admittance

HUMAN RESOURCES

- Success in recruiting personnel
- Employee retention
- Improvements in employee benefits and cost reduction

MANUFACTURING

- Increases in production and worker productivity
- Improvements in safety
- Reductions in operating costs and overhead expenses

RETAIL

- Increases in gross revenue, profit margins, and market impact
- Improvements in inventory turnover, speed to market
- Reductions in inventory, operating, and personnel costs

SALES

- Sales honors, awards, percentages over quota, rankings against peers
- Increases in revenue, profits, and market share
- New national accounts sales
- Expansion into previously undeveloped territories and markets

TECHNOLOGY

- Development of new technologies and their financial results
- Detailed results of implementation (e.g., revenue increases, cost reductions)
- Patents awarded
- Timely systems conversion, integration

Action Verbs

Using action verbs is important when writing your accomplishments.

🐦 Accomplishments are significant for any job seeker, but this is especially true for a SEAL. You need to emphasize recent accomplishments on your resume, which can make you appear younger, more in touch with today's business, more in tune with the challenges of your industry, and so on.

EDUCATION

Provide educational background starting with your most advanced degree or major, and remember to include the university or college name. Abbreviations are fine: BS, BA, MS, MBA, and PhD. Use the same fonts for school and company names. If you do not have a full degree, include those details by mentioning what degree you pursued and the number of years or semesters attended (or percentage completed, if available). As a SEAL, include your education at the bottom of your resume unless you feel there is grounds to move it up or it is customary in your industry to have it appear early on a resume.

🐦 It is acceptable to omit the dates from your education. However, if you have recently completed an advanced degree (e.g., Executive MBA), after many years of completing your undergraduate degree, including dates could have a beneficial impact—in this case, showing that you are not intellectually stale or resistant to learning new things.

Other Credentials

The following sections can add depth to your resume. You may not need every section below—just those representing strong qualifications for you.

1. Affiliations/Associations

Affiliations and associations can be impactful on a resume by indicating your involvement in your industry and the community. Include groups you are a member of. An Affiliations section may look like this:

American Marketing Association

Society for Human Resource Management

Health Care Administrators Association

American Red Cross

2. Appointments

Appointments are offices you held (generally in the last five years) and demonstrate involvement in both professional as well as civic organizations. Include only professional or significant charitable organizations—Middle School Bake Sale Organizer doesn't count! An Appointments section may look like this:

> Chairperson, American Management Association, 20XX–20XX
>
> Paul Harris Fellow, Rotary International, 20XX–20XX
>
> Regional Director—Rapid Response, American Red Cross, 20XX–20XX

3. Awards/Honors

This section reveals achievements, awards, and honors not connected to your career. Include accolades from college activities, professional service organizations, volunteer work, and so on. Examples include:

> Team Captain, Central Minnesota University Softball Team
>
> Up and Comer Award, Rotary International
>
> Volunteer of the Year, American Red Cross

4. Languages

The world is getting smaller. Being fluent or proficient in a foreign language can be a significant differentiator, depending on the kind of positions you are pursuing. A Language section generally appears this way:

> Fluent in Portuguese
>
> Proficient in Italian

5. Licenses

List all licenses relevant or required in your industry or the job description for your desired position. Don't list a real estate license if you aren't seeking a position in that industry.

6. Professional Training and Designations

🔨 If you have achieved an industry designation or significant certification in the last five years, list the date of achievement (use your professional judgment on how far back you go, but five to seven years is likely the limit). This helps dispel biases that you are intellectually stale, inflexible, or stuck in your ways. For designations and certificates outside your chosen time frame, you can elect to omit the date of achievement. However, if your designations and certificates have been continuously achieved over the course of years, you can choose to keep the dates as a reflection of your progression and desire to stay current with the industry.

Professional Training sections generally appear this way:

Dale Carnegie Corporate Strategy—20XX

Managing for Excellence, sponsored by the American Management Association—20XX

Selling!, a five-day program sponsored by Kaufman and Gentry Sales Training—20XX

If you've done more than five courses, just note the types along with who sponsored them, such as:

Completed sales, management, and computer skills programs sponsored by the American Management Association

7. Technical

Understanding technology is becoming indispensable in today's world. Include your proficiencies with technology here. A Technical section generally appears this way: C++, Cisco UCS, Commvault, VMWare, Windows Servers, Microsoft Active Directory, WordPerfect, PowerPoint, Microsoft Office, Microsoft Outlook, Adobe Acrobat

Use of Recommendations on a Resume

When properly used, recommendations, testimonials, and endorsements appearing on a resume can be impactful. These affirmations capitalize upon the persuasion principle of social proof mentioned earlier in this book.

Due to a resume's limited space, a statement of recommendation must be short, relevant, and direct. Consider putting recommendations in quotes, italics (for effect), or both. Testimonials and endorsements from others are more powerful than what you say about yourself.[118] Some recommendations can double as accomplishments (as in the first example below).

---

118 See also, Matt, "Brag Book."

For the recommendation to be effective, the person providing it must be identified by name and title. Get permission from this individual prior to including their recommendation on your resume.

Examples:

> *"Increased average profit on special orders by 17 percent, resulting in thousands of dollars in new revenue."*
>
> Letter of Appreciation from Elizabeth Jones, VP of Accounting

> *"Bonnie is a valued member of our team. Her expertise in cost-accounting strategies positively impacted our bottom line."*
>
> Elizabeth Jones, VP of Accounting

You can also close a resume with an impactful recommendation:
"Katy was clearly the most client-focused account manager we had on our team!"
> Bob Johnson, Vice President of Account Management

Information NOT to Be Included on a Resume

- Never put "References Upon Request" on a resume. It is naturally assumed that you will furnish references if asked.

- Never give reasons why you've left any of your previous jobs.

- Never list your career's salary progression on a resume.[119]

- 🦅 Avoid putting personal or legally protected characteristics on your resume. This would include age, marital status, length of marriage, ages of children, race, state of health, Social Security number, height, weight, and so forth. Some SEALs mistakenly include this information to be proactive in dispelling certain age biases. For example: "State of Health—Excellent." Although the motivation is admirable, omit this unnecessary information. It's generally accepted that much of it is often deemed irrelevant for hiring as a matter of law.

---

119 Yate, *Knock 'em Dead*, p. 48.

Testing the Impact of Your Resume

After your resume is complete, see if it makes the initial impression or impact you want. Give your resume to two or three objective colleagues who you can trust. Ideally, you want colleagues from the business world who hire as part of their job. Ask them to take ten to fifteen seconds to look at your resume. What do they remember?

If the "impact" points of your resume are not what you want them to remember, you may need to revise it. On the other hand, if your review group remembers what you want to communicate with your resume, it's ready for use! Have your "quality control" group do the same for your other job-search documents or online profiles, as well.

QR Codes

You can add a QR code to your resume (QR codes were discussed in the business card section). They can add a unique visual appearance to your resume and be a differentiator. Generally speaking, QR codes tend to appear on a resume either in the upper right-hand corner of the front page or bottom of the second page, but there is no placement rule. Use discretion and make sure the code does not distract from your resume's overall appearance.

Attaching Your Resume to Your Online Profile

When it comes to attaching your resume to your online profile (we'll discuss profiles in detail later), you have some decisions to make. If you are currently employed, it is recommended that you not attach your resume. Doing so opens you up to some awkward questions from your current employer or informs your employer that you are always on the market for other opportunities. Having a complete online profile should be sufficient to inform a hiring executive or recruiter about your professional qualifications.

If you are unemployed, it is entirely permissible to attach your resume. The potential exists that your resume could be printed off or electronically forwarded to a hiring executive by an internal-company recruiter or any other source. However, you may want to skip attaching your resume to your profile, as a conscious strategy. Remember, communicating with hiring executives is pivotal to your job-search success, and the desired goal. A well-constructed online profile creates interest on its own, triggering the hiring executive to communicate with you. After communication starts, then send your resume directly to the recruiter or executive. Not attaching your resume could be an effective job-search strategy that helps you get more inquiries, emails, and conversations.

Dealing with Employment Gaps on a Resume

Employment gaps on a resume can create anxiety. Fortunately, most employers understand the difficulties of the job market, the negative employment dynamics of a particular industry, or have experienced a gap in employment themselves.

Judgments regarding employment gaps have eased. According to a study conducted by CareerBuilder, 85 percent of hiring executives and human resource professionals "are more understanding of employment gaps" than they once were.[120] While there is an understanding that bad things can happen to good people, there are limits. If your gap is reasonably short and you have been productive in some way using or enhancing your skills, the gap is generally overlooked. But the longer the gap, the more negatively an employer views that gap. This can be scary.

Studies indicate that once your employment gap exceeds six months, your job search can become precipitously more difficult.[121] The unstated reasoning is if you have been unemployed for over six months nobody wants to hire you (especially when you have been actively looking for a job).

So, how can you get around this potential judgment and frightening statistic? Take comfort—there are ways:

- On your resume, list your dates of employment in years only, not month and year. It is honest and can cover your gap. However, be forthright if asked about actual dates of employment.

- Use a Showcase resume. Do what you can to emphasize your strongest selling points upfront on your resume. Hopefully, this will focus the employer on your skills, knowledge, and achievements and not on the employment gap.

- Become a consultant. You obviously have ability, so try to secure paid opportunities to advise companies in your area(s) of expertise. Show that you have remained active and are using your skills. (Refer to the Hire Yourself—Becoming a Consultant or Opening a Franchise section for more information.)

- Volunteer for a worthy cause or association. It may not be complicated work, but it is using your skills in some capacity. Examples: As an accountant, do the bookkeep

---

120 CareerBuilder, "Employers Share Encouraging Perspectives and Tips for the Unemployed in New CareerBuilder Survey," news release, March 21, 2012, http://www.careerbuilder.com/share/aboutus/pressreleasesdetail.aspx?id=pr684&sd=3/21/2012&ed=12/31/2012&siteid=cbpr&sc_cmp1=cb_pr684_ (accessed February 19, 2016).

121 O'Brien, Matthew. "The Terrifying Reality of Long-Term Unemployment," *The Atlantic*, April 13, 2013, http://www.theatlantic.com/business/archive/2013/04/the-terrifying-reality-of-long-term-unemployment/274957/ (accessed February 19, 2016).

ing for a nonprofit you are passionate about. As a sales professional, volunteer to do fundraising.

- Continue your education. This does not necessarily mean getting an MBA (although, clearly, that would be advantageous), but begin working toward a substantive industry designation.

- Be very cautious of the word "sabbatical" on a resume. It is an unusual word to the commercial private business sector. It raises the suspicion of long-term unemployment.

- Depending upon the circumstances, briefly address the employment gap in your cover letter. It could be that you chose not to look for a job, but you must have a very good reason. This information would come under the "Additional Information" section. (See Cover Letters and Other Written Communications.) Keep it brief.

- As a last resort, use the Functional resume format.

- Above all, never sacrifice your integrity.

Creating Your Own Resume

To grow, you must be willing to let your present and future be totally unlike your past. Your history is not your destiny.

—Alan Cohen[122]

An employer reads a resume for content and draws conclusions based on its appearance. If you are comfortable with your word-processing skills, create your own resume. If you are uneasy about creating your resume, seek out a resume-writing service. It is recommended to find a resume writer who is certified by a resume credentialing organization such as:

- CPRW (Certified Professional Resume Writer), designation sanctioned by the Professional Association of Resume Writers (www.parw.com).

- NCRW (Nationally Certified Resume Writer), designation sanctioned by The National Resume Writer's Association (www.thenrwa.com/).

- CARW (Certified Advanced Resume Writer) and CMRW (Certified Master Resume Writer), designations provided by Career Directors International (www.careerdirectors.com). They also have awards for resume writers.

Websites for the first two organizations provide a listing of resume writers by location. Designations of some kind (there are others) offer some assurance that the writer has the prerequisite level of expertise to create a resume to your satisfaction.

There are other talented resume writers who do not have a designation. Simply ask to see samples.

---

122 "Self-Limiting Beliefs," *Quotes from the Masters*, http://finsecurity.com/finsecurity/quotes/qm103.html (accessed February 19, 2016).

Most professional- and executive-level resumes cost from $250 to $1,000, or more. A well-written, professional resume is one of the best investments to make in yourself. The Appendix contains a few sample resumes for your review.

A resume is vitally important to a job search, and it must be well-constructed and impactful. However, it will not get you a job. It can only help you get noticed, help you get an interview, and then operate as a guide for hiring executives to ask questions during an interview. Don't overemphasize its role.

Too many job seekers erroneously believe that a "great" resume is the ticket to a great job. It's not! A resume is a tool . . . one of several.

Spend the appropriate amount of time building an impactful resume, but don't grind over its creation. Normally four to six hours spent on a resume, if you do it yourself, is adequate. Any more than that may be busywork disguised as being productive. Don't make this mistake. You have other important things to do! Once your resume is satisfactorily written, move on to other important tasks that can move your job search forward, such as networking, proactively marketing your professional credentials, and getting interviews. These tasks will shorten your search more than grinding over a resume's tiny details.

LinkedIn

Active participation on LinkedIn is the best way to say, 'Look at me!' without saying 'Look at me!'

— Bobby Darnell[123]

Please Note: LinkedIn changes its format, features, appearance, and functionality regularly. These changes can enhance the LinkedIn experience as well as restrict some of its functionality. This topic on LinkedIn was current at the time of writing.

LinkedIn is clearly the most used and effective professional networking website on the planet, with more than 467 million members in two hundred countries.[124] In the United States alone there are more than 128 million members. At present, LinkedIn adds "more than two new members every second."[125] "Over 25 million profiles are viewed on LinkedIn daily."[126]

In today's job market, it is imperative to your job search to have a complete and robust LinkedIn profile. In a recent survey of the HR professionals and recruiters, 65% cite a lack of skilled candidates in the market as the largest obstacle to hiring.[127] Human talent is the

123 Knyszweski, Jerome. "How to Use LinkedIn as a Student—And Nail That Dream Job," *LinkedIn Pulse*, April 28, 2015, https://www.linkedin.com/pulse/how-use-linkedin-student-nail-dream-job-jerome-knyszewski (accessed May 28, 2015).

124 Smith, Craig. "133 Amazing LinkedIn Statistics." Last updated November 17, 2016, http://expandedramblings.com/index.php/by-the-numbers-a-few-important-linkedin-stats/. (accessed November 28, 2016). *See also*, Smith, Craig, DMR, "200+ Amazing LinkedIn Stats" (Last Checked/Updated October 2016) http://expandedramblings.com/index.php/by-the-numbers-a-few-important-linkedin-stats/. (Downloaded November 28, 2016).

125 "About LinkedIn," *LinkedIn Newsroom*, https://press.linkedin.com/about-linkedin (accessed May 29, 2015).

126 Geoff, "Top LinkedIn Facts and Stats [Infographic]," (blog), *We Are Social Media*, July 25, 2014, http://wersm.com/top-linkedin-facts-and-stats-infographic/ (accessed May 29, 2015).

127 Jobvite 2016 Recruiter National Survey www.jobvite.com (accessed November 17, 2016)

lifeblood for every company. But there is a war for talent in the market due to the lack of well-qualified candidates.

Being in a candidate-driven job market is a good environment when you are looking for a job (should you be fortunate enough to be in that environment when searching for a new job). But how can you maximize being discovered for open opportunities? Answer: Your LinkedIn Profile.

LinkedIn is the overwhelming resource (87%) most frequently used by HR recruiters to identify and evaluate candidates.[128] By having a complete and robust LinkedIn profile, you significantly increase your chances of being contacted by an HR recruiter. In fact, "Users with complete profiles are 40 times more likely to receive opportunities through LinkedIn."[129]

Having a complete LinkedIn profile is **imperative** to your job search. A complete profile (its strength) and your discoverability through LinkedIn are connected. LinkedIn has five levels of profile strength:

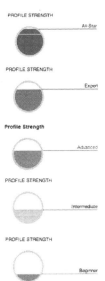

1. All-Star

2. Expert

3. Advanced

4. Intermediate

5. Beginner

Having an "All-Star" profile is a significant advantage in your job search. If your profile is incomplete, it won't register as high in searches as those that are more robust.[130] What makes your profile complete?

• Your industry and location

• An up-to-date current position (with a description)

• Two past positions

• Your education

128 Ibid. *See also*, Smith, Craig, DMR, "200+ Amazing LinkedIn Stats" (Last Checked/Updated October 2016) http://expandedram-blings.com/index.php/by-the-numbers-a-few-important-linkedin-stats/. (Downloaded November 28, 2016). This source indicates that 94% of recruiters use LinkedIn to vet candidates.

129 Foote, Andy, Why You Should Complete Your LinkedIn Profile, (December 7, 2015). https://www.linkedinsights.com/why-you-should-complete-your-linkedin-profile/ (Accessed November 22, 2016)

130 Reynolds, Marci. "How to Be Found More Easily in LinkedIn (LinkedIn SEO)," *Job-Hunt.org*, http://www.job-hunt.org/social-net-working/be-found-on-linkedin.shtml (accessed June 4, 2015).

- Your skills (minimum of 3)
- A profile photo
- At least 50 connections"[131]

It cannot be overemphasized. LinkedIn should be your primary online professional networking and job-search tool.

LinkedIn makes it easy to network, connect with colleagues in your industry, be contacted for opportunities, stay informed on industry issues and trends, research companies, and be alerted about job opportunities.

In many cases, your LinkedIn profile could be the first impression a hiring executive has of you. A strong profile is a must. It gives you credibility.

Before we begin discussions on specific topics, and if you already have a profile, go to your Profile page and turn off your Network Announcements. This white box is located down the right column of your profile and is normally located across from your Summary.

Notify your network?

No, do not publish an update to my network about my profile changes.   (No)

By doing this, your network will not be inadvertently alerted regarding changes you may be making. You can reactivate the announcements later if you choose.

Use of Keywords

It is estimated that there are more than a billion searches annually on LinkedIn.[132] Companies and recruiters search keywords to find candidates (in addition to people who search for a particular company or person).

Keywords are specific words or phrases that reflect your experiences and abilities, and are frequently buzzwords, or terms-of-art. You are undoubtedly familiar with the keywords of your industry (terms-of-art) and your abilities. Examples include "P & L" and "ROI" for commerce. Others include "pull-through strategies" for sales and marketing, or are specific

---

131 Ibid.

132 Stephanie Frasco, "11 Tips To Help Optimize Your LinkedIn Profile For Maximum Exposure and Engagement," Convert with Content (blog), https://www.convertwithcontent.com/11-tips-optimize-linkedin-profile-maximum-exposure-engagement/ (accessed June 10, 2015).

to a particular industry (like a professional designation). Your profile must contain certain keywords to get attention and communicate that you are qualified for a particular position.

Keywords can include the following:

- Position title
- Industries
- Professional designation
- Skills, knowledge, core competencies
- Industry terms-of-art (and abbreviations)
- Employer names (past or present)
- Licenses, certifications
- Location (state, city)
- Software and technologies you're familiar with
- Education (school names and degrees)

We will have an extended discussion about the use of keywords when we talk about optimization.

Your LinkedIn Profile - Sections

Before we begin our discussion on building an impactful profile ("optimization"), let's briefly introduce the major components of your profile.

1. Photo

Your photo is important. It shows that you are a real person. Since LinkedIn has a professional focus—and you are looking for a job—it is recommended to have a photo taken at a studio by a professional or, at minimum, a close-up photograph of you professionally dressed. According to experts, "profiles with a photo are fourteen times more likely to be viewed."[133] Moreover, having a photo makes you 36 times more likely to receive a message on LinkedIn.[134]

Here are some Do's and Don'ts when it comes to your LinkedIn photo. Many of

---

133 Smith, Jacquelyn. "The Complete Guide To Crafting A Perfect LinkedIn Profile," *Business Insider*, January 21, 2015, http://www.businessinsider.com/guide-to-perfect-linkedin-profile-2015-1 (accessed June 4, 2015).

134 Smith, Craig, DMR, "200+ Amazing LinkedIn Stats" (Last Checked/Updated October 2016) http://expandedramblings.com/index.php/by-the-numbers-a-few-important-linkedin-stats/. (Downloaded November 28, 2016).

these have been cited in a study by PhotoFeeler[135], while others should be common sense considering that LinkedIn is a professional networking site.

Do:
Be professionally dressed
The photo should be of your head and shoulders
Look directly into the camera. Make eye contact.
Smile

Don't:
No sunglasses (clear eye glasses are fine)
No fish
No pets
No golf course photos
No family portraits
No kids or grandchildren
No shopping mall Glamour Shots

It is highly recommended that your LinkedIn profile be professionally taken.

2. Name

Use the name you commonly go by. If your given name is Richard, but you go by Rich, use Rich. It is permissible to put both your given name and the name you use in quotation marks or in parentheses. If you have a common name, you may want to add your middle initial.

Professional designations appearing in the name field. There is a difference of opinion among commentators on this topic.[136] However, it can be to your advantage to put one (maybe two) notable professional designation behind your name. Designations should be significant to your industry, add to your credibility, or create a competitive advantage in the job market. Using one or two notable designations could increase the odds of having your profile viewed.

---

135 PhotoFeeler."New Research Study Breaks Down The Perfect Profile Photo, PhotoFeeler, May 13, 2014 https://blog.photofeeler. com/perfect-photo/. (accessed November 7, 2016)

136 Isaacson, Nate. "Professional Designations Are Great But They Are Not A Part of Your Name," *LinkedIn Pulse*, April 14, 2014, https://www.linkedin.com/pulse/20140414223601-23236063-professional-designations-are-great-but-they-are-not-a-part-of-your-name   (accessed July 16, 2015); Hanson, Arik. "Should You Put MBA Behind Your Name on Your LinkedIn Profile?" *LinkedIn Pulse*, May 29, 2014,   https://www.linkedin.com/pulse/20140529131058-18098999-should-you-put-mba-behind-your-name-on-your-linkedin-profile (accessed July 17, 2015).

3. Headline

Under your name is your Headline area. It is the first thing someone reads about you. You have 120 character spaces in your headline. Make it impactful (which will increase the number of views you receive) by describing yourself with keywords or short phrases that best describe your function. "What do you want to be known for?"[137] Or found for?

Avoid superlatives or flamboyant adjectives in your headline (The Industry's Best Sales Representative on the Planet).

The headline ultimately attracts viewers with the intention that they continue to read your profile and be impressed with your experience, skills, and accomplishments. When we discuss optimization, we will delve much deeper into the strategic use of your headline.

4. Location and Industry Sections

The Location and Industry sections appear below your Headline.

Kansas City, Missouri Area | Staffing and Recruiting

LinkedIn lists every significant metropolitan city in the country (more than 280 geographical location phrases at last count). Your location (or one very close) is likely listed.

It is important to put an accurate metropolitan city location on your profile. When employers and recruiters conduct searches, they often look for profiles of individuals who live in a particular city or region. Having no location or a generic "United States" makes you almost invisible to employers and recruiters who may need a qualified candidate located in a particular metropolitan area or region.

Be accurate when choosing an industry specialty. LinkedIn lists 145 industry phrases, so choose the one that best fits you. When employers and recruiters conduct searches, they may look for profiles from particular industries—ones from which they have made successful hires in the past.

Having an industry on your profile has the potential to get you fifteen times the amount of views than those who do not list an industry.[138]

5. Contact Information

LinkedIn allows you to provide contact information. Your Contact Info tab is located in the bottom right hand corner of the top section of your profile (where your name, photo and headline are located). It looks like this:

---

137 Whitcomb, *Job Search Magic*, p. 68.

138 "10 Tips for the Perfect LinkedIn Profile," LinkHumans, Slideshare, published July 1, 2014, http://www.slideshare.net/linkedin/10-tips-for-the-perfect-linkedin-profile (accessed November 11, 2015).

Contact Info

This is a good place to put your personal email address and perhaps your cell phone number. Only first degree connections can see this information.

6. Summary Section

The summary section is an area where you can write a narrative of your background, experience, and achievements. This is a biographical description of your career, so keep the content professionally relevant and use keywords.

There is a difference of opinion regarding how the content of this section should be presented. Some advocate that it is an opportunity for you to write in the first person and show personality.[139] Others might contend that it should be more in the third-person narrative. The choice is yours; however, make your decision based on how it will be best perceived by a potential hiring executive hiring for your level of position.

Your Summary section has a significant impact on optimizing your LinkedIn profile and will be discussed at length in the pages that follow.

7. Experience

This is reasonably straightforward. Think resume. Use relevant keywords. Remember that your LinkedIn profile and your resume must match in general content. According to LinkedIn, "add[ing] your two most recent work positions . . . can increase your profile views by twelve times."[140] Strategic use of the Experience section will be discussed with optimization.

⬥ As a SEAL, be consistent with your approach to dates. However you decided to handle dates on your resume, do the same on your LinkedIn profile.

8. Education

Your education should align directly with your resume. Start with your highest degree and work backward in reverse chronological order. As a SEAL, determine whether you want to include dates. Review the Education section of the Impactful Resumes portion of

---

139 Smith, Jacquelyn. "Here's What To Say In Your LinkedIn 'Summary' Statement," Business Insider, December 19, 2014, http://www.businessinsider.com/what-to-say-in-your-linkedin-summary-statement-2014-12 (accessed July 9, 2015).

140 Daniel Ayele, "Land Your Dream Job in 2015 with These Data-Proven LinkedIn Tips," *LinkedIn Blog*, January 29, 2015, http://blog.linkedin.com/2015/01/29/jobseeking-tips/ (accessed June 9, 2015).

this book. LinkedIn users "who have an education on their profile receive an average of ten times more profile views than those who don't."[141]

Additional sections of your profile. LinkedIn has additional sections to further customize your profile. Depending on the HR recruiter or hiring executive, these areas may have an impact on their impression of you. To find these additional sections on your profile, look under the area that has your photo, Headline, etc. and you should see: **Add a section to your profile – be discovered for your next career step.**

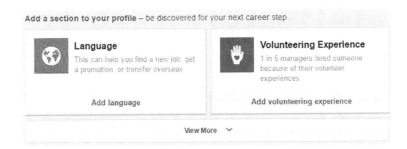

Click "View More" to see all of the sections that you can add to your profile. We'll discuss several of these additional sections.

9. Volunteer Experience and Causes

Many employers look favorably upon profiles of those who volunteer or are involved in civic causes—it speaks to matching the culture of the company. "In fact, according to LinkedIn, 42 percent of hiring managers surveyed said they view volunteer experience equal to formal work experience."[142]

10. Certifications

Listing certifications can enhance your value as a viable candidate for a position. Frequently a professional certification or designation is a significant differentiator from other job seekers.

11. Organizations

Listing your memberships in professional associations can have an influence on

---

141 LinkHumans, "10 Tips." *See also*, Smith, Craig, DMR, "200+ Amazing LinkedIn Stats" (Last Checked/Updated October 2016) http://expandedramblings.com/index.php/by-the-numbers-a-few-important-linkedin-stats/. (Downloaded November 28, 2016). This source indicates that 65% of job postings on LinkedIn require a Bachelor's degree.

142 Dougherty, Lisa. "16 Tips to Optimize Your LinkedIn Profile and Your Personal Brand," LinkedIn Pulse, July 8, 2014, https://www.linkedin.com/pulse/20140708162049-7239647-16-tips-to-optimize-your-linkedin-profile-and-enhance-your-personal-brand (accessed November 11, 2015).

employers because it reflects that you are in touch and following the industry. It can also be a source of networking and education.[143]

12. Skills and Endorsements

LinkedIn allows you to list fifty skills. Be reasonably specific and don't use all fifty. You don't want an HR recruiter or hiring executive view you as a "jack of all trades and a master of none." You may appear desperate if you list too many skills. How many skills are too many? When you feel you are starting to stretch to include a skill, you have likely reached the end. According to LinkedIn, listing 5 or more skills in your profile will get you up to 17 times more profile views.[144]

Endorsements are a nice LinkedIn feature. They add credibility and compelling nature to your profile as others agree with the skills you have listed (they can add others).

Endorse others. Remember, LinkedIn is a networking mechanism and a two-way street. The more you engage with others, the more they will engage with you.

13. Honors and Awards

List all notable Honors and Awards you have received, signaling to an employer that others have recognized you for your performance.

14. Ask for Recommendations

Remember that having others say good things about you is better than you promoting yourself.[145] "Recommendations are mini testimonials that people give you who have worked with you. You can request them via LinkedIn. It's another way to build credibility [for] you and your work. As appropriate, return the favor when someone gives you a recommendation."[146]

Many recruiters review recommendations as part of their evaluation protocols. As a minimum goal, get at least three recommendations posted on your profile from former bosses, colleagues, customers, or vendors you've interacted with.

15. Interests

This is a section where you can help improve the number of views you receive compared to other job seekers. List business interests using your keywords. Most job seekers don't

---

143 Yate, *Knock 'em Dead*, p. 86.

144 Smith, Craig, DMR, "200+ Amazing LinkedIn Stats" (Last Checked/Updated October 2016) http://expandedramblings.com/index.php/by-the-numbers-a-few-important-linkedin-stats/. (Downloaded November 28, 2016).

145 Matt, "Brag Book."

146 Frasco, "11 Tips."

do this. This is another place where LinkedIn looks for keywords when matching what a hiring executive or recruiter is looking for in a search for candidates.[147]

It is perfectly acceptable and encouraged to list your personal interests as well. It personalizes your profile. The point is to list both business as well as personal interests. We'll discuss the Interests section in more detail when we get to optimization.

16. Groups

LinkedIn groups are valuable, give you a platform to be an expert in an industry or topic, and help you gain insight and knowledge. "Your profile is 5 times more likely to be viewed if you join and are active in groups."[148]

HR recruiters and hiring executives search LinkedIn, and they also interact in LinkedIn groups.[149] With more than two million groups on LinkedIn,[150] there is no excuse not to join a group relevant to your industry or location. Eighty-one percent of users surveyed were in at least one LinkedIn group,[151] meaning hiring executives and recruiters—maybe even the one who will give you your dream job—are likely already members of, and might even be active in, a group. In a survey of LinkedIn users who found a job within three months of focused searching, 82 percent interacted with a group on LinkedIn.[152]

LinkedIn allows you to join 100 groups, so join those pertinent to your background, industry, and location. Determine a group's membership—larger ones offer more exposure. You will need to "apply" for membership to join a group.

Once you join a group, it is much easier to relate to people. You have something in common. Common ground is a good thing when starting a networking communication.

Groups occasionally send out updates to your email. Occasionally, job postings are contained in these emails. However, not all jobs posted to these groups go out in the group's emails. Routinely consult job sections of your different groups for new job postings.

17. Other Enhancements

You can also use a variety of media to showcase your skills (video presentations

---

147 See also, ibid.

148 LinkHumans, "10 Tips."

149 Lindsey Pollak, "How to Attract Employers' Attention on LinkedIn," LinkedIn Blog, December 2, 2010, http://blog.linkedin.com/2010/12/02/find-jobs-on-linkedin/ (accessed June 4, 2015).

150 Arruda, William. "Is LinkedIn Poised To Be The Next Media Giant?" *Forbes*, March 8, 2015, http://www.forbes.com/sites/williamarruda/2015/03/08/is-linkedin-poised-to-be-the-next-media-giant/ (accessed June 5, 2015).

151 Pamela Vaughan, "81% of LinkedIn Users Belong to a LinkedIn Group [Data]," *Hubspot Blogs*, August 11, 2011, http://blog.hubspot.com/blog/tabid/6307/bid/22364/81-of-LinkedIn-Users-Belong-to-a-LinkedIn-Group-Data.aspx (accessed June 8, 2015).

152 Shreya Oswal, "7 Smart Habits of Successful Job Seekers [INFOGRAPHIC]," LinkedIn Blog, March 19, 2014, http://blog.linkedin.com/2014/03/19/7-smart-habits-of-successful-job-seekers-infographic/ (accessed June 9, 2015).

including Slideshare, pictures or screenshots, and text documents). These are optional and not required to get you found by an HR recruiter or hiring executive. However, they can add credibility to your experience on the job. Upload a video if you do public speaking. If you're skilled in graphic design, showcase your portfolio. If you write, add an article or a chapter of your book. Consider adding anything unique or impactful to prove and reinforce your skills, experience, or achievements.

Keep Your Profile Current

Update your information and keep it current so it doesn't appear stale. According to LinkedIn, keeping your positions up to date on your profile makes you eighteen times more likely to be found in searches by recruiters and other members. [153]

Customize Your LinkedIn URL

Your URL is your LinkedIn address on the site. When on your profile, it appears at the very top of your computer screen. Your current LinkedIn URL is likely your name, in lowercase letters, and possibly followed by a series of numbers, slashes, and so on. It can look rather technical. LinkedIn allows you to customize the URL to make it much more visually appealing. By customizing your LinkedIn URL, it will be more appealing to the eye if you put it on your resume, business card, and so forth.

The first thing to consider is what you want the customized URL to be. For many, it could be as simple as capitalizing your name, deleting the numbers, and leaving it at that. The programming on LinkedIn will either accept the change or give you three suggestions. It is acceptable to put a position title after your name (e.g., "JohnSmithengineer"). Or, a professional designation (e.g., "JohnSmithCEBS").[154] Or a branding word (e.g., "JohnSmithintegrity"). Just don't get carried away with this. Keep it simple. Here are the brief click-by-click steps:

- Go to your LinkedIn home page.

- Click on your small photo (or icon if you don't have a photo) at the far upper right-hand corner of the page. You'll get a drop-down menu.

- Click "Privacy and Settings."

---

153 Smith, Craig, DMR, "200+ Amazing LinkedIn Stats" (Last Checked/Updated October 2016) http://expandedramblings.com/index.php/by-the-numbers-a-few-important-linkedin-stats/. (Downloaded November 28, 2016).

154 "Certified Employee Benefit Specialist"; see "About the CEBS Program," International Foundation of Employee Benefit Plans, Inc., https://www.ifebp.org/CEBSDesignation/overview/Pages/default.aspx (accessed November 12, 2015).

- On this page under Settings (right column), click the link "Edit your public profile."
- On the upper right-hand section of the page, you'll see the option to change your URL. Click the little pencil icon and make your changes. You have between five and thirty letters or numbers—no spaces, symbols, or anything like that.
- Click "Save" and you're done.[155]

Take note: LinkedIn is a dynamic site that changes frequently, adding some features and functions and taking others away. Be aware of programming changes and their possible implications on your profile and job search.

Introducing LinkedIn Optimization

Optimization is taking full advantage of how the LinkedIn algorithms and programming work to be discovered for what you want to be professionally known for or found for. It means effective use of your keywords, putting those keywords in the correct areas of your profile, proper use of repeating those keywords, profile completeness, adequate number of connections, and making your profile compelling. All of these elements, pulled together, optimize your LinkedIn profile for maximum effectiveness. An optimized LinkedIn profile makes you more discoverable and more desirable when an HR recruiter uses LinkedIn to find a professional with your skills and background. Since 87% of HR recruiters use LinkedIn to identify and recruit candidates, having an "optimized" LinkedIn profile could lead you to your next career opportunity.

How does it work . . . How does an HR Recruiter use LinkedIn to find candidates?

There are numerous ways an HR recruiter can use LinkedIn to locate candidates. To illustrate one common method, go to your LinkedIn home page or profile. Along the top next to the blue rectangle with a spyglass is the word Advanced.

Click on the word Advanced. "Advanced" means the Advanced People Search function for LinkedIn.

---

155 See also, Sue Cockburn, "Create Your Custom LinkedIn Web Address in 5 Easy Steps," *Growing Social Biz* (blog), September 30, 2015, http://growingsocialbiz.com/simple-steps-creating-your-customized-linkedin-url/ (accessed November 12, 2015).

You should now see a series of open boxes entitled: Keywords, First Name, Last Name, Title, Company, School, and Location running down the left side of the page among other qualifiers.

To illustrate how LinkedIn works and how HR Recruiters used the tool, put the word "insurance" in the Keyword box and the word "sales" in the Title box and hit the blue Search button. Your results will be hundreds-of-thousands of profiles appearing on the page. The example terms used were overly broad but it gives you a concept of how a recruiter uses LinkedIn by refining search terms to identify candidates.

The purpose of this section is to teach you how to optimize your LinkedIn profile so you are one of those top candidates!

The Goal of Optimization

Now that you have a general understanding of the functionality of the LinkedIn algorithms and programming, you need to know what you are striving for by optimizing your LinkedIn profile. Your goal, in descending order is: (1) to be the number one profile on the first page (the ultimate achievement), (2) to be on the first page, and (3) to be on the first three pages.

These goals can be achieved provided you have adequate career achievements and information and you follow the instructions for optimization. Depending upon your professional circumstances, you will likely need to evaluate your optimization goals by evaluating yourself to your city or metropolitan area. This is achieved by using the Location box (clicking the down arrow) on the Advanced Search page.

Location

Located in or near.

Country

United States

Postal Code

Lookup

Search Reset

Keyword Location

Where your keywords appear on your profile does matters. The sections listed below are the primary areas where the algorithms and programming look to match keywords.

1. Headline

2. Summary

3. Title

4. Experience/employment descriptions

5. Skills

6. Interests

There are advanced platforms that can be purchased from LinkedIn that could expand this list, but these are the primary sections where the algorithms and programming match keywords.

Headline

You have 120 character-spaces available to you in your headline, which is actually a lot of room. Since we know that this is a section where the algorithms and programming goes to match keywords, make sure they appear here.

The headline section provides an excellent opportunity for you to create a branding statement describing yourself. What do you want to be known for or found for? [156]

A convenient formula that works well for many job seekers is:

[Job function or title] + [A bridge phrase or action verb (e.g., "with experience in," or "with expertise in," "specializing in," "utilizing")] + [keywords: reference to products, services, skills, industry, and so on]

For example:

"Senior Sales Executive with Experience in Workers' Compensation, Pain Management, Leadership."

Or:

"Product Development Professional Applying Behavioral Research to Healthcare Technology."

Here are some real examples from LinkedIn profiles:

Sr. Sales Executive Specializing in Executive Leadership, Referenced Based Pricing, Stop Loss.

Healthcare Leader skilled in Key Account Growth, Sales, Strategy, Analytics, Problem-solving and Partnership Optimization.

When choosing keywords for your headline, use those that are skill, knowledge, products, and and services with which you have experience. Most HR recruiters will use keywords that are skills or knowledge based to identify candidates on LinkedIn. Then, during the screening process, they explore and evaluate soft skills (e.g. work ethic, communications skills, etc.). We'll mention your soft skills in just a moment in the Summary section.

This raises an interesting concept that you need to be aware of. As you build your LinkedIn profile, you occasionally need to think like an HR recruiter. What keywords would an HR recruiter or hiring executive use to find a professional like you? More often than not, the keywords you use will align with those used by an HR recruiter. However, that is not always the case. For example, some companies use the title Business Development to mean "sales". Other companies use that same title to mean marketing, branding, public

---

156 See, Whitcomb, Susan Britton. *Job Search Magic: Insider Secrets from America's Career and Life Coach.* (Indianapolis, IN: JIST Works, 2006), p. 68.

relations, and so on. If you happen to have one of those titles that is not generally accepted or representative of your function, you will want to use terminology on your LinkedIn profile that is more accepted and used by an HR recruiter. The point is to double check your thinking along the way.

Summary

You have 2000 character spaces available to you for your summary[157], which is a ton of room. Do not get "long winded" when writing your summary. Your summary is just that...a summary of your career not an autobiography. Think of your summary as the executive summary of a White Paper.[158]

An effective technique is to start your summary by re-stating your headline, word-for-word, and then expand upon it to include other keywords that would not fit or were of secondary importance in your headline (perhaps your soft skills). Below is the banner statements contained in the Summary of the two Headline profile examples:

Senior Sales Executive Specializing in Executive Leadership, Referenced Based Pricing, Stop Loss, Self-Funding, Product Distribution.

Effective Healthcare leader skilled in strategy, key account growth, sales, analytics, partnership optimization, team mentorship and problem solving.

Remember, LinkedIn is looking to match keywords and tracking the number of times they appear when ranking you against other similar profiles. By re-stating your headline you create an introductory statement (banner) running along the top of your summary. The HR recruiter does not think twice about it but you have taken advantage of the programming by stating keywords twice between your headline and your introductory banner-statement in your Summary.

After your introductory banner-statement, write one to three (maybe four) paragraphs that summarize your career experiences so far. This will include duties, responsibilities and will also include your keywords. As you write, be aware that this paragraph(s) must read smoothly. A good approach is to write the paragraphs then insert keywords as appropriate. It's also a good technique to write your summary paragraph(s) – and other sections – in a Word.doc then copy and paste into the appropriate section. This way misspellings and grammar errors will be caught. This is important. A survey conducted by Jobvite indicated that 72% of HR recruiters view typos negatively on social media.[159]

---

157 Foote, Andy, Maximum LinkedIn Character Counts for 2016, December 10, 2016 https://www.linkedin.com/pulse/maximum-linkedin-character-counts-2016-andy-foote. (Accessed November 22, 2016)

158 See, Kolowich, Lindsay, What is a White Paper, June 27, 2014 http://blog.hubspot.com/marketing/what-is-whitepaper-faqs #sm.0000lbm5cb9ke7e11nu1h1l4e63aj (Accessed November 22, 2016)

159 Jobvite 2016 Recruiter National Survey www.jobvite.com (accessed November 17, 2016)

The next component of your summary, following your career summary paragraphs, is your career accomplishments. These are your achievements of which you are most proud. Start with, "Career Accomplishments Include:" Then list your top three maybe four. If you are not sure whether to include a particular achievement, hedge towards not including it. You want these achievements to be your best ones.

This discussion on accomplishments fits directly into one of the tenets for optimizing your LinkedIn profile - Compelling. The concept of "compelling" will be woven in throughout the rest of this discussion as we address other topics and strategies.

Once you have your accomplishments listed in your Summary section, go to the Internet and copy and paste an icon and place it in front of each of your accomplishments. When choosing an icon, choose something dark, like a ● bullet-point or a black diamond ◆. These dark icons draw the eye of HR recruiters and highlights in their minds that you are good at what you do. Whatever icon you select, use it consistently throughout your profile. Using different icons makes your profile look jumbled or gaudy. Here are a couple of examples that appear in the Summary section of a couple of profiles:

Career Achievements include:

- Implemented cost savings strategies throughout a variety of initiatives resulting in a cost savings over 1 million dollars.

Career Achievements include:

- Recipient of 2014 Female Executives.

- Developed and executed business development, marketing and sales plan that yielded 30% year-over-year growth.

- Marketed and sold new business to large employers, generating 30% of the overall company revenue.

- One of six senior managers who re-engineered corporate-wide business practices resulting in over savings of more than $13 million.

Finally, at the end of your summary, provide your personal email address and cell phone number. This is a good strategy because people who are not connected to you cannot see your Contact Details (an additional feature to your profile).[160] You want to make it as easy as possible for an HR recruiter to contact you and providing this information at the end of your Summary makes it easy to do so.

---

160 Pearcemarch, Kyle, SEO for LinkedIn: How to Optimize Your LinkedIn Profile for Search (March 19, 2015) https://www.diygenius.com/how-to-optimize-your-linkedin-profile-for-search/ (Accessed November 22, 2016)

Title

The title area of your employment background is where LinkedIn looks for matching keywords. You have 100 character spaces for your title.[161] If you have a title that is unique to your company, make sure to also include a more descriptive terminology so the HR recruiter can determine your actual function.

Experience

This is your employment history and it is a section where you should heavily use your keywords. For each employer, write one, maybe two paragraphs describing duties, responsibilities, product knowledge, distribution, territories, target markets and so on... use your keywords. Beneath the paragraph(s), put: "Achievements or Accomplishments:" then, like you did in your Summary, list the important accomplishment you achieved in that position. This approach informs the HR recruiter of what your duties and responsibilities were and that you were successful in the role.

INCREASED SALES:

- 141% in 2006 over prior year
- 197% in 2005 over prior year
- 179% in 2004 over prior year

Follow this formula for each employment going back 15 to 20 years. In your Experience section, your career-level accomplishments listed in your Summary will appear again under the employment from which they occurred. This is fine. The HR recruiter will know from which employer your career-level accomplishments occurred. It is recommended to put your dark icon in front of each accomplishment like you did in your Summary.

Skills

List your keywords as skills, as appropriate. According to LinkedIn, the number of times you are endorsed for a skill has no weight on how many times the algorithms and programming recognize that particular keyword. In other words, having 30 people endorse you for a skill (keyword) does not mean the algorithms sees that keyword appearing 30 times on your profile. We will discuss an advanced technique using your Skills section in a moment.

---

161 Foote, Andy, Maximum LinkedIn Character Counts for 2016, December 10, 2016 https://www.linkedin.com/pulse/maximum-linkedin-character-counts-2016-andy-foote. (Accessed November 22, 2016)

Interests

The Interests section of your profile is an area where LinkedIn looks to match keywords. It is an often overlooked section where most job seekers list only personal interests. You can outrank a lot of competing profiles by including your business interests, using your keywords, in the Interests section.

Start with "Business interests include:" Then list your most important keywords. You can add your personal interests if you like after you list your business interests and keywords.

Interests

Business Interests: Wellness, Population Health, Tele-health, Consumerism, Employee Benefits, Technology, Team Building, Leadership, Sales, Business Development, Account Management, Strategic Planning, Project Management, Market Research and Intelligence. Personal Interests: Family, Friends, Traveling, University of Michigan Football

Keyword Stuffing

Keyword *stuffing* is abusively over using your keywords throughout your profile to increase your ranking.[162] It's a strategy designed to game the system. Sadly, this is a strategy too often suggested by some LinkedIn profile writers and career coaches. According to discussions with LinkedIn Customer Service, the algorithms and programming are now designed to detect this strategy and can actually reduce your ranking.

The far better approach (and the one promoted in this book), is to construct a profile using accepted and common sense optimization strategies that present your professional background and experience in a genuine and sincere manner to make the most positive impression possible on the HR recruiter.

This finishes the discussion regarding the first tenet of optimizing your LinkedIn profile regarding keywords. We will now move the discussion to the next tenet of optimization – Completeness.

Completeness

The more complete your LinkedIn profile is, the higher it will rank compared to other profiles. According to LinkedIn, "Only 50.5% of people have a 100% completed LinkedIn

---

162 See, Practices to Avoid When Optimizing Your Profile For LinkedIn Search. https://www.linkedin.com/help/linkedin/answer/51499/practices-to-avoid-when-optimizing-your-profile-for-linkedin-search?lang=en (Accessed November 23, 2016)

profile."[163] Consequently, by having a complete profile you can outrank many other competing profiles.

Profile completeness is very important. The LinkedIn algorithms and programming display search results (How you rank compared to other profiles) based on the following:

1. Profile completeness (All-Star, 100%)

2. The number of shared connections

3. Connections by degree(1st, 2nd, and so on)

4. Groups in common

Profile completeness is the "trump card" with the LinkedIn algorithms and programming.[164] The other factors of ranking do not matter if your profile is not complete. If you need a refresher of what constitutes a Complete Profile, here are the components:

• Your industry and location

• An up-to-date current position (with a description)

• Two past positions

• Your education

• Your skills (minimum of 3)

• A profile photo

• At least 50 connections"[165]

You are already well-down-the road to completeness (and compelling) as you work on your profile using keywords. However, at last count, LinkedIn has 17 additional sections that can be added to your profile beyond those that are most commonly used. They include:

Language

Volunteering Experience

Volunteering Opportunities

Honor and Awards

Test Scores

---

163 Foote, Andy, Why You Should Complete Your LinkedIn Profile, (December 7, 2015). https://www.linkedinsights.com/why-you-should-complete-your-linkedin-profile/ (Accessed November 22, 2016)

164 Ibid. ("Profile Completeness is a trump card in the search engine.")

165 Ibid.

Courses

Patents

Causes you care about

Supported Organizations

Projects

Personal details

Certifications (Professional Designations)

Publications

Interests

Contact information

Organizations (Professional Associations and Affiliations)

Posts

We have already discussed the Interests section and its importance regarding keywords. We will now selectively discuss some of these additional sections leaving the others to be self-explanatory.

Language

If living in the United States and English is your native language, do not list it. It is assumed that you are fluent. This section is used for foreign languages.

Volunteering Experience, Volunteering Opportunities, Causes you care about, Supported Organizations, Organizations

There are a couple of considerations regarding these sections. First, volunteering experience is favorably viewed by employers, but it must be substantive. Standing behind the card table selling brownies at the Cub Scouts meeting doesn't count. However, being a volunteer Red Cross First Responder does. Second, avoid any reference to any organization or cause that could be viewed as controversial. This would generally mean anything regarding politics, religion, race, and so on. Of course there are exceptions if your career is in politics, religion, and race relations.

Honors and Awards

It is perfectly acceptable to re-state your accomplishments and achievements in the Honors and Awards section. This is especially true if the achievement actually results in an award. Repetition of your achievements affirms in the mind of the HR recruiter that you are a well-qualified job seeker.

Personal details

Avoid providing any personal information that would be inappropriate for an HR recruiter to ask in an interview. Marital status and year of birth are two notable ones.

Connections

The more connections you have, the better the probability you will rank higher than other profiles.[166] Your ranking is, in part, influenced by how closely connected you are to an HR recruiter (or anyone else looking). The difficult part is you have no idea who could be looking on LinkedIn and how closely connected you are to them.

The best strategy to combat against or take advantage of this connection factor is to increase your connections and join industry relevant groups. Try to get connected to as many professionally relevant people as possible. These are professionals that can hire you or help you. This would include colleagues and peers at other organizations including clients, vendors, competitors, and so on. If you want to work for a particular company, seek connections within that company. Strive to get a minimum of 500 professionally relevant connections (possibly more depending upon your professional circumstances). The more professionally relevant connections you have, the higher the probability that you will be more closely connected to the HR recruiter who is searching on LinkedIn. The closer the connection, the higher you will appear in the ranking of profiles.

To help identify possible connections, go to the Advanced People Search function previously discussed. Put in the name of a company in the Company field that is in your industry or one you are interested in. Click "Search." As necessary, further refine the list by adding a title that a peer or hiring executive at that company could have. You may need to further refine your search by location. Depending upon how many connections you already have and other factors, you might be able to invite those people to connect with you. CAUTION: LinkedIn does not endorse the extension of invitation unless there is a relationship to that person. In practice, however, the policy is relaxed so long as you have some viable rationale for the request. Also, do not extend invitation until after you have optimized your profile! This will increase the likelihood of people accepting your invitations and make a positive first impression when they review your profile.

---

166 Pearcemarch, Kyle, SEO for LinkedIn: How to Optimize Your LinkedIn Profile for Search (March 19, 2015) https://www.diygenius.com/how-to-optimize-your-linkedin-profile-for-search/ (Accessed November 22, 2016)

You are allowed to join up to 100 groups on LinkedIn.[167] Since your ranking is influenced by the number of common groups you have with an HR recruiter, it is very important to join relevant and well-populated groups, especially those groups that are in industries you belong or are interested.

🔱 Fully appreciate that your network has value and is an area of evaluation when a hiring executive or HR recruiter looks at your profile. An evaluation of the number of contacts in and quality of your network creates a "Network Value Score." By analogy, it's like your credit score when applying for a mortgage. The higher your "Network Value Score," the more valuable you become as a quality candidate for the position.

If you are new to LinkedIn or have been inactive, work to get five hundred connections. The number of connections you have appears on your profile until you exceed five hundred. After that, it appears as "500+." As a SEAL, you want hiring executives viewing your profile to conclude that you have a network of professional colleagues. It can add to your professional value proposition. If you're staying within your field, it is not uncommon for hiring executives to see how many common connections you have with each other—the more the better. And it is not uncommon for hiring executives to reach out to these common connections and inquire about you as well. Hence this is another good reason to stay active with your network.

Compelling

A profile is compelling when it intellectually or emotionally moves the HR recruiter to contact you. There are several factors that can make a profile compelling. They include: your knowledge and skills, accomplishments, endorsements, recommendations, the overall appearance and completeness of your profile, and anything else that makes you unique in the eyes of the HR recruiter.

Your profile can be compelling based on your knowledge and skills. You know things or have done things in your career that an HR recruiter is looking for or is impressed by. You have experience and a skillset needed by the HR recruiter. This can range from knowing and having experience with a particular software programming to having Profit and Loss ("P&L") experience with a large organization. There are thousands if not millions of things an HR recruiter could look for that is knowledge or skill based.

Documented accomplishments are clearly compelling. The most influential accomplishments are those that can be quantified with numbers, percentages, dollars signs,

---

167 General Limits for LinkedIn Groups, https://www.linkedin.com/help/linkedin/answer/190/general-limits-for-linkedin-groups?lang=en (Accessed November 23, 2016)

savings (in time and money), and the list goes on. Accomplishments can heavily influence an HR recruiter to contact you.

The number of endorsements you have for a sought-after skill can influence the compelling nature of your profile. If an HR recruiter finds a profile with 99+ endorsements for a sought-after skill or experience, it is a clear indication that the professional could be a qualified candidate.

An advanced technique is to list one professional character trait you possess as a skill. Examples would be work ethic, perseverance, honesty, and so on. Then, get as many connections to endorse you for that character trait as possible. Having a professional character trait listed as a skill and having an adequate number of endorsements is a differentiator from other profiles and will get noticed by an HR recruiter. Endorsements for a sought-after character trait open the door to what kind of person/professional you are as seen through the eyes of others. This enhances the compelling nature of your profile.

Recommendations can influence the compelling nature of your profile. Once your profile is identified as a "probable" qualified candidate by an HR recruiter, the number and content of the recommendations can influence the HR recruiter to contact you. As a general rule of thumb, try to get three positive recommendations for each employer going back to at least two to three employers.

And finally, the overall completeness and appearance of your profile can be a compelling factor. There are millions of well-qualified job seekers who fail to appreciate the career enhancing power of a LinkedIn profile. Potentially life-changing opportunities pass those people by though their failure to have a complete and professionally appearing LinkedIn profile. However, to your benefit, you will have a complete, professional, and compelling profile that will open your career to opportunities that others will not have (or ever know about).

Put it to the Test

After you have revised your profile and optimized it, put it to the test. Get on LinkedIn and run an Advance Search on yourself. Put in one keyword or phrase that you are using in your profile along with your title. How do you rank (remember, you may have to limit your search criteria to your metropolitan area)? Did you appear on the first page? On the first two or three pages? Try another one of your keywords. How did that one work? If you are not coming up on the first three pages, double check to make sure you have all of the elements of a complete profile. Then, look at the profiles that appeared in front of you and see if you can make improvements based on what those candidates put on their profiles.

Selective borrowing is permitted. Make revisions and try it again. Do what you can to improve your ranking to appear on the first page or the first three pages, if possible.

Understand that regardless of the revisions you make and the optimizing strategies you use, you may only be able to improve your ranking so much. Don't get frustrated. You can only do so much with the algorithms based on the information on your profile. But, whatever you do, don't go overboard! Your profile must still appear professional and informative. Optimizing is a great strategy and it will improve your ranking, but creating an awkward-looking profile for ranking purposes defeats the ultimate objective . . . impressing an HR recruiter or hiring executive.

Strategies for Your LinkedIn Profile When You are Unemployed

If you are unemployed, what do you put on your LinkedIn Profile? Do you announce your availability or would doing so reduce your attractiveness as a candidate? Fortunately, you have several strategic options.

As you consider the options that follow, the primary consideration is this: How would an HR recruiter or hiring executive react to the strategy you use for the level of position you are seeking? After we discuss the strategic options, we'll discuss factors that could influence your decision on which strategic approach to take.

Put an End Date on your last Employment. Your first option is to list an end date on your current employment. It's honest and your profile is up-to-date. HR recruiters will draw the conclusion that you are currently unemployed.

Announce your Unemployment in your Headline. As you know, the headline is the area immediately below your name. It is acceptable to use your headline as an advertisement of your availability: "Currently Seeking New Opportunities," or "In Transition," among others.

However, there is a more effective approach since the LinkedIn algorithms and programming searches the Headline for keywords. Create your Headline with your keywords "Seeking Opportunities." For example, "Banking Professional Specializing in Commercial Lending, Seeking New Opportunities." This strategy capitalizes on your keywords and announces your availability.

Announce Your Availability as a Statement in Your Summary Section. Another option is to include a statement of your availability early in your Summary section. Your statement could be as simple as "Actively Seeking New Employment."

As you know, your Summary section is also an area where the LinkedIn programming and algorithms look to match keywords. There is a strategic advantage of adding a sentence or two with keywords about position types, industries, types of companies that would interest you. For example, "Actively seeking a new opportunity as an account manager in the employee benefits industry." This can help tighten your search but be aware that it can also reduce potential opportunities. After you make this statement, continue with the rest of the Summary in traditional fashion.

List Your Availability as Your Current Employment. The consideration with this approach is that LinkedIn programing and algorithms look at position titles and position descriptions for matching keywords. So simply putting "Open to Opportunities" as your title does not take advantage of the programming. A better approach is stating an actual title or job function followed by "seeking opportunities." For example, "Sales Operations Professional Specializing in Healthcare Seeking New Position." You have 100 character spaces in the title area which should give you ample room to use this strategy. You could re-word your headline and put it here as well.

For the Company Name, you can put "Unemployed." But, that sometimes can carry a negative stigma – though the weight of that stigma has faded in recent years. Instead, consider a more positive approach, such as putting "Exploring a Career Move," "Seeking New Position," or "In Transition" as your current employer.

Your position description provides some unique opportunities. If you resigned from your previous employment, the first sentence of your description could read something like this:

"Currently seeking a new position after voluntarily leaving [Past Employer] in good standing with recommendations."

OR

"Actively looking for a new job in event planning after resigning my position at [Past Employer] with strong job performance evaluations."

If you were laid off, you could state the description something like this:

"Was subject to a company-wide lay off affecting [XX number employees, the entire marketing department, X number of departments]. Release was not performance related."

If you were terminated for performance, it's probably best to leave that unspoken and use the position description space for other strategies.

For the rest of the position description space, create the messaging to put you in the best light. According to LinkedIn, there is now a 200 character minimum and a 2000 character maximum in the position description area.[168]

The content of the position description could be a brief statement of your abilities and knowledge using keywords. It could function as an abbreviated cover letter. You could also re-work your elevator speech and put it here. The key consideration is to use the space wisely, not be lengthy, and consider how an HR recruiter would react to what you write. When pulled all together, it could look something like this:

Title: Account Manager Seeking Opportunities in Employee Benefits

Company: Exploring A Career Move

Description: Was subject to a company-wide lay-off affecting over 100 employees at Insurance Company. Release was not performance related.

Seeking an account management position to benefit an insurance organization with proven skills in client service, ACA compliance, implementation, renewals, and claim resolution. (Then customized content based on your best judgment.)

Be a Consultant. You can list your current employment as consulting and your title as a consultant. Taking this approach is accepted "code" that you are unemployed but doing consulting projects to stay active and engaged.

The key to this strategy is the use of your keywords. Knowing that the LinkedIn programming and algorithms look at position titles; describe your title using keywords. For example:

"Security Technology Consultant"

Or,

"Workers' Compensation Cost Containment Consultant"

You can also shorten and manipulate the wording of your headline (you have 100 character spaces).

For company name, many use their last name or initials followed by "Consulting." You

---

168 Foote, Andy, Maximum LinkedIn Character Counts for 2016, December 10, 2016 https://www.linkedin.com/pulse/maximum-linke-din-character-counts-2016-andy-foote. (Accessed November 22, 2016)

have a lot of latitude for the name of your consulting practice, just be professional in the naming.

Your professional description should contain your keywords, as previously discussed. Using your keywords in your position description will help you when an HR recruiter or hiring executive searches for you.

Do Nothing At All. The final option is do nothing at all and if asked about your profile, go with "I forgot." This is not ideal, but the option is available to you.

Which Strategy would be Best for You?

The correct strategy(ies) depends on your unique professional circumstances. You may choose a select combination of approaches.

If you work in an industry where it is common to hire on a project basis, contractor-to-hire, or consulting basis, announcing your availability using these strategies makes good sense.

The level of your position or positioning on the corporate organizational chart for the position you are pursuing also has an influence on your strategy. Speaking generally, these "announcement" strategies may be more acceptable to lower, mid-range, sales to management roles rather than true senior management or C-Level positions. The size of the organization you are targeting could be a consideration as well. Smaller more entrepreneurial organizations may be more receptive to the announcement strategies. Exercise your professional judgement as to whether or which strategy(ies) to use. Your strategy hinges on how you believe an HR recruiter or hiring executive for your desired position could respond.

Job Alerts

LinkedIn can send you job-alert emails based on "job description profiles" you can create on LinkedIn. You will receive an email alert when a posted job matches the job description profile you create.

To receive these email alerts, start by accessing one of your LinkedIn pages (Home page, Profile, etc.) and click the Jobs tab.

| Home | Profile | My Network | Learning | Jobs | Interests |

You will now see a page title, "Jobs you may be interested in."

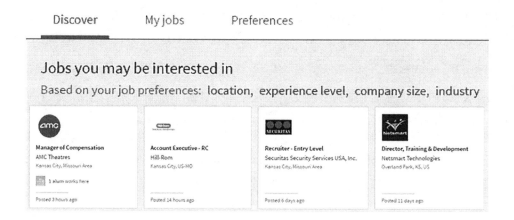

These are posted openings on LinkedIn that the programming believe you might be qualified for based on the information contained in your profile (This is yet another reason to have a complete and robust LinkedIn profile). On that page you will see a message from LinkedIn: "Whenever we uncover new jobs where you'd be a top applicant, we'll show them here." Click on any of the job(s) of interest to you to read more or to apply.

To create email job alerts, go to the top of the page where you see "Keywords, titles, or company names" and fill in the box with the criteria you are focused on. Location will be filled in based on your city. Once you have filled in the information, click "Find Jobs."

You will now see a page with listed jobs. Down the left column, you can refine your search parameters. You will also see at the top of the column an option to "Create Job Alert."

Get notified as new jobs become available.

Create job alert

Manage job alerts

Location ∧

- [ ] Kansas City, Missouri (1304)
- [ ] Overland Park, Kansas (533)
- [ ] Independence, Missouri (219)
- [ ] Lenexa, Kansas (190)
- [ ] Olathe, Kansas (188)

  + Add

Company ∧

- [ ] trustaff (208)
- [ ] Navajo Express (162)
- [ ] State Farm Agent (125)
- [ ] Hogan Transportation Companies
- [ ] Jackson Nurse Professionals (78)

  + Add

Date Posted ∧

Any Time (3689)

Past 24 Hours (168)

Past Week (630)

Past Month (2474)

Job Function ∧

- [ ] Management (1129)
- [ ] Manufacturing (1035)
- [ ] Sales (779)
- [ ] Health Care Provider (737)
- [ ] Business Development (536)

  + Add

Industry ∧

- [ ] Transportation/Trucking/Railroad
- [ ] Hospital & Health Care (573)
- [ ] Staffing and Recruiting (551)
- [ ] Insurance (459)
- [ ] Financial Services (242)

  + Add

Experience Level ∧

- [ ] Entry level (2449)
- [ ] Associate (444)
- [ ] Not Applicable (389)
- [ ] Mid-Senior level (268)
- [ ] Director (31)

  See more

Title ∧

- [ ] Registered Nurse (302)
- [ ] Truck Driver (233)
- [ ] Team Member (128)
- [ ] Delivery Driver (127)
- [ ] Travel Registered Nurse (105)

  + Add

When you click "Create Job Alert," you will be taken to a page where you are asked "How often do you want to get alerts for this search?" and "How would you like to get alerts? Make your selections and hit "Create alert."

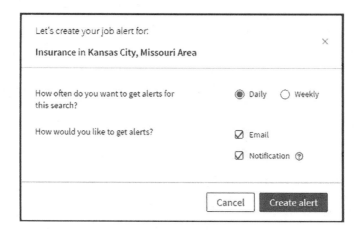

You can repeat the process for other opportunities you are interested in. LinkedIn allows for several saved searches. The exact number of searches you can save depends on the type of account you have (Basic or Premium). Your saved searches will be kept under the "My jobs" tab.

When you look into several jobs in one week, the LinkedIn programming concludes that you are a job seeker (Although the exact number is guarded by LinkedIn as proprietary, seven is the number often used by career coaches.) When that happens, you should automatically begin receiving emails from LinkedIn about jobs similar to the ones you researched.

Remember, LinkedIn is a dynamic site that frequently changes to enhance its capabilities and functionality. Be aware of these changes and how they affect your use of the site.

The Open Candidates Feature on LinkedIn

LinkedIn has a feature where you can signal recruiters that you are open to new opportunities. This feature is called "Open Candidates."

How to access the Open Candidates Feature. To access this feature, click the "Jobs" option at the top of your LinkedIn profile.

From there you have three options: Discover, My Jobs, and Preferences. Click "Preferences."

Discover   My jobs   Preferences

Scroll down a bit and begin answering the questions about location, experience, industries (LinkedIn will offer suggestions), company size, and availability. When you activate the feature you are also given an Introductory section with 300 character spaces.

Discover   My jobs   Preferences   Looking for talent?   Post a job

Let recruiters know you're open

Share that you're open to new opportunities and let your next job find you.

On

What kind of jobs are you considering?

Title

+ Add title

Job type

☐ Full-time   ☐ Part-time   ☐ Contract   ☐ Internship   ☐ Remote   ☐ Freelance

When can you start?

Anytime

Introduction (300 characters or less)

What else should recruiters know?

Who can see your Open Candidate profile? Only recruiters who have paid for and use LinkedIn's premium "Recruiter's Platform" (Prices begin at around $8,000 per license) can see that you have filled out the Open Candidates questionnaire.[169] Your current employer and its affiliates should not be able to view your Open Candidates profile. However, LinkedIn provides this disclaimer "We take steps to not show your current company that you're open, but can't guarantee that we can identify every recruiter affiliated with your company."

Naturally, if you are unemployed, there is no risk. Even if you are employed, the risk of discovery is reasonably small. Besides, it is not illegal, immoral, or unethical to be open to a new job that can enhance your career experience. Most employers know that the job

169 Uzialko, Adam, LinkedIn's Open Candidates: How to Search for a New Job, Quietly, October 6, 2016, http://www.businessnewsdaily.com/9468-linkedin-open-candidates.html (Accessed November 25, 2016)

market is a free agency market. Employees, especially today, look to maximize their career experience and that can mean pursuing new jobs when the time is right.

Strategies for using the Open Candidate feature. For most job seekers, using the Open Candidates feature is a very good idea. Recruiters can screen potential candidates not only based on qualifications, but those that are open to new opportunities. This shortens their work and can place you towards the top of their contact list! According to LinkedIn, "open candidates" are more likely to be contacted by recruiters[170]. Use your Introductory section of the questionnaire to emphasize skills/background and accomplishments. Remember, you only have 300 characters spaces so you have to be very succinct. For example:

"Account management professional seeking a position with a health insurance organization with proven skills in client service, ACA compliance, implementation, renewals, and claim resolution. Promoted 3 times, 95% client retention, recognized with client services award, have client recommendations"

If you are unemployed, there is virtually no reason for not using this feature. The only rare consideration (employed or unemployed) would be perception based on the level of position you are seeking. Would a senior-level hiring executive, board of director, or possibly a retainer-only search firm pause to reach out to you because you are an Open Candidate on LinkedIn? Very unlikely (hopefully), but it is worth a moment of thought.

Consider Upgrading Your LinkedIn Account

Consider upgrading your account to the premium level during your search. The prices are reasonable, and the benefits are worth it. With a premium account, you can send InMails to reach more people on LinkedIn.[171] There are other advantages as well, including being able to see who's looked at your profile, how you compare to other applicants applying for the same position, coming up more often in searches, and so on.[172]

---

170 Bell, Karissa, LinkedIn will now help you secretly tell recruiters you want a new job , October 6, 2016, http://mashable.com/2016/10/06/linkedin-tell-recruiters-you-want-a-new-job.amp. (accessed November 7, 2016)

171 "InMail—Overview," LinkedIn Help Center, https://help.linkedin.com/app/answers/detail/a_id/1584/~/InMail---overview (accessed June 24, 2015).

172 Gyanda Sachdeva, "Unlocking Your Competitive Edge with the Power of LinkedIn Premium," LinkedIn Blog, December 18, 2014, http://blog.linkedin.com/2014/12/18/unlocking-your-competitive-edge-with-the-power-of-linkedin-premium/ (accessed June 9, 2015).

Measuring the Effectiveness of Your LinkedIn Profile

Having a complete LinkedIn profile, implementing optimization strategies, and making your profile compelling are necessary steps to maximizing the use of your LinkedIn profile in your job search. But the true effectiveness of your profile is the number of views it gets.

If you are in a full-blown, active job search utilizing all the tools at your disposal, one measure of success is getting a minimum of twenty profile views a week. This is not a scientific number but rather a minimum threshold number to use as a benchmark for the progress of your LinkedIn profile and your job search as a whole. If your profile views fall below the minimum twenty, reevaluate your efforts to keep those profile views above twenty. Keep in mind that although LinkedIn profile views are important, they are not interviews. Interviews are the purest measure of the effectiveness of your job search, and the only way to get a job.

What do you do with your LinkedIn profile after you get a new job?

Once you land a new job (and you will), you have a couple of choices with your LinkedIn profile. First, you can create your background/experience section in the same fashion as previously instructed for your new position.

There is another approach you can consider. Understand the construction of your profile has been focused on you. It has been written to showcase you as a professional with the purpose of a job search. When you get a new job, you may want to shift that focus to your new employer. This is achieved by putting a paragraph in your current employment that describes the company, its products, services value proposition, etc. You can often get this information from the company website or LinkedIn company page.

After you insert the company description, follow the same advice as previously instructed with a paragraph about your duties, responsibilities, followed by accomplishments as they occur.

Remember, LinkedIn is a dynamic site that changes frequently, adding some features and functions and taking others away. Be aware of programming changes and their possible implications on your profile and job search.

Part VI

Cover Letters and Other Written Communications

Dost thou love life, then do not squander time, for that's the stuff life is made of.

—Benjamin Franklin[173]

Some employers focus on a cover letter, while others will bypass it and go straight to the resume. If the resume is strong, some employers will then go back and read the cover letter. Regardless of how an employer treats the letter, make sure that you invest an appropriate amount of time writing an impactful cover letter (don't grind over details, and don't rush). A well-written cover letter immediately begins to differentiate you from other job seekers by highlighting strong points in your background and providing a sample of your writing ability. SEALs occasionally have stronger written communication skills than younger job seekers.[174] A well-written letter can also serve as a customizable template for different job opportunities.[175]

---

173 Franklin, Benjamin [Richard Saunders, Poor Richard, pseud.]. *The Way to Wealth.* July 7, 1757, *American Literature Research and Analysis*, http://itech.fgcu.edu/faculty/wohlpart/alra/franklin.htm (accessed February 19, 2016).

174 Adams, "Older Workers, There's Hope"; Wilson, "Why Millennials Are Often Poor Writers."

175 Claycomb and Dinse, *Career Pathways*, Part 4.

Types of Cover Letters

In general, cover letters fall under three categories:

A **letter of application** is used to match a specific employment position.

A **letter of inquiry** is written (frequently to HR) when you are exploring whether the employer may have a possible open position within the company.

A **marketing letter (or email)** is written to quickly grab the hiring executive's attention. The goal of this "attack" strategy is to showcase your qualifications and create enough interest so the hiring executive reads your resume and engages you in conversation. You are proactively marketing yourself directly to a potential hiring executive who could likely hire you for the position you seek (regardless of whether there is a known or posted opening).

The Cover Letter Success Formula

The kind of cover letter doesn't matter on this particular point: Getting your cover letter read increases the odds that your resume will be read. Be concise. With your cover letter (as well as all your written communications), proofreading is mandatory. Executives are reading not only for content, but for sentence structure and how you express your thoughts. Spelling or grammar errors broadcast that you either don't pay attention to detail or are careless. Have someone who's unfamiliar with your letter read it. You could also let your writing sit overnight. Some claim that reading it backward helps. And when it comes time to send your letters, don't send the same one to every executive. Having a template is fine, but customize each one. And don't mention salary, compensation, or benefits in a cover letter.

To maximize your effectiveness when writing cover letters, use the following approach, which has proven effective over the course of time:

- Create interest (first sentence)
- Match (next)
- Showcase an accomplishment/qualification (next paragraph)
- Provide additional information (paragraph three and perhaps four)
- Close

Here's an in-depth look at how to do this:

Create interest

You must quickly get the attention and interest of the employer. Personalizing the letter with their name (found by searching LinkedIn or the company website, or by calling the company) will go a long way. Adding a "RE:" line (meaning "regarding") lets the executive know what your letter is about and what position you're interested in. Generating interest increases the time the executive spends on your letter. All too often, people do the opposite by beginning their letters with something similar to the following:

I am writing you today regarding any potential need you may have for a director of operations. I believe I have the qualifications you are looking for.

This type of opening sentence is ineffective, if not boring. Instead, begin your letters with something effective, relevant, and even thought provoking. Some examples are:

1. **Mention a personal or professional referral.** *Our mutual friend, Peter Huggins, suggested that I reach out to you.* Mentioning a common acquaintance is one of the most effective ways to capture a reader's attention (using the persuasion principles of social proof and liking).

2. **Come out swinging with one of your top achievements.** *For the last four years, I have been ranked as one of my company's top ten sales representatives for overall sales production.*

3. **Identify yourself by a unique or highly sought-after skill or knowledge base.** This uses the persuasion principle of scarcity. *I am a software engineer with a Microsoft Master's Certificate and five CCIEs from Cisco.*

4. **Refer to a statistic.** *According to the most recent polling, 43 percent of small businesses will explore private health-care exchanges for their company's health insurance needs, up from 21 percent just a year ago.*

5. **Offer to solve a business problem.** *If you need to decrease your company's operating expenses by 20 percent, without layoffs, I have a track record of doing just that.*

6. **Ask a relevant business question.** *Have you found it difficult to increase company revenue during this economic downturn? If so, that is my specialty.*

7. **Mention a recent company event or a significant news release.** *Congratulations on your acquisition of Plate Co., Inc.! I understand this could increase your market share significantly.*

8. **Use a quotation.** *Jeremy Johnson of the American Marketing Association recently found that redefining target markets can increase effectiveness by almost double.*

9. **Cite a relevant industry trend.** *It is a well-known fact that health-care reform is causing a silent exodus of tenured physicians from private practice. I have a track record of recruiting these doctors into onsite clinics.*

Match

After you have the hiring executive's attention, hold it by very briefly identifying your function, which must match one the company already has—even using their exact wording, if possible. Consider using the "word cloud" technique (mentioned in Essential Job-Search Topics and Tools) to do this. "Matching" makes you relevant and encourages the hiring executive to read on.

Here are a couple of example phrases:

As an industrial engineer with over fifteen years of manufacturing experience . . .
I am a senior-level account management professional with a specialty in wellness and care management . . .

Depending on your writing style, this matching statement could be placed at the end of the "create interest" paragraph, added as the first sentence of the "showcase" paragraph, or appear in a short paragraph by itself.

Showcase an accomplishment/qualification

The accomplishment paragraph is even more important after you have created interest and matched a known company role. Make this paragraph impactful by using bold lettering sparingly to focus the executive on key points, but do not repeat your resume. Make your accomplishments relevant by identifying the position's most important requirements, link your qualifications to them, and then show your accomplishments in each or most of the job functions. In other words, tell a prospective employer you can do the job and you have a track record of doing it well. These "showcase" techniques can also help to get your resume read.

If you want to pursue job opportunities as a director of operations (just as an illustration), start with your Master Job Description combined with research on similar open positions (or a job description from the employer). You may find a job description like this:

Director of Operations

Candidate must have at least ten years' experience managing multisite locations. Individual will have experience with the following: process-management systems, personnel management, performance improvement, and emergency-response plans.

So, when writing your letter, use the exact wording to demonstrate your skills in the listed job requirements. This paragraph of your letter could look like this (portions bolded for clarification):

In the last fifteen years, I have worked as a director of operations for three manufacturers in the plastics industry. During my most recent position at See Through Plastics, LLC, I had success in the following areas:

- *Managed four manufacturing facilities in four separate regions of the country. Exceeded production and profit goals for the last five consecutive years.*

- *Designed and implemented a process-management system that improved production efficiency by 32 percent and increased product output by 20 percent.*

- *Created a workplace-accountability matrix with floor supervisors that decreased absenteeism of workers by 15 percent while improving productivity per worker by 21 percent.*

- *Worked with company auditor to develop an auditing system that revealed resource and time inefficiencies. Program saved 12 percent on resource orders in the first year and reduced fulfillment time by over 20 percent.*

- *Worked with safety consulting firm to create and implement a state-of-the-art emergency-response plan for catastrophic events and business interruption. Plan has been duplicated by other manufacturers.*

To keep your letter concise, only use bulleted items that address the position's most important requirements. In the above example, the job seeker may only use two or three of the five accomplishments.

In rare instances, there will be unique situations where accomplishments can be less important. This occurs when you may be one of relatively few in your field or area with a certain skill, certification, or knowledge that becomes an important element of your candidacy. Showcase your unique qualification in this paragraph.

Provide additional information

In the following paragraphs of the letter, elaborate on your experience, skills, background, and achievements. This is where you have a fair amount of latitude on what you want to showcase. Choose those topics you feel are the most relevant or impressive to the employer. Once again, inform the employer what you did, in addition to how this produced positive results.[176]

> *I am a motivated sales professional with a positive track record of opening new territories. At Ins. Company, I took over a three-state virgin territory with no sales or business contacts. I researched and identified broker-dealers, set appointments, traveled, and made sales presentations. Within the first year, I generated over $1.2M in product sales and exceeded goals by over 300 percent.*

🦜 This is also a place where you can weave in statements that address and counter possible age biases.

Another approach is to add a strong recommendation. This paragraph should be indented and single-spaced. To realize this technique's full impact, identify the person providing the recommendation by name and title. Here's an example:

> *My supervisor, Susan J. Smith, Director of Operations, Cyban, Inc. states:*
> *Sandra has a strong work ethic. She is organized, resourceful, and can work successfully without supervision. She is flexible and will roll up her sleeves to get the job done!*

Remember, it is always more influential when others speak well of you than when you promote yourself.[177]

🦜 Another technique you can use in this section is to reveal a professional insight about yourself to personalize the letter. It must be something relevant or important to the employer. These statements can work to defeat age-related biases (e.g., that you are worn out or potentially unenthusiastic about work). This paragraph can start with a phrase such as: "I am passionate about . . . ," "I am professionally rewarded when . . . ," "I continue to be intrigued by . . . ," and so on. For example:

> *I am passionate about wellness. I get a great deal of satisfaction knowing that the*

---

176 See also, Safani, "Tell a Story."

177 Matt, "Brag Book."

wellness services I promote to clients will have a personal impact on the health and well-being of that employer's employees.

🦭 You may choose to add some information about your personal life that could have relevance to the job and defeat an age bias. As mentioned previously, younger hiring executives occasionally want to know about you as a person and a professional.

I am competitive professionally as well as in my personal life. In fact, I routinely compete in local tennis tournaments . . . successfully, I might add!

Use these paragraphs to inform the employer about any other piece of information relevant to your job search, such as relocation.

I will relocate to Portland in the next sixty days as a result of my wife's promotion.

Close

Conclude your letter by using a brief closing statement, followed by your intention to follow up:

Based on my track record of successful operational efficiency, I believe I have the qualifications and accomplishments to make a positive impact on ABC Inc. I look forward to discussing this opportunity with you, and I will contact your office next week.

Don't restrict yourself to paper cover letters. Other effective methods include marketing emails (See Proactively Marketing Your Professional Credentials and the Appendix), as well as videos and YouTube (discussed later). Use each of these, as appropriate, in your search to gain greater visibility with employers and increase opportunities for interviews.

Cover Letters and Career Transition SEALs

🦭 For SEALs making a transition from one career focus to another, or possibly changing industries, consider adding a paragraph informing the employer exactly how your skills translate or are directly transferable to the job opportunity.[178] This explanation of transferability must be succinct. If it isn't, the employer may conclude that you are

---

178 Leanne, *How to Interview*, p. 104.

struggling to draw the connection between your skills and the job. In that case, you lose. This information about your transferability of skills should be a part of the third or fourth paragraph. For example:

- "There is a strong correlation of my skills as a . . . and your open position for a . . . "
- "My skills and experience as an employee benefits account manager are directly transferable to your need of an internal benefits human resource specialist. [Now explain why] . . . "

Cover Letters and Recruiters

When you are contacted by a recruiter for a specific opportunity, the following technique can differentiate you from other job seekers since you will be competing against other well-qualified candidates.

Here's the scenario and how to gain a potential edge:

- You have been contacted by a recruiter regarding a specific opportunity. You are interested and qualified, and the recruiter is willing to submit your credentials to the employer.

- Ask the recruiter if there is a job description or job posting. If so, get it and read it. In the same conversation or a follow-up call, tell the recruiter that you are going to send him or her a brief cover letter (by email) regarding the position. Most, if not all, recruiters will accept the letter. Ask the recruiter, at his or her discretion, to include the cover letter as a part of your submission to the employer. Here's why: Many recruited candidates don't bother with cover letters because they think a recruiter's involvement makes a cover letter unnecessary. Differentiate yourself from your competition and showcase your accomplishments and qualifications by writing a cover letter (remember to use the word cloud technique, which could help). Employers will note that you took the time and effort to write the letter, and draw the conclusion that you must be more interested than some of the other candidates who did not. And when the letter gets read, you have differentiated yourself even more.

Thank-You Letters

The primary purposes of a thank-you letter are to express your appreciation; reiterate your relevant background, qualifications, and successes; and differentiate you from other job seekers. Most hiring executives appreciate a thank-you correspondence after an interview.[179] And "some employers may expect a job interview thank-you card."[180] However, it has been said that only 20 percent of all job seekers take the time to write a thank-you note.[181] If so, writing a thank-you note can differentiate you from a majority of other job seekers. And not sending a thank-you note may reflect negatively on your candidacy.[182]

An important secondary purpose is to make sure the hiring executive remembers you. In a survey by *TheLadders*, a combined 76 percent said a thank-you note was "somewhat important" or "very important" to their hiring decision.[183] That's three out of every four! Therefore, capitalize on this opportunity to reinforce your skills and accomplishments. Write a thank-you note after every interview. And keep it short. This is a letter, not an interview transcript.

To maximize the impact of your thank-you letter, use the following approach:

1. Express your appreciation
2. Match
3. Emphasize past achievements
4. Close

Let's look at each step in more detail:

Express your appreciation
Thank the hiring executive for their time. Then build rapport, depending upon the circumstances. Your first paragraph could look something like this:

> *I appreciate you taking time out yesterday to meet with me regarding your implementation consultant position. I enjoyed learning how you derived the concept behind your state-of-the-art system. [This is a compliment, using the persuasion principle of liking.] As we discussed, my knowledge in this area could assist your*

179 Accountemps, "Farewell to the Handwritten Thank-You Note? Survey Reveals Email, Phone Call Are Preferred Methods for Post-Interview Follow-Up," news release, June 14, 2012, http://accountemps.rhi.mediaroom.com/thank-you (accessed February 19, 2016).

180 "Do Employers Expect a Job Interview Thank You Card?" CVTips, http://www.cvtips.com/interview/do-employers-expect-a-job-interview-thank-you-card.html (accessed February 19, 2016).

181 Helmrich, Brittney. "Thanks! 22 Job Interview Thank You Note Tips," *Business News Daily*, March 11, 2016, http://www.businessnewsdaily.com/7134-thank-you-note-tips.html (accessed April 19, 2016).

182 "Nothing Says 'Hire Me' Like 'Thank You': Thank-You Note Etiquette," CareerBuilder, http://www.careerbuilder.com/JobPoster/Resources/page.aspx?pagever=ThankYouNoteEtiquette (accessed February 19, 2016).

183 "Give Thanks or Your Chance For That Job Could be Cooked," *TheLadders*, http://cdn.theladders.net/static/images/basicSite/PR/pdfs/TheLaddersGiveThanks.pdf (accessed February 19, 2016).

department with the challenges it will face in the coming months.

Or perhaps more like this:

> *Thank you for meeting me on Tuesday regarding the regional sales position. I appreciate your time. And, by the way, good luck to your son during tryouts for the starting quarterback position!*

Match

Because you were interviewed, you should know what the hiring executive is looking for in the position. Briefly restate and match your qualifications to that need(s).

> *During our plant tour last week, I was very impressed with your use of robotics in the manufacturing process. I can honestly say I have never seen such an impressive after-market manufacturing plant! With over fifteen years as an industrial engineer from nearly identical manufacturing environments, I am well-suited for the challenges of this position.*

Emphasize past achievements

Express your interest in the position, and link two or three job requirements with your accomplishments. For maximum impact, try to make them relevant to company needs, a position's special qualifications, or topics mentioned in the interview. Your paragraph could look something like this:

> *I am interested in joining your company in an engineering operations capacity. As we discussed, my recent accomplishments include:*
>
> - *Implemented a manufacturing process improvement system resulting in an $800,000 savings.*
>
> - *Designed and implemented an inventory-auditing system that increased turnaround time 30 percent and reduced spending by 12 percent.*
>
> - *Developed and implemented a "Visions" business plan that reduces operating expenses and forecasts budgets for a variety of business operations, including equipment and technology upgrades and new facility construction.*

Close

Here, express your continued interest and outline your plan to contact the hiring executive. Here's an example of this final paragraph:

What I achieved for Sinc Company, I can do for you. I will follow up with you in ten days, as you requested, to discuss additional steps.

Thank-You Letter When You Are Not Selected for the Job

This letter builds bridges for the future and is a very strong networking technique. It will differentiate you from others and create a favorable impression with the hiring executive. There are two good reasons for doing this. First, it can leave the door open for future opportunities with the company. It is not uncommon for employers to revisit previous candidates when new opportunities become available.

Additionally, since professionals within an industry often run in the same circles of influence, the letter distinguishes you and could lead to other business relationships with the hiring executive. Writing a professional correspondence after a decision not to hire shows the hiring executive your character and professionalism. You don't know where, when, or in what way your paths may cross again. The letter helps ensure the next engagement is positive—be it business or personal. You can also follow up by email if you choose (see Proactively Marketing Your Professional Credentials for tips on how to professionally structure an email).

Something to Think about

Some suggest that sending hard-copy cover letters, resumes, and thank-you letters is no longer as effective as it once was. People think, "It's all done by email these days." Perhaps that's true, but consider this: How many emails did you get in your last position? A lot, right? There are some hiring executives who receive two hundred or more emails a day (maybe yours was one of them). Obviously, not all of these emails are from job seekers, but the point is these hiring executives are busy people who receive lots of emails.

In your last position, how often did you receive a personal letter (not junk mail)? Probably not very often.

Here's the concept: Due to the sheer volume of emails that a hiring authority receives, one possible technique to differentiate yourself (which is a goal in your job search), is to send a cover letter, resume, or thank-you note by US mail. *That which was old may be new again.* It's an idea you may wish to explore with some of your target companies and target contacts.

A variation of this approach is to send the cover letter by US mail and if there is no response, then follow up with an email message referring to the hard-copy letter you sent. Include a copy of the letter as an attachment or a summary of the letter's contents in the body of the email.

Another Idea

If you decide to send a cover letter, resume, or thank-you letter by US mail, consider investing in customized envelopes. Since there is a lot of usable, open space on an envelope, consider noting two or three of your top achievements in the envelope's lower-left corner. How often does a hiring executive see this? Probably rarely . . . and that might be just the differentiation you need for him or her to open the envelope.

Use your best discretion on how receptive a hiring executive at your level would view these techniques.

Some Final Words about Written Communications

As you know, communication skills (written, verbal, and listening) are highly sought after.[184] Being able to write effectively and persuasively is a very important element in your job search, and it will be evaluated (as well as whether you've proofread your materials). What you write about, how you communicate it, and the caliber of your sentence structure, word choice, grammar, and punctuation are evaluated against other job seekers. By following the Cover Letter Success Formula and proper thank-you letter writing techniques, you can feel confident that your written communications will differentiate you from other job seekers, grab the attention of the employer, and result in a higher success rate.

Have someone unfamiliar with the documents review them. Using an effective writing formula will be rendered useless if there are spelling, grammatical, or punctuation errors.

The Appendix has sample letters for your review.

Shifting Gears

So far the topics we have been discussing have been preparing you to engage in job-search activities that lead to interviews by helping you establish the right mindset and set up templates and to-do lists for success. At most, these preparatory activities should take two weeks (as a *maximum*)—ideally much less. Anything beyond that could be just busywork or

---

184 Hanson and Hanson, "What Do Employers *Really* Want?"

a diversion for you to avoid the necessary work of engaging the job market and beginning your job search in earnest.

We are now going to shift gears into topics related to generating job leads and interviews.

Part VII

Professional Networking

Everything you want is just outside your comfort zone.

—Robert Allen[185]

Hidden Job Market

As you engage the marketplace in search of a new job, accept this statistic: It is widely believed that "at least 70 percent, if not 80 percent, of jobs are not published."[186] These jobs are often filled by companies before the need to advertise or post the opening online arises; they are referred to as the Hidden Job Market. Much has been written about the Hidden Job Market.[187] It is real.

The Internet and social networking have dramatically changed the nature of job searching. As a result, networking techniques and strategies (as well as how you will land your next career position) have taken on a whole new meaning.

Why don't employers advertise their open positions? For some it is a matter of company policy that they must post all job openings, so they do. However, many companies choose not to advertise for any of the following reasons:

185 "Quotes on Initiative," *Leadership Now,* http://www.leadershipnow.com/initiativequotes.html (accessed May 28, 2015).

186 Kaufman, "A Successful Job Search."

187 *Get Hired Fast! Tap the Hidden Job Market in 15 Days* by Brian Graham, *Cracking the Hidden Job Market: How to Find Opportunity in Any Economy* by Donald Asher, and others.

- The sheer amount of respondents (with the vast majority wholly unqualified) makes for time-consuming work sifting through countless resumes.

- For truly specialized positions, there are few or no qualified candidates.

- Employers want well-qualified, interested, and affordable candidates without the hours of effort to locate them through advertising. This easing of the hiring process is part of the value recruiters bring to employers.

- Some employers choose to fill positions by word of mouth and networking.

How can you tap the Hidden Job Market effectively and efficiently? Follow the strategies and techniques in this book. Take a proactive approach to your search (don't just sit at home and apply for jobs online). Network both online and face-to-face.

There will be more about networking in the following pages. But, understand and appreciate this truth: Networking works, but it can take time. "Those who give, get," is said to be the philosophical foundation to effective networking.[188] When you help others find what they want, they will remember you and return the favor (persuasion principle of reciprocity).

Networking

Networking is an essential part of building wealth.
—Armstrong Williams[189]

Networking for a job involves connecting with people you know and then the people they know to lead you to a job. It also includes reaching out professionally to those you don't know for the same purpose.[190] It generally involves three types of contacts:

1. Those people who can lead you to others who can assist you in your job search.

2. Those people who can introduce you to someone who can hire you.

3. Those people with the authority to hire you.

---

188 Vlooten, Dick van. "The Seven Laws of Networking: Those Who Give, Get," *Career Magazine*, May 7, 2004, http://www.sciencemag.org/careers/2004/05/seven-laws-networking-those-who-give-get (accessed April 14, 2016).

189 Williams, Armstrong. "A Few Simple Steps to Building Wealth," *Townhall*, June 13, 2005, http://townhall.com/columnists/armstrongwilliams/2005/06/13/a_few_simple_steps_to_building_wealth/page/full (accessed May 28, 2015).

190 Claycomb and Dinse, *Career Pathways*, Part 7.

Job-search networking can take place in a wide variety of situations including face-to-face, online through sites focused on professionals (LinkedIn), or people's social interactions (Facebook and Twitter), professional associations, alumni events, and even the casual dinner gathering with friends.

It is estimated that between 60 and 80 percent of all jobs are found by networking.[191] Furthermore, surveys indicate that job seekers who are referred to a hiring executive have a one in seven chance of landing a job offer compared to one in one hundred if they apply online.[192] Getting referred to a job is a function of networking. So, statistically speaking, your next job will come as a result of your networking efforts.

This next statement is very important and goes straight to the heart of professionally networking for a job: It's not how many people you know, but rather how many people know you. Ponder that for a moment to understand the concept. How many people know you well enough that they would refer you to someone else or possibly go out of their way to help you, even if it's in a small measure? It's this kind of relationship networking that drives a job search.

Fear of Networking

🦭 Unfortunately, many SEALs hesitate to take full advantage of networking because they're intimidated or are afraid of being viewed as pushy, annoying, or self-serving. Put those feelings aside. Networking is not about arrogant self-promotion. Instead, it's about building relationships. When you think about networking as building relationships—or creating professional friendships—many of your fears will disappear.[193]

Besides, when you network you are interacting with people, setting appointments, having conversations, helping others, having fun, and so on.[194] Remembering these things helps reduce any feelings of isolation and gives you something to look forward to (your scheduled appointments!).

Accept this next statement as gospel truth: Whether your networking is formal or informal, online or offline, there are people out there who want to help. It's your job to get out there and let them!

---

191 LinkedIn, "Using LinkedIn to Find a Job"; Beatty, "The Math Behind the Networking Claim"; Rothberg, "80% of Job Openings."

192 Jobvite, "Jobvite Social Recruiting Survey Finds Over 90% of Employers Will Use Social Recruiting in 2012," news release, July 9, 2012, http://www.jobvite.com/press-releases/2012/jobvite-social-recruiting-survey-finds-90-employers-will-use-social-recruiting-2012/ (accessed November 10, 2015).

193 Phillips, Simon. *The Complete Guide to Professional Networking: The Secrets of Online and Offline Success.* (London: Kogan Page Limited, 2014), p. 1.

194 See also, ibid., p. 50–51.

Why Networking Is So Effective

Do the thing you fear and the death of fear is certain.

—Emerson[195]

There are several reasons why networking is an effective way to find your next opportunity:

1. It taps into the Hidden Job Market.

2. It decreases the time it takes to land a new position. Networking is a proactive job-search tactic. People you know or have been referred to are more likely to speak or meet with you personally. The more communications you have, the closer you get to a job offer.

3. It reduces competition. Job postings tend to draw a pile of resumes. It's been referenced that for every online job posting, there are 118 applicants.[196] Networking makes you the preferred candidate of a much smaller candidate pool.

4. It introduces you through a common connection and expands your current network. People do business primarily with people they know and like.[197] As your network expands, so will your opportunities as you meet more and more people.

5. It helps you practice for interviews and builds self-confidence. Networking creates phone conversations, lunch dates, and research interviews. These are opportunities to practice your interview skills. This will boost your self-confidence, awareness that your job search is moving forward, and feelings of success as you improve overall, leading to better interviews. Having confidence translates into better communications, which creates more interviews, eventually leading to more job opportunities.[198]

Types of Networks

Conceptually there are two job-search networks: personal and professional. Your personal network includes family, friends, neighbors, and doctors, as well as your dentist, financial

---

195 "Ralph Waldo Emerson Quotable Quote," Goodreads, www.goodreads.com/quotes/60285-do-the-thing-you-fear-and-the-death-of-fear (accessed May 28, 2015).

196 Smith, Jacquelyn. "7 Things You Probably Didn't Know About Your Job Search," *Forbes*, April 17, 2013, http://www.forbes.com/sites/jacquelynsmith/2013/04/17/7-things-you-probably-didnt-know-about-your-job-search/#71fe2c6e64e6 (accessed February 12, 2016).

197 Byrne, *Attraction*, quoted in Kurtzberg and Naquin, *Essentials*, p. 35.

198 Moynihan et al., "A Longitudinal Study," quoted in Kurtzberg and Naquin, Essentials, p. 30–32.

advisor, accountant, and members of church, civic, or philanthropic groups you attend. Everyone else you interact with in your personal life is also included here. Websites in your personal network include Facebook and Twitter, among others.

Your professional network is developed from your career and consists of people who are work colleagues, connections at other companies, former bosses, senior management, association contacts, and so on. As mentioned before, LinkedIn is the leading professional networking website.

Both networks can be extremely powerful in directing you and connecting you to potential job opportunities. Deciding which network will yield the most leads is personal and depends upon your circumstances. Your networks could perform equally well.

Each one of your contacts connects you to their network. And any member of that network could know about an available opportunity. Let's say you have solid relationships with twenty people in either your personal or professional network. Now let's say they each know twenty people. That's four hundred people you can get to know reasonably quickly without much effort.

For some people, twenty connections is a very low number. It's possible that your network, especially on the professional side, could be in the hundred-plus range. You do the math on how large your extended network can be—chances are, you'll be pleasantly surprised.

Evaluating the Strength and Quality of Your Network

Prior to actively networking, take some time and evaluate your current network. It's been noted that as we get older, our networks usually get smaller. This can have a negative impact on your search overall.[199] Are there enough quality, relevant contacts to drive your job-search efforts?

Give yourself one point for each of the following questions that you can answer yes to:

1. Is your professional network comprised predominantly of people within your industry or position type?

2. Does it contain connections who can lead you to other connections who have influence, perhaps even potential hiring executives?

3. Do you feel your professional network is large enough?

---

199 Maderer, Jason. "Here Are 5 Tips for Job-Seekers Over 50," Futurity.org, June 18, 2015, http://www.futurity.org/older-adults-employment-jobs-944902/ (accessed February 12, 2016).

4. Are you a member of enough industry-specific LinkedIn groups, associations, or relevant local groups?

5. Do you feel your network can help you?

How did you do?

5 points: Great job on your network!

4 points: Your network is excellent but could stand some improvement.

3 points: You need to spend time building your network.

2 points: Your network needs serious attention.

0 or 1 point: Get your network a lifeline, stat!

If you need to improve your network, put in extra time and effort to get introduced and connected to others who can enhance the strength and quality of your contact base. The more time and effort you devote to your network, the quicker it will grow . . . and the quicker you'll connect with your next opportunity. Start with your strong connections (your Cabinet, who are your inner circle of trusted contacts—more on this in just a moment) and ask for their assistance. They will be most willing to help, but contacting them and asking to be introduced to their network contacts will take time. Many will help, some won't. Either way, thank them for their time and move ahead.

Who to Connect and Network With

The point of networking for a job is connecting and communicating with people who can help you or hire you. So, who would that be? Below is a list of "targets," along with "help" or "hire" designations to get you thinking:

1. Hiring executives from competing companies or from your current or past employers (hire you and help you)

2. Peers and colleagues, selectively chosen, from your current company or past employers (help you)

3. Hiring executives from vendors, customers, suppliers, or business partners from your current or past employers (hire you and help you)

4. Peers and colleagues from these vendors or business partners (help you)

5. People who are "centers of influence"—these could be contacts from a wide variety of

sources, including personal, philanthropic, civic, and nonprofit organizations (help you)

Many other connections exist—just make sure these possible connections can move your search forward. No matter the type, most of these people can be identified and contacted through a search of LinkedIn.

LinkedIn

LinkedIn has dramatically influenced networking during a job search. Here are some cautionary strategies and notes to keep in mind:

1. **Use good judgment when connecting or extending invitations.** Determine whether a potential connection could be helpful or a center of influence for you. Connect with those who are in your industry or field of interest.

   Extend invitations to peers in your industry and those one to two levels above your title or function. Going above one or two levels may stretch the logical relevance of connecting.[200]

   Whenever possible, customize your invitation for a better response and success rate. If you extend an invitation that is not accepted, it's okay. Try not to take it personally. Instead, create an Excel spreadsheet of those who did not respond, and include a hyperlink to their profile. If you upgraded your LinkedIn account, you can still reach this person for future communication as needed or appropriate.

2. **Join Groups.** As previously mentioned, there are over two million LinkedIn groups.[201] Statistically, there are groups that will apply to you—join them. Consider the LinkedIn *Over 50 Job Seekers* group.[202] Once you are in a group, it is easier to connect and get introduced to people of interest to you.

3. **Follow target companies.** Look up the company page for any company you are interested in. Click the "Follow Company" tab. All activity from that company's page, including job postings, will appear on your LinkedIn home page. This is a great feature to track the company's activities and potential hiring needs.

4. **Use the "Discover Jobs in Your Network" feature.** LinkedIn now informs you

---

200 See also, Yate, *Knock 'em Dead*, p. 83.

201 Arruda, "Is LinkedIn Poised."

202 Found at https://www.linkedin.com/groups/8368426/profile (accessed February 12, 2016).

of job openings at companies where you have LinkedIn connections. If a position becomes available that interests you, see if you can get a referral from someone you know who works for the employer.

LinkedIn conducted a six-month study of senior-level professionals (vice president titles and above) and their use of LinkedIn during their job search. The results clearly indicated that these senior-level professionals knew "the value of building and nurturing professional relationships in order to be successful in their job search"[203] (networking). The study found that "80 percent were sending connection requests, 50 percent were participating in groups, 40 percent were engaging on LinkedIn via shares, likes, and comments."[204]

Do your best to keep track of changes to LinkedIn's system, as these changes could affect your profile (and job search as a whole).

Create Your Professional "Cabinet"

The President of the United States has a Cabinet. It is a select group of trusted advisors composed of the Vice President and other prominent government officials of the executive branch, totaling sixteen (not including others who are a part at the President's discretion).[205] You also need to create a Cabinet of trusted advisors. Here is a definition to guide your thinking, selection, and development process:

A professional (networking) Cabinet is a select group of people in your professional life who you can trust and call upon, knowing that they will undoubtedly help you in any way reasonably possible. This would include providing you with advice, introductions, mentorship/"tough love," referrals, insight, and recommendations, among other things. It is a reciprocal relationship; they know they can count on you to do the same for them.

Let's examine a few components of this definition:

A select group—Your Cabinet will likely be small, comprising five to ten people, perhaps a few more if you can create and maintain close relationships. It's likely that your Cabinet will be people with whom you have developed (or are currently developing) a close relationship.

Professional life—Your Cabinet is a group of people in your professional life. These people may be your friends, but the foundation of the relationship started in your professional life.

---

203 Ayele, "Land Your Dream Job."

204 Ibid.

205 "Constitutional Topic: The Cabinet," U.S. Constitution Online, http://www.usconstitution.net/consttop_cabi.html (accessed November 10, 2015).

Trust—These people must be trustworthy. They are, in large part, confidants to whom you can be vulnerable regarding professional matters.

Undoubtedly help—These are people you can count on and who have your best interests at heart. These people are your "go-to" inner circle.

In any way reasonably possible—You must understand and appreciate that there are limits. Like the President's Cabinet, each member has an area of expertise. This is also true with your Cabinet. Your Cabinet will likely consist of professionals who have unique abilities, insight, connections, and so on. In fact, over time you want to have a reasonably diverse Cabinet.

A reciprocal relationship—As with any network, the relationship must be a two-way street to be productive. You must be willing to give when your Cabinet member needs you.

A Cabinet is a very important networking group to create and have. It is the group you can rely upon in a pinch. They are your network's foundation. How many people do you know who you can contact almost immediately and ask for help with full confidence that you will receive it? If that number is not at least seven to ten, you need to grow your Cabinet.

Create Your Sales Company

The next layer of your network is your "Sales Company." The words used to describe these network contacts were chosen by design.

Sales. As you know, salespeople promote the products and services of the employer. They sell the benefits of those products and services. They assist buyers. They are ambassadors for their employers in the market. They also provide feedback to their employer. By analogy, you want to create a layer of connections who will assist you, promote you, and be your ambassadors in the job market when given an opportunity.

These are the people you have good professional and collegial relationships with. You have interacted with them professionally, and perhaps socially, on some level. These are people you are reasonably sure (though not completely, like your Cabinet) will help or lend a hand if the opportunity presents itself. Put into percentages, your Cabinet is 100 percent sure to help. Your Sales Company is 60 percent and above. It's more likely than not. There are no scientific percentages, but connections in your Sales Company are those people you can call on who are likely to help. This help can take many forms, including:

"I'll keep my eyes open."

"You might want to read this article on XYZ Company."

"You may want to network with Kipp Sawyer."

"Call Ruth Moore, my boss. We're looking!"

Always be a professional networker. Thank everyone who responds and offer to help them if they need anything.

Company. The word "company" is chosen for its military definition. A military company is one hundred to two hundred soldiers.[206] Therefore, picking the midpoint, your Sales Company should number around 150 contacts. The 150 number also has some scientific basis—it happens to be the Dunbar Number, created by British anthropologist Robin Dunbar. Based on his studies, he theorized that there is a numerical limit to the number of individuals with whom a stable interpersonal relationship can be maintained. That number is 150.[207]

The point is this: You want to have around 150 connections in your Sales Company.

Let's think through the power of what this could mean for your job search. Let's assume that you have a healthy network—ten Cabinet members and 150 in your Sales Company. Now, let's assume that only 40 percent of your Sales Company actually provides assistance to you in some form (remember the 60 percent number—so we are being pessimistic about the level of help for this example). Let's do the math: 40 percent of 150 is sixty, plus ten (Cabinet members are 100 percent reliable) gets you to seventy. You have seventy sales reps, advisors, promoters, and ambassadors out there helping you and promoting you in some measure. Think about that for a moment . . . that's a lot! Are you beginning to grasp the importance and power of a healthy network?

The Peripheral and Pruning

Outside your Cabinet and your Sales Company are the rest of your connections. The people you know, are acquainted with, or simply connected to on LinkedIn. They are peripheral, but still important!

All human relationships ebb and flow. People enter your life and stay or fade away over time for any one of a thousand reasons. This will be true with your network. The people in

---

206 "Operational Unit Diagrams," United States Army, http://www.army.mil/info/organization/unitsandcommands/oud/ (accessed November 10, 2015).

207 Konnikova, Maria. "The Limits of Friendship," *The New Yorker*, October 7, 2014, http://www.newyorker.com/science/maria-konnikova/social-media-affect-math-dunbar-number-friendships (accessed November 10, 2015).

your network will migrate between or out of your network circles. Cabinet members move to the Sales Company and vice versa. Some retire or pass away. New connections appear on the scene. Maintain and cultivate relationships and be aware of what you have with your Cabinet and Sales Company.

Then there are times when you need to prune your network. This is when the relationship with the connection has diminished in value to a point where there is no mutual (professional) benefit for the relationship. It would be like a director of robotics being connected to a person who has become a pastry chef. The connection is just not there, at least not on a professional level. From a job-search perspective, these would be connections who can't hire you, help you, or be a center of influence for you.

On LinkedIn, these are the connections you may choose to "remove." When you do this, the connection is not alerted that you have severed the connection. And, more often than not, your circle of professional acquaintances is or has become divergent enough that it will go completely unnoticed. There'll be no hard feelings.

Spreading the Word—Asking for Help

Having access to a network will not help you find a job until you get the word out about your situation. Start by making contact with your strong connections (your Cabinet and short list). Initial contact can be either by email or by telephone. A personal call is always best even if it's done after an email (or LinkedIn InMail).

Focus your networking on connecting and exchanging information. This enhances or builds a relationship that, over time, becomes mutually beneficial. Maintaining professional friendships is a give-and-take process. Take time to catch up on family, mutual friends, industry trends, and so on, if a connection is strong. After that, segue to the topic of your job search. Do not ask for a job (especially if your connection is in a position to hire). Trust in the fact that if your connection can hire you or refer you to someone who can, they will. Instead, enlist your contact as an information source, ally, or a lookout for your job search. Ask for information, insight, and advice. One useful and safe approach is to ask your networking contacts about target companies that you are interested in.

🦭 You have probably heard that you should never bash your former employer in an interview. That same rule extends to networking contacts as well. Most don't want to hear it. There will be some who will want "the dirt," either because they are competitors or they are simply prone to gossip. Don't fall for it! Keep your comments professional, and use your Exit Statement.

Be as specific as possible about the type of position, company, or industry you are interested in (more on this in a moment). Aimless or generic networking requests are often vague, and your networking contact will struggle to remember what you need. Providing specific information is easier for your networking contact to remember—and to recall that it was you.

When reaching out to a new connection, inform him/her how you are connected. Use a referral's name or common association membership whenever possible. Then, with humble sincerity, professionally inform the connection of your situation. Like a strong connection, enlist this new connection as an information source or lookout for your job search. Don't forget to provide this person with your contact information.

If you are unemployed, consider sending your resume to your connection if given permission to do so. In your cover email, restate or inform the connection of the types of opportunities you would be interested in. Do not include any salary information. Grant permission for the connection to pass along your resume to others if it would be appropriate, in their opinion, to do so.

 For every connection you make, be sensitive to their time. Make the connection, have the conversation, but do not overextend your welcome—some SEALs tend to do this. This can be especially true when they (or you) have nothing better to do than network. That doesn't mean your contact has the time. They will help if they can, but be aware of when to wrap it up. Boring or overloading a connection with information does not help your job search.

When you speak with a networking connection, be present in the moment. Give your full attention to the conversation. Focus. Listen. Avoid distractions. Strive to form a relationship that goes below the surface. This could take some time and a few engagements, but it's worth it. Having a few deep networking relationships is far more beneficial than a lot of superficial ones.

Networking in a Local Market for a Local Position

For local, general (non-industry-specific) job searches, network with those who are dependent upon networking for their livelihood. These people include real estate agents, financial planners, stockbrokers, mortgage lenders, bankers, and insurance agents, among others. These people interact with the public every day and are frequently privy to information from these interactions that could lead to a job opportunity.

Another group to network with are those involved in civic organizations, and philanthropic and fundraising activities. These people often interact with local business leaders and hear about certain openings.

Get Busy! (And Keep Momentum in Networking)

⬧ Some SEALs struggle to get out of the gate when it comes to networking. This could be because their network is not developed, their network has grown cold from lack of contact, or they fear coming off wrong when making contact. But remember, networking is how most jobs are found.[208] The thing to realize is most everyone is willing to help if you give them a chance! Networking is an ongoing process. Here's the goal—especially if you are just starting your search: Fill your calendar with a minimum of twenty-five appointments in the next two to three weeks, slightly more than one per day or five per week. Network every day in some form. Talk to someone, preferably someone new (this is a great help so you don't slow down after an initial flurry of quick contacts). These can be scheduled telephone calls or face-to-face meetings for coffee, breakfast, lunch, or something else. Get busy making contact! When you book twenty-five appointments, reach for the brass ring and book twenty-five more. When you achieve that goal then move on to the next. Get the idea? And . . . don't stop! As your search progresses, time commitments will erode the amount of time you can network. That's okay. There are only so many hours in a day. And it could be a good indication that your search is progressing (if you're getting interviews). But, overall, don't stop reaching out completely.

Maintaining Your Network

To network successfully, remember that you are building mutually beneficial relationships. That means giving freely to others, as well as receiving. Try to give without expecting to receive anything in return, whenever appropriate. Nurture these relationships. Avoid being a hit-and-run networker, disappearing after you get what you want.[209] With an appropriate level of communication, you will create a network that will benefit you and your network for years to come, and perhaps a lifetime.

Professional Associations

Professional associations are one of the most powerful networking tools you have. One of the best things you can do to shorten your job search is to join and be (reasonably) active in a professional association. Associations exist to promote the interests of the industry it serves *and* the careers of its members—through networking!

---

208 LinkedIn, "Using LinkedIn to Find a Job"; Beatty, "The Math Behind the Networking Claim"; Rothberg, "80% of Job Openings."

209 "Job Networking Tips," HelpGuide.org, http://www.helpguide.org/articles/work-career/job-networking-tips.htm (accessed November 3, 2015).

Some of the most connected and networked professionals you'll ever meet will belong to professional associations. These people get a "charge" out of being connected in your industry. So, as you discover them, connect with them, network with them, and (professionally and diplomatically) leverage them as a resource for your job search.[210]

Professional associations are mostly volunteer organizations. With the exception of a select few positions in large national associations, an association depends on its members volunteering to help. This is achieved through various committees tasked with certain functions. With your job search in mind, which committees could bear the most fruit from networking? Two committees in particular can be most helpful:

Membership Committee—This committee gets you involved and interacting with potential new members as well as current members. It's a terrific committee to be involved with for easy introductions and networking.

Program/Speaker Committee—This committee identifies and approaches industry leaders to speak at association events. Being involved with this committee is a great way to get connected to thought leaders in your industry. Being known by these movers and shakers improves your influence in the industry, not to mention your ability to name-drop by knowing them (persuasion principle of social proof).

Finally, being a member of a professional association gives you access to the membership directory. This directory can easily be used to identify professionals in your industry for networking (as well as identifying companies for any marketing purposes). Properly handled, your membership in an association will frequently, though not always, gain you a brief networking conversation with another member, because you can reference the membership both of you have in common.

The more deeply connected you are (or can become) in professional associations, the greater your chances of tapping into the Hidden Job Market and shortening your job search.

Association/Industry Conferences

Association and industry conferences are great events for job-search networking. They present an opportunity to meet face-to-face with industry colleagues and hiring executives. You can learn which companies are potentially hiring. Occasionally you can get insider information on companies of interest to you. If you are a seasoned professional who has attended professional conferences, you know there is as much covert recruiting and informal interviewing taking place as actual business interaction with potential clients and customers.

---

210 Yate, *Knock 'em Dead*, p. 86.

Conferences can be expensive once you factor in the registration fee, travel, and lodging. However, attending and investing in one major industry conference is a good job-search strategy.

Discover whether the sponsoring organization has local chapters. Some do, and they frequently hold monthly or quarterly meetings. Local chapter meetings tend to be breakfast or after-hours meetings. The cost for these local meetings is usually little or nothing, if you are a member of the organization. Attend as many as possible and build your network. Use the following strategies to get the most out of attending a professional conference and further your job search:

1. **Do research using lists of attendees and exhibitors.** Every industry conference requires you to register. Registrants often get lists of the attendees and exhibitors (potential employers) in advance. Look at both lists for any hiring executives who will attend. This is invaluable information for you. Make it a goal to meet and speak with them. Research the executives on LinkedIn, and see if you have anyone in common who can introduce you via email or LinkedIn before the conference.

   Research the companies that will be at the conference as well. Come to conferences prepared. Your research will edge out your (frequently unprepared) competition. Check out each company online, as well as their jobs page, if one exists. See if they are looking to hire someone with your skills and background. Also, find out from the conference materials when the exhibit hall is open. You'll probably do most of your job-search networking while other potential job seekers are aimlessly wandering the booths just "checking things out."

2. **Come prepared with your elevator speech, resume, and business cards.** Be ready to use your elevator speech. Bring plenty of resumes, but only offer one if asked. Put each resume in an envelope with your name on it so it can be transported easily (and discreetly) in a suit or portfolio. Business cards are a must, especially for circumstances that don't allow for an extended discussion about employment.[211] Make the contact, have a good conversation, and exchange business cards. You can communicate more fully later and supply a resume (if appropriate). Make sure you put a short note on the back of each business card you receive so that you can remember something about the person or your conversation with them. This is a lifesaver when following up later.

3. **Keep your attire conservative, and employ a solid conference game plan.** First impressions are critical, so conservative business attire is a requirement. Being

---

211 Ayres, "Resume Business Card."

overdressed is better than being underdressed. Dressing in conservative attire portrays professionalism and taps into the persuasion principle of authority. Survey the layout of the conference before you arrive (using the conference materials). Map out the companies that interest you, and put them in order of your personal preference—high interest to low interest. Keep in mind that your order may have to change if a lower-priority company has a booth very close to a higher-priority one. As a matter of convenience, you may drop in on a lower-priority company before the higher-priority one. When you arrive at the conference, see if any new companies registered too late to be included in your materials, and see if any of them need to be added to your "company hit list." If you see someone you know at a conference, saying hello is fine, but clinging to them is not.[212] You're here to expand your network and connect to your next job, not waste precious time socializing.

4. **Remember:** Every conversation is an interview. Use your elevator speech, and remember the three keys to kicking off a good interview or conversation: make eye contact, offer a firm handshake, and show enthusiasm. Be prepared with a few questions for the person you are speaking with. If in doubt, "What do you think of the [conference] so far?"[213] works well. You can also use the section on Icebreaker Questions, mentioned later, to help you.

    You are most likely being interviewed from the moment you speak with a company representative or hiring executive, but don't bring up the topic of open positions right away. That may make things awkward. Read the situation before asking. Most people will understand your ultimate goal and will offer help, either at the conference or during post-conference communication.

5. **Following up is crucial to your success.** You'll likely use email to do this, and contacting every relevant connection you made at the conference may take a lot of time. But you never know which connection will lead to your next job. Use all of the business cards you collected and create a brief follow-up email (or LinkedIn InMail) to each. This is where the notes you recorded on the back of each card pay dividends.

The idea of walking into a conference filled with strangers can be intimidating. This is completely understandable, and you are not alone in that feeling. However, networking

---

212 Weiss, Tara. "Find Your Job by Going to a Conference," *Forbes*, March 24, 2009, http://www.forbes.com/2009/03/24/conference-job-seeking-leadership-careers-networking.html (accessed July 10, 2015).

213 Ibid.

is very important to your job search. Follow the steps in this section. Research. Plan your strategy. Bring your business cards and practice your elevator speech. And then meet people. After the first few tries, initiating conversations will get easier. Before you know it, you won't be able to wait to talk to the next person!

Icebreaker Questions for Conferences and Events

Often the most intimidating part about networking at a conference or event is starting a conversation. After making an introduction, it's uncomfortable to deal with that awkward moment of silence. The trick to overcoming that awkwardness is to be prepared with a handful of conversation starters—icebreaker questions.

When engaging in a conversation, be present and focus. Use open-ended questions starting with "what" and "how" whenever possible. Start all networking conversations with the idea of creating a "conversation surplus" for the other person. Let them fill the "conversation bucket" with information about them. Be a good, interested listener. Only speak of yourself when they ask. Otherwise, keep the focus on them. Let them create the surplus in the conversation.

More often than not, a networking conversation balances out and ends up being equal in terms of the sharing of information and time spent in conversation.

If the conversation ends with a significant surplus in your fellow attendee's favor, that's fine. Praise yourself for being a good listener. You don't know how that seemingly lopsided conversation might benefit you in the future.

Here are some good icebreaker questions to spur conversation:

- What do you do? (Follow up with a request for their opinion [their "take"] on an industry issue, trend, event, or something else.)
- What motivated you to come to this conference/event?
- What do you think of the lineup of speakers?
- What did you think of the last speaker?
- What are you finding most interesting [or valuable] about this conference?
- Attendance looks good. Do you come every year?
- What's keeping you [or your company] busy these days?

Once the conversation begins and the initial discomfort dissipates, an engaging conversation can start to develop. As a good networker, always offer to help a contact whenever you can with the understanding that they will do what they can to help you. Remember, in networking, "those who give, get."[214]

Goals of the Networking Conversation

Your primary goal in a networking conversation is to display and utilize professional networking techniques. Yes, you are networking with the purpose of advancing your job search, but you will gain more traction and advance your search further by being patient and strategic.

This is done by actively listening, asking questions, offering insight, and so on. Avoid a making a statement about your situation until the contact asks a question about you. By being present, professional, and engaging in conversation, you have built rapport. Then when you state your situation, there is more likelihood the contact will help you!

Listen carefully and learn—what you discover may help advance your job search (you never know). You could also pass on to others what you discover and possibly help them in a myriad of ways.

As a part of your networking communications, you are looking for three kinds of information (from each networking encounter, if possible):

Advice. This is any kind of insight you can receive about anything related to your job search. The topics here can be wide and varied. As a general theme, most people respond positively to a request for advice. It's a compliment that you are interested in their thoughts and expertise.

Information. This is anything related to the market, including jobs as a whole, trends, companies that are hiring, receiving funding, introducing new products, downsizing, and so on.

Referrals. This is enlisting every contact into your Sales Company, if they would be willing to help, as much as they're able. You want to have your networking contact communicate with you about job opportunities or refer or introduce you to other contacts.

Realize that these networking goals or requests are not "asking for a job." It is really requesting help in the form of information that can advance your search.[215]

---

214 Vlooten, "The Seven Laws."

215 See also, Phillips, *Guide to Professional Networking*, p. 50–51; Pete Leibman, "9 Keys on How to Email a New Networking Contact During a Job Search (written by Career Expert, Pete Leibman)," *CareerMuscles* (blog), January 6, 2011, https://careermuscles.wordpress.com/2011/01/06/9-keys-on-how-to-email-a-new-networking-contact-during-a-job-search-written-by-career-expert-pete-leibman/ (accessed November 10, 2015).

Face-to-Face Networking as an Introvert

Networking can be more challenging if you are introverted. Meeting new people face-to-face just does not come as easy to you as it does to others. Fortunately, there are some very practical strategies you can use to defuse much of the anxiety of networking. They are:

- Remind yourself of the value networking brings to your job search. Sixty to eighty percent of all jobs are a result of some form of networking.[216] Psyche yourself up the best you can.

- Go to smaller events. Avoid conferences or association events that are attended by the thousands; look for opportunities where the attendees are more in the hundreds, instead.[217]

- Focus on groups where you have a common interest or common purpose. For example, if you're a nurse in workers' compensation, look for a group that comprises nurse case managers. Conversation will be easier because you have knowledge of and interest in the topics of conversation. These types of functions often have educational sessions, which give you a reason for being there if you feel the need to state one.

- Before attending a function, create a list of three or four icebreaker questions. Use the previous section on icebreaker questions as a guide. Preparation is key. At an event with unfamiliar people, you may become distracted by your surroundings and forget a few things—having your list of questions will make conversations with other attendees much easier.

- Finally, know how to close a conversation. When the conversation has run its course and the silence begins to feel awkward, have a closing line that will politely allow you to move on. For example, "It has been a pleasure speaking with you. I'm sure you have others to meet as do I. Do you have a card?"

When properly done, networking will open doors to opportunities. To be a successful networker, give far more than you ever expect to receive. Over time, you will discover that you have received more than you gave.

---

216 LinkedIn, "Using LinkedIn to Find a Job"; Beatty, "The Math Behind the Networking Claim"; Rothberg, "80% of Job Openings."

217 Townsend, Maya. "The Introvert's Survival Guide to Networking," *Inc.com*, http://www.inc.com/maya-townsend/introvert-networking-guide.html (accessed November 4, 2015).

A STORY OF INSPIRATION

Like many others I was "that" person over fifty (fifty-seven actually) who was having a hard time getting noticed and landing a job—for the reasons we all know well.

As a part of my job search strategy, I decided to attend a three-day conference. I had attended this conference before when I worked for a former employer. I registered by phone and told the person I spoke with about my situation and got a nice break on the cost (never hurts to ask).

After reviewing the list of attendees and sponsoring organizations, I made an action plan of companies I wanted to visit. While working my plan, two organizations really stood out. One was in the telehealth space. The other was a new technology firm now playing in healthcare. Both organizations were smaller, which was what I was looking for.

I approached the booths and asked who the highest ranking person was. It was the CEO for both. I used an elevator pitch to initiate conversations. It quickly became clear that both organizations had needs that matched much of my thirty-year healthcare career. I diplomatically gave them several ideas that really resonated with them. The next day I came back with a few more ideas—they were both eating it up!

I did NOT bring up employment with either organization at this juncture. They were there to promote their organization and I did not want to distract them from their missions (nor did I want to appear hard up for a job).

A few months before the conference, an industry colleague of mine, also over age fifty and in a job transitions, told me that he struck a 1099 arrangement with a company for a fifteen-hour a week gig at a below market hourly rate. Of course, he gave them more than fifteen hours (but never billed more than fifteen hours). He wanted the firm to fall in love with him, which it did. Six months later they offered him a full-time position with a very competitive compensation package! That sounded like a pretty good plan to me, if needed.

A week after the conference I reached out to both CEO's and set up follow up calls. When I steered the conversation to possibly joining forces, both organizations were interested in me. However, both had financial constraints at the moment and perhaps later in the year would be a better time to discuss the topic.

I wanted to strike while the iron was hot. If three months went by, they would probably forget who I was!

So, I borrowed a page from my industry pal's playbook and offered each organization a 1099 arrangement with a very competitive hourly rate for ten-fifteen hours a week. The line I used on each was "you're getting a major league pitcher for a minor league contract." I was making it easy for them to say YES. All I needed was a chance to get my baseball uniform on and show them I could pitch no-hit baseball!

It worked! BOTH said yes and I was back in the game!

Here are a few take-aways I got from my experience that perhaps can help you:

- Get over your fears, have courage, and put yourself "out there."
- Attending the conference and meeting people face-to-face was key for me. It was networking.
- Offer what you know and who you know for free and steer clear from the topic of employment until after the conference.

You can succeed! Persevere and whatever you do, don't stop trying.

M.B.
Age 57

Part VIII

Social Media and Networking: Twitter and Facebook

There is in this world no such force as the force of a man determined to rise.

—W. E. B. DuBois[218]

Social media has drastically changed how you conduct a job search. The big three online professional/social sites are: LinkedIn, Twitter, and Facebook. We have already discussed LinkedIn. It is clearly the most prevalent online professional networking site. We will now explore using Twitter and Facebook as components of your job search.

Twitter

Twitter has quickly become part of the arsenal used by employers and recruiters to reach qualified job seekers. According to a recent survey by Jobvite, an unprecedented 52 percent of recruiters are using Twitter for their search activities.[219] Getting dialed into Twitter can help you in your job search. The percentage of job seekers using Twitter continues to increase year after year. In 2011, 26 percent of job seekers used Twitter, which increased to

---

218 Pine, Joslyn. Ed., *Book of African-American Quotations*. (New York: Dover Publications, 2011), p. 51.

219 "2014 Social Recruiting Survey," *Jobvite*, https://www.jobvite.com/wp-content/uploads/2014/10/Jobvite_SocialRecruiting_Survey2014.pdf (accessed June 1, 2015).

45 percent in 2015.[220] This is likely due to its increasing effectiveness and its use by younger generations who grew up with the technology. In fact, research shows that 23 percent of Internet users surveyed, age eighteen or over, used Twitter in 2014, with an increase in every age bracket.[221]

One very unique feature about Twitter that enhances its job-search value is that you can follow anyone you wish, including companies, target contacts, thought leaders, HR, corporate recruiters, and more, without requesting permission (unlike LinkedIn and Facebook). This openness can be a profound resource for gathering information, identifying job leads and opportunities, and communicating with those who can help you and hire you.

If you are new to Twitter, here are some pointers to get you started:

Create Your Twitter Username (Handle). This is nothing more than a name that appears as you tweet (slang for posting a message). You're permitted fifteen characters for a name or handle. You can use your own name, nickname, or any other descriptive name—so long as it is professional.

Set up Your Twitter Profile. Your profile is limited to 160 characters including spaces, so you must be succinct but impactful with your description. Review your elevator speech, branding message, and business cards. Then formulate your professional profile. Explore other Twitter profiles for ideas if needed.

Add a photo, likely the same as the one that appears on your LinkedIn profile. Since your Twitter profile is so short, add a link to other sites, most notably LinkedIn.

Here are a couple of partial example profiles to get you thinking:

Award-winning care management sales professional . . .

Accomplished operational management executive . . .

Once you have an account, establish a handle, and write a profile, you are ready to go! Now that you're set up, here are some steps to using Twitter in your job search:

Create a second account if necessary, then follow target companies and people. For job seekers with established personal Twitter accounts, it's recommended to create a

---

220 Adams, Susan. "4 Ways to Use Twitter to Find a Job," *Forbes*, November 30, 2012, http://www.forbes.com/sites/susanadams/2012/11/30/4-ways-to-use-twitter-to-find-a-job/ (accessed June 16, 2015). Sunberg, Jordan. "How Job Seekers Use Social Media and Mobile in 2015." http://theundercoverrecruiter.com/job-seekers-social-mobile-2015/ (accessed January 29, 2017)

221 Duggan, Maeve, Nicole B. Ellison, Cliff Lampe, Amanda Lenhart, and Mary Madden, "Demographics of Key Social Networking Platforms," Pew Research Center, January 9, 2015, http://www.pewinternet.org/2015/01/09/demographics-of-key-social-networking-platforms-2/ (accessed June 16, 2015).

second one solely for your job search. Identify and begin following target companies of interest to you. This can be a way to gain an edge over other job seekers, as well as a great source of information to further your search, since most major or established organizations have a corporate Twitter account. A growing trend is using Twitter first to announce open positions.[222] Following industry thought leaders, hiring executives, human resource professionals, recruiters, and so on can help as well.

Use hashtags well. Twitter uses hashtags (the # symbol) as an index or filing system of sorts. It's a way to search Twitter for topics or specific information. You can use this indexing system to look for job leads. Below is a short list of hashtags that can lead you to possible job openings:

#jobs
#jobsearch
#employment
#resume
#careers
#nowhiring

Think creatively about how to use hashtags, and you may discover hidden openings. You can use the hashtag indexing system to narrow your search by location or function.

For example:

"#Dallas" + "#jobs"—jobs in Dallas

"#jobs" + "#sales"—jobs in sales

"#jobs" + "#accounting" + "#omaha"—accounting jobs in Omaha

Use Twitter job search engines. Use job search engines such as TwitJobSearch (twitter. com/twitjobsearch), JobCritters (www.jobcritters.com), and CareerArc (www.careerarc. com) to stay well informed and up-to-date on the latest job postings from target companies and search firms.

These sites allow job seekers to choose from over six thousand job categories and then be notified when a job fits chosen parameters. It's similar to receiving an Indeed.com or LinkedIn job alert.

Create content. Once you have established yourself with any social media platform

---

222 Dickler, Jessica. "Get Your Holiday Job—on Twitter!" *CNNMoney*, October 21, 2010, http://money.cnn.com/2010/10/21/pf/job_openings_on_twitter/ (accessed June 4, 2015).

(LinkedIn, Facebook, Twitter, or a personal blog—discussed later), you need to learn about posting and interacting. Posting is actually a form of publishing, whether you do it as an author (using your own information or ideas) or commenting on what others have done.

Twitter only gives you 140 characters (links and spaces included). Abbreviate words, and be brief and to the point. To spark your thinking, below is a list of ideas and topics that you can post about:

- Write an article (consider breaking into parts and posting as a series)

- Reference or forward someone else's article (forwarding is called "retweeting" by Twitter)

- Comment on a business or industry trend

- Express an opinion (stay within professional, safe boundaries)

- Ask a question, seek advice, request feedback

- Comment on an article or book you read and link to it in your comment

- Your job-search progress (carefully worded and well-timed)

Consult the section on blogging, mentioned later, for additional information. Remember to think before you post—your tweets and other social media posts reflect directly on you as a job seeker, and people will form opinions about you based on them.

Overall, Twitter's use and acceptance can be industry specific. In other words, some industries may use it more than others. Regardless, Twitter is gaining wider acceptance by employers every year. Twitter is a job-search tool that should be seriously considered and used as part of your strategy, but its impact will depend on your use and your industry's acceptance and use of it.

🔱 For some SEALs, getting a Twitter account and using it for a job search is a bit of a stretch. That's understandable; the choice is yours. Your search will not be significantly handicapped if you choose not to use Twitter. There is one interesting tactic you can employ if you do use Twitter: Follow any hiring executives at companies you are interested in. Hiring executives will see that you are following them on Twitter if they are paying attention. And who knows? That attention could lead to an interview.

Facebook

When it comes to Facebook, the lines between social and professional networking have blurred. Facebook has historically been viewed as a purely social networking venue for "kids." That has changed. As younger professionals enter the job market and advance their careers, many have repurposed Facebook into a professional networking tool, with a personal touch. Many SEALs have Facebook accounts and use them to stay in touch with friends and family. Facebook is now frequently viewed as a job-search tool that showcases the "whole person," not just the professional.

Companies have caught on. Most larger, established, and forward-thinking companies now have a corporate Facebook presence. They use Facebook to attract job seekers and check their backgrounds.

As a job-search tool, Facebook is similar to LinkedIn. You will discover similarities as we discuss Facebook. Some of these points will be shorter because concepts have already been more thoroughly covered in the LinkedIn section. Similarities include:

Profile. Like LinkedIn and Twitter, you need to create a professional Facebook profile. It appears under the "Timeline" heading. Align your Facebook and LinkedIn profiles.

If you already have a Facebook account and you have been using it socially with your friends, make absolutely sure that all posts and photos are acceptable to the professional viewing audience (hiring executives, corporate HR, executive recruiters, and so on).

Similar to LinkedIn, use keywords and industry terms-of-art to enhance your "findability." Consider linking to or mentioning your LinkedIn profile. Make sure they are consistent with employment, dates, and so on.

Classify your friends. This is similar to tagging your connections on LinkedIn. Go to your friends list and put the cursor over the rectangle next to the name. From there you can create a "New List." Create a list for your professional friends/contacts. The benefit of this is that you can post information directed only to your professional contacts. As you add professional friends, classify them to this list. Depending on the number of friends you have, it could take you a while to do this, but it is worth it. Be sure any professional contacts you add are relevant to you.

"Like" and follow target company pages and search firms. By doing this, you will receive information about job openings, announcements, news releases, and so on. This is very similar to following a company on LinkedIn.

Use Facebook to do more than follow. You can search within Facebook on a wide variety of topics (likes, interests, groups, and so on); it's like a search engine inside Facebook.

Post relevant content. Similar to Twitter and LinkedIn, post relevant content and pass along good information as it should come your way. Remember to think and be smart about what you post.

Protect your Facebook privacy. To ensure what you are sharing with the public and potential employers during a search is appropriate, convert any post that is either Public or visible to Friends of Friends into strictly Friends Only posts. To do this, choose "Settings," then "Privacy" from the left part of the top of Facebook. For any shared posts that are Friends of Friends or Public, click "Limit the Audience" when you see "Who can see my stuff?" Facebook will then warn you that even though you may change your posts to Friends Only, they'll still be visible to friends of anyone tagged. Continue by clicking on "Limit Old Posts." Make sure all your future posts are still set to Friends Only. Always keep in mind anything you post online needs to be a good representation of yourself, and that your job-search audience can (and may) see it.

Some final words on Facebook. Traditionally viewed as a purely social site, Facebook is now a significant tool and resource for a job search. Will Facebook ever surpass LinkedIn as a professional networking site? Who's to say? It's certain Facebook is another way that today's job seeker can advance and shorten a job search.

A Caution about Online Networking/Posting

Online networking and posting is a powerful job-search strategy and tool. Properly used, it can and will advance your job search. It can also be a tremendous time-waster! It is very easy to get caught up clicking away and connecting with others who have only a remote chance of advancing your job search, but "you never know." Or you can end up having delightful online communications that make you feel good—which is okay—but really do not serve any job-search purpose, but "you never know," right? Wrong.

Be careful! Before you know it, two hours of your precious time can be gone, and your search hasn't budged one inch. The advice here is simple: Be aware of the purpose of what you are doing and the amount of time you are spending on online professional and social media sites. Don't go overboard posting content. If you catch yourself asking whether your activities on online networking sites are advancing your job search, you've likely crossed the line into busywork disguised as a job search.

What Employers Find on Social Media

As discussed, it is undeniable that social media will play a role in your job search. The significance of that role depends largely on how much you use social media. But employers also use social media.

A study conducted by the Society for Human Resource Management found that 52 percent of employers evaluate job seekers using social media.[223] This trend will likely continue to grow. That means more and more companies use your social profiles to get a sense of you as a person. What they find about you will influence their hiring decision.

To help you more fully appreciate how social media will affect your pursuit of a job, CareerBuilder.com asked more than 2,100 people in charge of hiring to explain exactly how social media factored in to their decision-making.

In the CareerBuilder survey, employers who chose not to pursue a job applicant after researching social media sites indicated the following reasons:

- Job seeker posted inappropriate pictures—46 percent

- Found evidence of job seeker's use of alcohol or drugs—40 percent

- Job seeker made negative remarks about previous employer—34 percent

- Inappropriate comments made about race, gender, religion, and so on—29 percent[224]

🦭 Many of these discoveries are of lesser concern to most SEALs. Professional, mature adults don't participate in many of these activities because they know what information is appropriate for public view and what is not. It is one of the blessings of life experience and maturity. But that is not to say you should drop your guard. If you ever pause and ask yourself whether you should post something, that pause is likely a sign that you should not.

However, over 30 percent of hiring executives discovered information that improved a job seeker's candidacy, including:

- Job seeker's background matched qualifications of position—42 percent

- Candidate's personality impacted them positively—38 percent

- Professionalism—38 percent

- Creativity—36 percent

- Communication—37 percent[225]

---

223 Rossheim, John. "Social Networking: The Art of Social Media Recruiting," Monster, February 11, 2015, http://hiring.monster.com/hr/hr-best-practices/recruiting-hiring-advice/job-screening-techniques/recruiting-using-social-media.aspx (accessed August 26, 2015).

224 CareerBuilder, "35 Percent of Employers Less Likely to Interview Applicants They Can't Find Online, According to Annual CareerBuilder Social Media Recruitment Survey," news release, May 14, 2015, http://www.careerbuilder.com/share/aboutus/pressreleasesdetail.aspx?sd=5%2F14%2F2015&id=pr893&ed=12%2F31%2F2015 (accessed June 1, 2015).

225 Ibid.

According to CareerBuilder, the research clearly indicates that employers utilize social media to gain additional insight into job seekers' behavior and personality outside the interview. They use all tools available to help assure a good hire. Which means you should make certain your social media profiles are as effective in your job search as they can be.

Part IX

Working with Recruiters

Just begin and the mind grows heated; continue, and the task will be completed!

—Goethe[226]

According to surveys conducted by the American Staffing Association, over 90 percent of employers have or would use an executive recruiter to fill open positions.[227] This section will cover how to find recruiters (search firms) who fit your industry or position and how to work with them effectively to enhance your search.[228]

What Recruiters Can and Cannot Do for You

Recruiters can be a terrific resource during a job search. However, they should not be your leading source for landing your next job, simply because they are hired and paid by clients

226 "Johann Wolfgang von Goethe Quotable Quote," Goodreads, http://www.goodreads.com/quotes/316359-just-begin-and-the-mind-grows-heated-continue-and-the (accessed June 11, 2015).

227 "Top 5 Reasons to Use Staffing Firms as Your Primary Hiring Strategy," DISYS, http://www.disys.com/top-5-reasons-to-use-staffing-firms-as-your-primary-hiring-strategy/ (accessed June 19, 2015); See also, "Get Help With Hiring . . . And More: Working With Staffing Firms: What's in It for Me?" CareerBuilder, http://www.careerbuildercommunications.com/staffing-firms/ (accessed June 19, 2015).

228 See also, Claycomb and Dinse, *Career Pathways*, Part 6.

to find well-qualified candidates, not find jobs for job seekers.[229] That being said, the search and placement business is a billion-dollar industry,[230] and job seekers get identified and placed by recruiters every day. In fact, networking with recruiters can lead you to open positions that other job seekers will never know about. According to a survey conducted by LinkedIn, only 18 percent of job seekers think of search firms when looking for a new job.[231] Recruiters "are not top of mind."[232] This creates an opportunity for you. By identifying and contacting executive recruiters, you are tapping into a channel of potential opportunities that most job seekers neglect. The trick is to be found and have the right qualifications at the right time. Here is a non-exhaustive list of the benefits of aligning yourself with a recruiter:

1. They can introduce you to job opportunities with their clients.

2. They often have insight on opportunities with their clients before they are made public.

3. They can help you determine your market value.

4. They frequently can provide you with much more information about the position, company, and culture than what you can discover on your own.

5. They can prepare you for interviews and inform you about hot buttons to hit upon and landmines to avoid.

6. They can give advice on how to manage the interview process, often because they are a consultant on the types and timing of communications with the employer.

7. They can provide insight and advice during offer negotiations.

8. They can counsel you through the resignation process (should that apply to you).

There are also things that a recruiter cannot or will not do for you:

1. Hold your hand and become your nursemaid during your job search.

2. Get you a job. Remember, recruiters are hired to find qualified candidates for their clients, not find you a job.[233]

---

229 "Don't Do That!—Mistakes To Avoid When Working With Recruiters," *True Source* (blog), November 2012, http://www.true-source.com/2012/11/dont-do-that-mistakes-to-avoid-when-working-with-recruiters/ (accessed June 9, 2015).

230 "Employment and Recruiting Agencies in the US: Market Research Report," IBISWorld, March 2015, http://www.ibisworld.com/industry/default.aspx?indid=1463 (accessed June 11, 2015).

231 LinkedIn Talent Solutions. "2015 Talent Trends: Insights for Search and Staffing Recruiters on What Talent Wants Around the World," p. 17, https://business.linkedin.com/content/dam/business/talent-solutions/global/en_us/c/pdfs/global-talent-trends-staff-report.pdf (accessed November 23, 2015).

232 Ibid.

233 True Source, "Don't Do That."

3. Unless you become a viable candidate in an active search with the recruiter, they will not spend an inordinate amount of time with you discussing your resume, the job market, interview strategy, and other free advice.

The key to working with recruiters is knowing what to expect from them and controlling your own expectations. Recruiters can be a valuable resource, but the responsibility of your search lies with you and your efforts.

Retainer and Contingency Search Firms

Before we discuss how to target and contact recruiters, it's beneficial to have a basic understanding of the two types of search firms you're likely to encounter as a professional-level job seeker: retainer and contingency. We'll briefly describe the differences and then move on to how to engage and work with them.

If a firm works on a retained basis, they are generally paid an upfront fee to begin search activities. Then, at certain predetermined points along the search timeline, the firm is paid another installment. Final payment is usually made upon completion of the search assignment.[234] Fully retained searches are generally used for senior executive and C-level positions with larger organizations.

A contingency firm is paid differently. As the name implies, their fee is contingent and is earned only when a referred candidate is hired by a client. It is strictly pay-for-performance.[235]

It used to be said that contingency firms are paid for performance while retainer firms are paid for process, regardless of whether or not the position gets filled. In large measure, it is this "pay for performance rather than process" that has led to the continued growth of the recruiting industry's contingency side. In fact, many retainer firms now conduct contingency searches to compete for the revenue flow of clients who prefer a contingency arrangement. Contingency firms also conduct retainer searches and function in similar ways, with the same (and sometimes more) resources, blurring the distinction between the two types. What this means for you as a job seeker is that it doesn't matter how the firm is paid. What does matter is whether the firm can match you to an open position with one of its clients.

---

234 Hallowell, Kirk. *The Million Dollar Race: An Insider's Guide to Winning Your Dream Job.* (Austin, TX: Greenleaf Book Group Press, 2013), p. 112.

235 Ibid., p. 111.

Contract or Project Firms

Both of these types of firms are prevalent in the technology field. These firms lease the employee to a company for long periods of time (occasionally up to and over a year). Generally speaking, these assignments are paid on an hourly basis or on a contract arrangement. These contract positions can result in permanent employment or a renewal of the project employment contract.

How to Find Recruiters

Identifying and contacting recruiters is not as difficult as you might think. Below are three effective methods. We recommend that you use all three. They are:

1. Calling hiring executives in your industry
2. Calling colleagues in your industry
3. Researching recruiters online (most notably, using LinkedIn)

Let's discuss these approaches in detail.

Calling Hiring Executives

One of the best methods for identifying recruiters is to reach out to hiring executives and ask for referrals. Think about it: Who better at identifying and referring you to potential recruiters than the executives who hire them, right?

This method has three major advantages. First, it is an easy call to make. You are asking for help, and most people will help you if they can (networking). Asking for referrals to recruiters is a safe and reasonable topic for your call.

Second, this method will lead you to the industry's top recruiters. Connecting with them will expand your reach for potential opportunities.

Finally, and most importantly, you will be speaking with hiring executives who could have an opportunity (such as the type described in the Hidden Job Market section earlier) or know of one in the industry. Hint: It's extremely helpful here to be ready with your elevator speech.

How do you go about calling these hiring executives? Here are the steps:

1. Identify companies that interest you.

2. Research and determine who the likely hiring executive is for the position you would be interested in.

3. Pick up the phone and make a call. Engage the hiring executive in a conversation, explain your situation, and as part of the conversation, ask whether he or she could identify the names of a few recruiters and pass them along to you.

This technique is effective because it's a *call* to the hiring executive. The ultimate goal is to speak to the executive and have a voice-to-voice conversation; avoid using email, as it dilutes this technique's effectiveness.

Because this technique is such a powerful way to network with hiring executives, here is a script you can modify:

Introduction:

"[First name of the hiring executive or Mr./Ms.], this is (state your name). I'm a clinical nurse manager with thirteen years' experience in the population health management industry. I am looking to make a career move, and I would like your advice and assistance regarding my search."

Confirm you have the right contact:

"If I have it right, you are the hiring executive (or use the executive's title) for case and nurse managers. Here's what I'm looking for . . . I am looking for the names of recruiters I can contact who specialize in (title of your position). I am hoping that you could refer me to a few recruiters you like."

Assume the hiring executive will help:

"Do you know of any recruiters who you feel good about? Maybe some good ones you've used in the past?"

Show appreciation and (maybe) ask one question:

"Thank you. Let me ask you since I have you on the phone: What do you think the effects of health-care reform will be on the population health management industry?"

If you're unemployed, close and offer to send your resume:

"Again, thank you. I appreciate your help. If it's okay, I'm going to email my resume to you just so you have it. Feel free to forward it to others as you deem appropriate."

For anyone who helps you, send a thank-you email. Depending upon the conversation, it could be appropriate to send a LinkedIn invitation.

There are a couple of reasons why calling hiring executives for referrals to recruiters is a powerful technique. First and foremost, it gets you talking with hiring executives, which could lead to a job opening with that company! Second, hiring executives typically approve the payment of recruiting fees. Therefore, when you call a recruiter later saying you were referred by one of their paying clients, that will help get their attention, and they should take or quickly return your call. The recruiter does not want to say that they did not speak with you if the hiring executive asks later.

When properly executed, this approach will get you several names of recruiters who likely specialize in your industry or position type. If you hear the same names being held in high regard, you've likely discovered your industry's best recruiters. On the flip side, you may discover which recruiters to avoid.

Most importantly, you have connected with hiring executives in the industry. Those contacts can pay big dividends in your career in the short or long term.

Calling Your Colleagues in the Industry

The advantages of contacting your own industry colleagues are many. You can have open and frank discussions regarding recruiters. You will be able to create a list of several recruiters who call your colleagues. You might learn about a few recruiters you may elect not to contact. And networking with colleagues may result in job leads.

These calls are easy to make. The hazard is you can easily get tied up in long conversations that eat up your time and distract you from your real goal of getting a new job.

Researching LinkedIn and the Internet

Search LinkedIn for recruiters. By using the keyword feature, you may limit your search to recruiters with a specialty that matches your background, experience, or interests. Search your LinkedIn groups for recruiters.

Another fast way to obtain names of your industry's recruiters is to search the Internet. There are online services that maintain nationwide databases of recruiters. One particular website and organization where you can describe a recruiter by industry and location, and find one to match your profile, is www.mrinetwork.com.

Another way to compile a list of recruiters tailored to your industry is to search through the *Directory of Executive & Professional Recruiters* (Kennedy Publications). Updated annually, this publication is classified by geography and specialty.

For local searches, the local business journals frequently include names of search firms in their *Book of Lists.* The firms are listed by the number of recruiters and the specialties of each firm.

Contacting a Recruiter

If your first contact with a recruiter is by email, keep it short but impactful. Identify your role or function (title) and highlight a couple of accomplishments. Do not send a lengthy email! Recruiters are time sensitive, and the mere appearance of a long email will most likely discourage them from reading it. Attach a copy of your resume. Ask for a call, but follow up with the recruiter in a couple of days if you have not heard back.

If your first contact with a recruiter is a proactive call, start your conversation by getting their attention. Begin your conversation (or voice message) with an attention-getting statement. The most impactful approach is to name the person who referred you, if you have one. Another way would be to mention an accomplishment: "Bob, my name is Linda, and I am an award-winning marketing professional with seventeen years of experience in the commercial real estate industry. I am exploring a career move, and I would like discuss how we might be able to work together."

Stay in routine contact with the recruiters you feel can help you. This can be done with a call or email. Most all recruiters will permit this kind of routine communication. The key here is to keep your name in front of the recruiter without becoming a pest. Turning off a recruiter is closing a door to a potential opportunity. It's a fine line that really turns on the level of position you are seeking. Contacting a recruiter once every three or four weeks is adequate.

Finding a Recruiter Who Can Help You

When talking with recruiters, ask questions. Here are some questions to ask a recruiter to find out if the two of you are a match, either now or in the future:

- In what industry do you do most of your work?
- What types of positions do you fill?
- Based on my background, am I a viable candidate for you?
- Can I send you a LinkedIn invitation? (If you fit within the recruiter's specialty)

When there is not a match with the recruiter's specialty

If the recruiter tells you they can't be of assistance, ask for the names of any other recruiters they may know who can help you. If they don't know of anyone, do not be disappointed. They may not have contacts who specialize in your area of interest. You could also ask the recruiter for general assistance, but be sensitive to the recruiter's time! Here are a couple of questions you could ask:

- What is your opinion of the job market?

- If you were in my shoes, what would you be doing to advance your job search?

When there's a match between your background and the recruiter's specialty

If there is a match between your background and the recruiter's specialty, provide and volunteer any information requested by the recruiter, especially a resume if you have not already provided one.

Even if there is a match between your background and the recruiter's specialty, understand that most of the time, they will not be able to help you immediately. This is simply a function of timing. They may not have an active assignment that fits your background, geographic location, or other factors. But just because they cannot place you today does not mean that they cannot place you in the future.

Recruiters can be a rich resource for your job search and the industry you work in. To foster a good relationship with recruiters, it is good etiquette (and networking) to offer your network of connections (both online and on LinkedIn) who may help them in any way. Developing this kind of relationship with a recruiter is priceless. Recruiters have long memories. Helping a recruiter can benefit your career greatly in both the short and long term.

Some Final Advice Regarding Recruiters

Remember that recruiters work for the employer, not you. They will call you if and when they have a potential opportunity that fits your qualifications.

- Connect with recruiters who specialize in your industry or position type—preferably both.

- Stay in touch with recruiters, but don't become a pest.

- Always return a recruiter's call promptly. Evaluation begins with your responsiveness—and recruiters almost always have a reason for calling.

- Always give referrals. Ask if you can help the recruiter. Even if you're not interested in a particular opportunity, try to help the recruiter find someone who might be qualified.

- Never "Decline" an InMail message from a recruiter. Some recruiters have a professional policy of never again contacting job seekers if they decline a message. It's better to respond and say you're not interested than to decline.

- And, if you are contacted by a recruiter, never ask the recruiter to identify the client unless that information is volunteered by the recruiter.

- Never lie about anything in your professional background, go around a recruiter to contact an employer about an opportunity without permission, or use a recruiter to elicit a counter offer from your current employer.

Targeting the right recruiters and connecting with them can be an effective channel to appropriate job opportunities and job-search advice.

Part X

Proactively Marketing Your Professional Credentials

Far better it is to dare mighty things, to win glorious triumphs, even though checkered by failure, than to take rank with those poor spirits who neither enjoy much nor suffer much, because they live in the gray twilight that knows not victory nor defeat.
—Theodore Roosevelt[236]

Networking will generate job-search activity. However, there is another technique that you should also use to maximize your exposure to the job market—proactively marketing your professional credentials.[237] When you use both networking and proactive marketing, you will be utilizing what are generally viewed as the two most effective job-search techniques available. Earnest and properly executed use of both approaches will significantly shorten your job search.

Proactively marketing your professional credentials will differentiate you from the vast majority of other job seekers regardless of age, but it requires initiative and perseverance.

These proactive marketing techniques will create activity in your job search in the form of conversations, networking, referrals, leads, and interviews by diving straight into the heart of the Hidden Job Market.

We are about to discuss two techniques for proactively marketing your professional

236 Theodore Roosevelt, "The Strenuous Life," (speech, The Hamilton Club, Chicago, IL, April 10, 1899), http://www.bartleby.com/58/1.html (accessed May 28, 2015).

237 Claycomb and Dinse, *Career Pathways*, portions of Part 5.

credentials (which will also aid your networking efforts). The first is a cold call. It involves you calling a prospective hiring executive and presenting yourself as a well-qualified job seeker. You will then, as needed, make follow-up communications through additional calls or email correspondence. This approach requires courage, perseverance, and the emotional strength to accept some verbal rejection. However, it is arguably one of the quickest ways to get interviews in the Hidden Job Market. Why? Because you are presenting yourself as a solution to a hiring need before an opening is advertised.

🪶 Proactively marketing your credentials directly to hiring executives works to defeat age-related biases by showing your energy and passion toward your career, that you are not "above" calling an executive, and that you're willing to do the work to achieve a goal (defeating the biases of low energy, entitlement mentality, and lack of commitment/poor work ethic, respectively).

For some, the idea of making cold calls as part of a job search is very uncomfortable, too pushy, or too aggressive. This technique is not for everyone. There is an alternative.

This second technique can be equally effective and initially easier to execute. It requires that you create and send an impactful email to a hiring executive, *followed by telephone calls* and *additional* emails. The follow-up calls are more of a warm call since you have reached out to the hiring executive after an email correspondence.

Regardless of which approach you take, it is absolutely necessary that you pick up the phone and call executives who could potentially be hiring! At the outset, make sure your voicemail message at home is appropriate and your cell phone greeting is professional.

Taking full advantage of these techniques and tapping into the Hidden Job Market requires that you identify employers of interest, identify the hiring executive, and communicate a compelling message about your abilities and how you can benefit the employer's organization.

Here are the steps to creating and executing an effective proactive marketing plan:

1. Identify your target companies (your short list of companies, to start with).

2. Determine the hiring executive's identity.

3. Research the hiring executive's telephone number and email address.

4. Write a compelling call script and email cover letter about your credentials.

5. Execute, starting with either a call or email.

The Work

The technique of proactively marketing your professional credentials is an effective method of identifying job opportunities and can significantly shorten your job search once executed. This method strikes straight into the heart of the Hidden Job Market. Proactive marketing takes effort, but it is one of the most effective ways to uncover opportunities that may not even exist *except* in the mind of the hiring executive or in confidential conversations among senior managers or even board members.

Your proactive efforts could represent the most labor-intensive commitment of time you invest in your search. It may take three to five days of solid research time for you to identify target companies, the right (or probable) hiring executive, and his or her current email address and phone number. It is recommended that you make the commitment of time to do this work early in your job search (and do it early in your day).

The proactive method requires a shift in your thinking. You are now looking for a company you want to work for, instead of a job . . . so to speak.[238] As you discover and learn about interesting companies, put additional marketing effort toward these companies, perhaps a drip email and call strategy (discussed later).

As you identify those "high-interest" companies, follow them on both social media (LinkedIn, Twitter, and so on) as well as more traditional news sources (press releases, Google alerts, and more). Connect with relevant employees and executives on LinkedIn. Consider asking for a research interview(s), which is another technique mentioned later. The more you can learn, the more you network, and the more you make them aware of your professional credentials, the greater your chances of getting an interview. Review Getting Off to a Successful Start to ensure you're organizing your research properly.

Determine Your Target Employers

There are now a variety of methods and sources to identify target employers. They include:

1. Competitors of your current employer
2. Companies where your LinkedIn contacts work
3. Companies you can identify by reviewing profiles on a LinkedIn group
4. Association membership lists
5. Industry conference attendee lists and vendor lists
6. Clients, suppliers, and distributors of your current/past employer

---

238 Whitcomb, *Job Search Magic*, p. 273–274.

7. Books of Lists with major employers by industry type (most metropolitan areas have them)

8. Purchased lists (services that sell databases of companies and contacts) including:

   - www.infousa.com
   - www.hoovers.com
   - www.standardandpoors.com
   - www.listgiant.com
   - www.goleads.com
   - www.vault.com

Start with your short list of targeted companies. Then collect information on one hundred more companies. It may sound like a lot, but it might be the only one hundred companies (plus your short list) you'll need to research to get an offer (or two). If you exhaust the original group of companies, research one hundred more as you deplete your original list.

Identify the Hiring Executive

This is a process of research. You are looking for the executive who has the authority to hire you—not HR. This executive can be identified in several ways:

   - Company website
   - LinkedIn
   - Call the company and ask

If you are in doubt, contacting two or three executives in the company is fine. Always contact the most senior executives—those who are one to two levels above your current position.

Research the Hiring Executive's Email Address

This can be tricky, but the best way is to review the company website. Go to the contact page and look for an email address. If there is not one there, go to the news and events page. Normally a press release for the company will have the marketing employee's email address. That can give you the formula that companies use for their email addresses. If you cannot find an email anywhere on the website, just use the website address and put an @ symbol before it.

Another way is to look up employees of the company on LinkedIn through an advanced search. Sometimes employees provide their company email address, which will give you the email formula you need.

As an alternative, use different forms of the hiring executive's name and then the company web address or the email address you found on the website in the Google search. For instance, most companies might use the formula firstinitiallastname@xyz.com. Google that and see if you have any results. If not, try different formulas: firstname.lastname@xyz.com. You can usually find email addresses this way because people sometimes use a work email address for personal use. Check out www.hunter.io. It could be helpful.

Below are some different formulas you can use to search for email addresses:

1. jsmith@xyz.com
2. john.smith@xyz.com
3. smithj@xyz.com
4. john@xyz.com
5. johns@xyz.com
6. johnsmith@xyz.com

Using the Telephone

Some SEALs hesitate to proactively market themselves and their credentials using the telephone. To get a job in today's world, you must utilize every resource and technique available to shorten your job search. The telephone must be part of your job-search arsenal.[239] To help ease the physical use of the telephone, consider investing in a hands-free headset or use a Bluetooth device on your cell phone. This will free up your hands so you can write, and you won't have to hold the phone to your ear with your shoulder. Being hands-free will have a positive effect on your tone of voice and keep you more relaxed when making calls.

The Positive Impact of Using the Phone

There are several good reasons why you need to make calls to hiring executives as a part of your job search. Almost every point under "The Advantages of a Self-Motivated Job Search" can be achieved by using the phone during your search. Using the phone also helps you:

1. **Differentiate yourself.** Calling a hiring executive to discuss your background and

---

239 Claycomb and Dinse, *Career Pathways*, Part 5.

possible opportunities sets you apart from other job seekers. Employers value initiative. Proactive effort works to overcome age-related biases, such as lack of initiative or being tired.

2. **Create a positive mental impression.** When you are on the phone, the only variables that count are: your background, qualifications, enthusiasm, and positive phone voice.

3. **More quickly establish a relationship.** Your call personalizes the engagement and communication. According to a study by the University of Michigan on hiring managers, 60 percent of most hires are made based on personal chemistry.[240] A conversation helps build that chemistry (using the persuasion principle of liking), which can lead to an interview.

4. **Create urgency.** By calling an employer, you create the perception that you will not be on the market long. The hiring executive will see that you are taking your job search seriously and are researching future opportunities thoroughly. All of this helps you create value (using the persuasion principle of scarcity).

5. **Gather information to be more prepared for possible interviews.** An initial phone conversation with the hiring executive may help you learn what issues are important to that company or executive. You can then prepare answers to possible interview questions based on that information.

Excuses for Not Using the Phone in a Job Search

(If you have no inhibitions about using the telephone to call hiring executives as a part of your job search, you can bypass this topic.)

Over the course of time, every excuse imaginable has been raised about why not to use the phone. These excuses basically encompass the following:[241]

1. **"It's beneath me."**

   Check your ego at the door and think of these calls as nothing more than networking calls with a purpose (and a script). Accept the fact that virtually everyone (including those you will call) has faced unemployment or a career transition at some point. It was as uncomfortable for them as it is for you now. They understand what you are doing and going through. Most will help if they can. Using the telephone to connect and network is not beneath you, but rather shows what you're made of.

---

240 DiResta, interview by Canters, "How to Blitz."

241 See also, Claycomb and Dinse, *Career Pathways*, Part 5.

2. **"I have better uses for my time than leaving a bunch of voice messages."**

Actually, you don't. Leaving voice messages and playing a little phone tag is all part of the process. You must show persistence. You may have to call someone several times before speaking to them. A hiring executive takes note of persistence—as long as you don't cross the line and become an annoyance. As a general guideline, make three attempts. If you do not get a response, it's safe to move on.

If you keep missing an employer who has called back, ask to schedule an appointment that is convenient for both of you. Ask if the hiring executive's administrative assistant can contact you to set up the appointment.

3. **"I have sent so many emails and resumes, and I've networked extensively. They'll be calling me!"**

Conducting a job search is about using every avenue available to you to advance your search. This means taking the initiative to reach out to hiring executives. Failing to do so simply prolongs your job search.

4. **"My resume, background, and qualifications are strong. Once the word really gets out, they'll call me!"**

Maybe, maybe not. When a hiring executive takes the time to read your email and looks at your resume, it is easy to get sidetracked or distracted. The executive has business priorities to attend to. You need to do something to bring your value back to the forefront. One simple phone call will make a remarkable difference.

5. **"They could hang up on me!"**

This excuse is ridiculous, and so what if they do? Regardless, it is so rare that it is almost not worth mentioning. When was the last time you hung up on an industry colleague asking for help? You would not do that, and neither will they. You are asking people for their assistance. They will not hang up on you.

6. **"I don't want to be rejected."**

This excuse, for some SEALs, can significantly slow a job search because at the root of the excuse is fear. Fear, whether real or perceived, is a formidable emotion. If this is an obstacle for you, call upon your courage to overcome it. Read the virtues to practice during a job search at the beginning of this book.

No one wants to be rejected. Although you will encounter the word "no" or a statement such as "I don't think I can help you" or any number of responses that will not advance your job search, don't get discouraged. Rejection is an inescapable part of the process. But bear in mind: Rejection is not personal, it's business.[242] They are not rejecting you as a person. And every "no" gets you one step closer to a "yes."

Here is the reality: You will either use the phone in your job search or you won't. But if you do, you will reap significant rewards that will positively affect your job search and your career.

If you choose not to use the phone, the following things will likely happen (and you probably know what they are):

1. Your job search will take longer.
2. You risk settling for any job (just to be employed).
3. You risk slipping into a passive job search relying on posted job openings.

Getting Started: Making Calls

Since we have dealt with the obstacles to making proactive calls to hiring executives, it's time to get started.

Phone Zone

This is a quiet place free of distractions where you can focus and concentrate on the task at hand. It can be your home office or den, where the risk of interruptions and background noise (including kids and pets) is minimized. Prior to making calls, remove all unnecessary paperwork and nonessential items from your work surface or desktop. The only things you need are:

- Your call list.
- Your script for leaving a voice message.
- Your presentation of what you will say when you speak to the hiring executive.
- A script for answering common responses or objections.
- A copy of your resume.
- Success stories.
- Pen, paper, maybe something to drink.
- Your enthusiasm.[243]

---

242 Thompson, "6 Virtues to Practice."

243 Whitcomb, Job Search Magic, p. 348.

Phone *Phear*: The Pre-Game Jitters

It is perfectly normal to have some anxiety about calling hiring executives. For some of us, it happens. Your entire job search won't collapse because of one case of the nerves. In fact, a healthy dose of nerves is an indication of an outstanding performance to come! Below are some tips to turn nervousness into focused effort:

1. Script and practice the delivery of your message. Know what you are going to say (more on that in a moment).

2. Concentrate on delivering your message/script with confidence. You are on the phone. They cannot see you.

3. Remember that you know everything about the subject at hand: You! In other words, there won't be a question you can't answer.[244]

4. Adopt the attitude that every hiring executive you will call has a possible opening. Never assume that it is a bother that you called or the answer will be "no."

🦭 Here is a suggestion that helps most SEALs: When it comes time to start making calls, generate five calls in succession (without breaks) as efficiently and effectively as you can. Remarkably, once you break the ice and create a rhythm, the reluctance fades. Progress is being made. Once you get the feel for it, you will be surprised how many quality calls you can make.

The Marketing Call Script

The following is a sample script to use when speaking to a hiring executive:[245]

Introduction

The introduction identifies who you are. If you can, reference a mutual business colleague or business association. That common ground often helps break the ice.

"Mr. Tyrrell, my name is Gene Watson. I was referred to you by Bob Johnson."
"Mr. Tyrrell, my name is Gene Watson, and I am a care-management sales professional. I don't believe we've spoken before; however, we both belong to the (care-management association)."

---

244 See also, Claycomb and Dinse, *Career Pathways*, Part 5, "Phone-phobia."

245 See also, Beshara, *Job Search Solution*, Chapter 4, "Getting Face-to-Face Interviews"; Yate, *Knock 'em Dead*, Chapter 7, "Making Contact."

If you do not have a common reference point:

"Mr. Tyrrell, my name is Gene Watson. I am a care-management sales professional and I am currently (or formerly) with (Company Name)."

Ask permission to continue the call
Hiring executives are busy, and they will appreciate the thoughtfulness.

"I realize that I've called you out of the blue. Did I catch you at a good time?"
OR
"I hope I can get a few minutes of your time?"

Get their attention
Similar to your elevator speech and cover letter, make a clear statement about one of your showcase accomplishments. Grab the hiring executive's attention.

"I am a care-management sales professional, and for the last four years I exceeded sales quotas by 27 percent. My sales have been achieved by selling through fee-for-service consultants, payers, and directly to larger companies."

"I am an underwriting-management professional, and with my previous employer I rewrote the underwriting guidelines, which resulted in the growth of our block of business from $25M to $80M over four years."

Purpose for the call
Now that you have introduced yourself and gotten the hiring executive's attention, state the reason for the call . . . to set up an interview.

"I'm looking to make a career move, and I would like to explore with you, either in person or over the phone, how I might further the success of (Company Name)."

Relate to the employer (optional)
If possible, try to make a statement that relates to the employer. This can be a statement specific to the company, a trend, or an issue facing the industry.

"By the way, I understand that you have just rolled out a new cost-containment service line."
"As we both know, the new regulations that take effect next year are going to complicate business."

If you do not have enough information about the company or industry, you can omit the "relate" portion of the script.

Close

Close the script with a request for an interview (the ultimate purpose of the call).

"I am available (to meet with you or speak with you in more detail) in the afternoons next week. Which day would work best for you?"

OR

"I can make myself available Tuesday morning or after 3 p.m. on Thursday. Which time frame might work best for you?"

OR (a less assumptive approach)

"I am available generally in the afternoons next week if you would be interested in meeting (or speaking) further."

The purpose here is to get an interview. And the key to success is to ask for one!

After you finish the script

Once you finish speaking the script, you will likely encounter a moment of silence. The hiring executive is processing what you have said. This is not the kind of call they receive every day. Remain quiet.

The hiring executive will respond with one of two things: a question that indicates interest (a "buying sign") or an objection/deflection. If the response is a question, this is good. Provide a short, responsive answer. There could be a follow-up question, which is great. Provide a response. However, at some point you need to again request an in-person or phone interview.

"Mr. Tyrrell, it sounds like we might have some things to discuss. Let's schedule an appointment to (talk in more detail/meet in person)."

OR

"Mr. Tyrrell, it appears that there may be an opportunity where I can bring some value to your company. When could we schedule a time to speak in more detail?"

Objections

If you get an objection (or deflection), it will likely be one of the following:[246]

1. *"I don't have any openings."*
More often than not, this response is truthful. The first priority of any smart hiring executive is to achieve company goals through people and be on the lookout for talented professionals. Offer to send your resume. If it gets read, another opportunity within the company could be a possible fit. And, most importantly, ask a question—get the hiring executive talking if you can. It is this part of the engagement where you build rapport.[247] Something as simple as:

"I understand. May I forward my resume to you in the event something changes? One question: What do you see as the industry's most important trend right now?"

OR

"That's all right. Can you think of someone else you could refer me to who might have a need? Your referral will be appreciated by both of us."

2. *"Can you send me your resume?"*
The response here is to agree but ask a question to hopefully get an interview or further the dialogue and continue to build a professional relationship. Responses could include one of the following:

"I will! However, my resume is just a paper representation of the value I can bring to (Company Name). When could we sit down and discuss my background so you further understand what I can bring to the table? I can make myself available to your schedule."[248]

OR

"I will! What job title or opportunity should I refer to when I send it?"

OR

"I will! What specific skills or experience are you looking for?"

---

246 See also, Claycomb and Dinse, *Career Pathways*, Part 5, "Phone-phobia"; Yate, *Knock 'em Dead*, Chapter 7, "Making Contact."

247 Beshara, *Job Search Solution*, p. 54.

248 See also, ibid.

3. *"I really don't have time to talk right now."*
"I understand. Is it possible to schedule a brief ten-minute call later?"

4. *"You'll need to talk to Human Resources."*
This may or may not be a brush-off, but at least you have a name in HR, and when you make contact, be sure to name the hiring executive who referred you. Respond with something simple, like:
"Great! When I speak to HR, who should I ask for? And what position should I tell them you asked me to contact them about?"[249]

Ask One Question after the Objections

If you can, ask one question after you respond to the hiring executive's objection(s). A good method to initiate this question is: "Let me ask you a question." There are myriad questions you could ask, but choose one that is germane to the conversation.

Rejection

A very important point to remember when you make these calls: You will be rejected eventually (in one form or another). You need to keep telling yourself that people are not rejecting you as a person. Most of the time, it is the situation with the company—they aren't hiring, they don't employ people with your background, or something else. So each time you are rejected, renew your positive attitude with the next call. With each rejection you get, you are closer to an affirmative response (an interview!). It's a process of elimination.

> *I can summarize the lessons of my life in seven words: never give in; never, never give in.*
> —Winston Churchill[250]

Screening

As you make calls, you will undoubtedly encounter a gatekeeper—a person whose function is in part to protect the hiring executive's time. For many SEALs, you had this type of

249 See also, Asher, Donald. *Cracking the Hidden Job Market: How to Find Opportunity in Any Economy.* (New York: Ten Speed Press, 2011), p. 136.

250 Cornerstone Coaching LLC, "What Winston Churchill Can Teach Us About Inevitable Success," (blog), February 26, 2014, http://www.cornerstoneadvisoryservices.com/blog/what-winston-churchill-can-teach-us-about-inevitable-success (accessed May 28, 2015).

person doing for you what this gatekeeper is doing for someone else! Be ever so kind and polite to these people. Befriend them if possible. As a general rule, they will have one question for you:

"What is this regarding?"
When speaking with the gatekeeper, be straightforward and honest. If applicable, refer to the hiring executive by first name. Something like:

"I am an executive sales professional in the care-management industry. I am exploring a career move and it has been suggested to me to reach out to Bob. Is he available?"

Voicemail

Most of the time, you will get the hiring executive's voicemail. Use the opportunity to leave a brief message. The voicemail could go something like this:

"Bob, this is Kevin Johnson, and I am an operations professional who successfully saved my most recent employer over $5M in operating costs by streamlining our customer-relations call center. I would like to connect with you at your convenience to further discuss my background and how I can contribute to the success of (Company Name). I can be reached at 123-456-7890."

How many voice messages should you leave? There is a fine line between being persistent and becoming a pest. Only you can make that determination. However, three to four would likely be the maximum. Remember that you can reach out to the hiring executive by email and LinkedIn InMail as well and blend your contact methodology.

Email Marketing Your Professional Credentials

An alternative approach when proactively marketing your professional credentials is to initially reach out to hiring executives by email. With reference to the Cover Letter Success Formula, write a compelling email cover letter. Marketing emails essentially follow the same formula, with some distinct differences that should be observed to increase effectiveness. These differences include:

Subject Line. Good use of the subject line is vital. It must be short and impactful. A poor subject line would read: *"Accountant looking for work."* A good subject line would read: *"#1*

Provider Technology-Sales Representative." A very good approach is to use your Headline from your LinkedIn profile and modify it as needed.

Inside Address. This is a communication sent by email, not by the US Postal Service. Do not put an inside address in the email. A date is unnecessary as well.

Attaching a Resume. Here you have to make some decisions. Some companies have servers with robust firewalls that screen out all unfamiliar emails with an attachment. You can either send an attached resume or not. If your email that had a resume attached is returned with an undeliverable kickback, try again without the resume attached. Another consideration is your current employment status. If you are unemployed, it is recommended that you attach a copy of your resume. If you are currently employed, think through whether you want to provide a copy of your resume. You may decide to be selective and send a copy to some companies and not to others.

When it comes to attaching a resume, customize the name of the document. At a minimum, use your first and last name with a space between each (e.g., John Smith.docx). A better approach would be your name plus a branding statement (e.g., John Smith Lean Six Sigma.docx). Or, add a position type or function, (e.g., John Smith Senior Engineer. docx).

Close. Your close should be different due to the "reply" function with emails. It is recommended that you ask the recipient to act in response to the email. An example of a good close would be: *"If you have an interest or a need for a proven account manager with a documented track record of success, please reply or call me."*

Telephone Number. Always put your telephone number in your marketing emails. The hiring executive may want to bypass the reply button and speak to you directly. Give them a way to do so.

The Appendix has examples of marketing emails for your review, including a suggestion about using video (which will be discussed below).

Sending Your Marketing Emails

Once you have identified your target companies, identified the (probable) hiring executive, obtained an email address, and written a compelling marketing email, it is time to send them.

Send each email individually. DO NOT send a mass email and waste your time and effort.

Instead, copy and paste your template email, and then customize each email as needed. Spell check. Give it one last look for appearance, and send. When you get an undeliverable message on an email, don't get discouraged or distracted. When you've completed sending the other emails in your original batch, address the kickbacks. Double-check the spelling and the email formula. Call the company to confirm the email address, informing the person on the phone about the email address you used and that you received a kickback. This approach frequently works.

Email Marketing through LinkedIn

Sending marketing emails as LinkedIn InMails is acceptable. However, since the number of InMails you begin with is limited, try reaching hiring executives first through their company email and use LinkedIn InMail as a secondary strategy if reaching the executive through company email proves futile.

Follow-Up Calls

After you send your marketing emails, wait a day or two and see if you get responses. Obviously, you want to immediately follow up on any emails you receive indicating interest. After a day or so, you will need to start generating *calls* to the hiring executives you sent emails to. You will use virtually the same scripts previously provided with a reference to the email you sent to the hiring executive. Your voice message should also reflect that you sent an email a few days prior.

These calls should seem more like a warm call, and they should be easier to generate, since you have already reached out to the hiring executive. You are now simply following up. Remember, the ultimate purpose of the call is to get an interview.

Drip-Email Marketing

An effective strategy when marketing your professional credentials is "drip" marketing, which is when you send messages to a hiring executive over a period of time. The drip concept is to send a marketing email and then systematically contact the same hiring executive with additional emails containing different information. The goal is to generate interest from the hiring executive to secure an interview.[251]

---

251 Hill, Paul. *The Panic Free Job Search: Unleash the Power of the Web and Social Networking to Get Hired.* (Pompton Plains, NJ: Career Press, 2012), p. 203.

There are several important points to be aware of when using this technique. Be very organized, record who you have contacted, with what information, and when. Space your drip emails at least two or three days apart. Do not send a resume on the first contact.[252] Wait until you get interest or some positive response from the hiring executive before submitting a resume (or better yet, get an interview scheduled and then send your resume).

There is a variety of information you can select for your drip messages. Start with a description of your professional credentials and then follow up with emails containing:

1. A recommendation or endorsement.

2. A list of references—especially if there is a chance that the hiring executive might know one of them.

3. A short success story.

4. A short list of accomplishments, especially if they may resonate with the hiring executive.[253]

5. Positive comments from job performance reviews.

6. An abridged summary from a personality assessment.

7. A list of marquee clients or distribution-channel partners (or contacts) if you're in sales or account management.

If you are asked for a resume, this could be a good sign. However, think about telling the hiring executive that you are making some revisions, and reply with another drip message. Make yourself irresistible. Then, a day or so later, provide a resume and ask for an interview. Remember, the purpose of drip marketing is to generate interest and secure an interview.

Most job seekers who use the drip-marketing approach find it easier to execute and less stressful than follow-up phone contact (you will still need to call the hiring executive, though!). However, overall effectiveness depends on the hiring executive. Some may respond more favorably to a follow-up call because they recognize and appreciate the initiative. For others, it makes no difference.

Blend the email marketing and phone contact approaches. Follow your business instincts on the number of contacts and method(s) you use. Show persistence, but again, don't become a pest. If you are not getting a response after several overtures between calls and emails/InMails, move on (See When All Else Fails . . . , mentioned later).

---

252 Ibid., p. 205.

253 Ibid., p. 205–206.

The Research Interview

This job-search technique can yield promising job leads. A research interview is a very brief conversation, either by telephone or face to face, with an employee who currently works for a target company. The point of the conversation is to ask open-ended questions that elicit responses regarding their experiences working for that company.

The reason why the research interview works so well is twofold. First, people like to talk about themselves and share their experiences with others. Just assure your contact that the conversation is confidential.[254]

Second, as a general rule, people like to help others. Once you establish confidentiality and show genuine interest in their responses, people tend to speak openly. Once people realize that their experiences and opinions are the focal point of the call, without a hidden agenda, the information will flow.

Here's how to set up and conduct a research interview:

1. Identify an appropriate number of target companies in which you have a sincere interest.

2. Identify an appropriate contact within each target company. Use LinkedIn to get referred to that person if possible.

3. Call, email, or use LinkedIn InMail and request an appointment by clearly stating the purpose for the conversation (to learn about the company). If appropriate, mention a contact the two of you have in common, or the person who recommended you reach out to them. Establish an appointment time for a fifteen- to twenty-minute conversation.

4. Prepare, in advance, four or five open-ended questions on topics of interest to you. The key is to get them talking about themselves, the company, their position, and so on. As a rule, stay away from the topic of salaries and compensation.

5. Since you set up the appointment, be the one to call. Be prompt and ask your contact whether it is still a good time.

6. Conduct the research interview by asking your questions. Keep things to fifteen to twenty minutes to be mindful of your time and respectful of theirs. If you start to run over, acknowledge it; frequently the contact will say it is okay to continue.

    It is not uncommon for people to ask about your job search as a part of this conversation. This is where the magic of this approach often happens. They will

---

254 Hallowell, *Million Dollar Race*, p. 107.

volunteer information about internal openings (can you say Hidden Job Market?), lead you to network to others inside or outside the company, mention job leads with other companies, and so on.

7. Always write a thank-you note or email. Send it promptly after the conversation.

   If there happens to be an open position within the company, ask whether your contact could refer you to the appropriate person.[255] Also (and this is important), ask whether the company offers referral bonuses to employees for referring qualified job seekers. If so, this creates an obvious incentive for your contact to refer you. According to recent surveys, nearly two-thirds of companies encourage employee participation in recruiting by offering referral bonuses. These bonuses often exceed $1,000.[256]

A research interview is a great strategy. It is an easy and comfortable call to make (similar to calling hiring executives about recruiters), and the topic is safe and reasonable for the company employee.

Using Videos or YouTube in Your Job Search

Embedding a short video (or YouTube link) into email messages to hiring executives is unique, effective, and can differentiate you from others, *if done correctly*. As a SEAL, this means you need to be familiar with how to do this (with training, if necessary). You will impress an employer with your technology skills as well as the content of the video.

First and foremost, your video must be professional. If it is not, you can significantly harm your job-search efforts. If you decide to pursue video, consult the section on Webcam or Skype Interviews. Many of the same considerations listed there will apply to your video (your attire, look into the camera, and so on).

The purpose of the video is to introduce you as a professional, create interest with the hiring executive, and differentiate you from other job seekers. Used for this purpose, it is not a lengthy video resume. Therefore, keep your video short; the recommended length is a minute to a minute and a half.

The video personalizes you. The hiring executive can see you, pick up on your personality, and learn about your background. The video operates as a first impression, which is very important (see First Impressions later in this book). Remember to smile.

---

255 Ibid., p. 107–108.

256 "Bonus Programs and Practices," *WorldatWork*, June 2014, http://www.worldatwork.org/adimLink?id=75444 (accessed June 1, 2015).

What do you talk about? After introducing yourself, discuss your qualifications, accomplishments, and professional traits. A logical starting point is your elevator speech. Start out strong with an attention-getting statement. This could be your biggest accomplishment or qualification, or you could reference an industry trend. Refer to the attention-getting recommendations listed previously. Many of those will work here. (As you may have figured out already, many of the concepts and techniques of a job search weave together, interrelate, and complement each other.)

It is imperative that you script, memorize, and practice what you are going to say. Then make sure you can deliver the speech in a conversational tone and manner (just like your elevator speech). This video will be viewed by hiring executives and recruiters. It must be perfect!

Where you shoot the video can have an impact on its effectiveness and the hiring executive. For example, if you are targeting positions that will require air travel, consider shooting the video at a quiet area of an airport (the key here is the setting must clearly *be* an airport). If you are in manufacturing, consider shooting the video on the floor of a manufacturing facility.

Putting high-level graphics into the video can make it distinctive. You can voice-over while the graphics are on the screen. Frequently, companies that design and create websites could help you produce a video with graphics.

When All Else Fails . . .

There comes a point when it becomes apparent that a hiring executive is simply not going to respond to your messages (emails or calls). If this happens, there's one last thing you can do before you "close the briefcase" and move on. Send one last short email describing your background and ask the hiring executive to please pass along your information if he or she becomes aware of any openings that would be a match. This technique enlists the hiring executive as a resource who could be helpful to your search.

Here is an example to get you thinking when composing your email:

Anita,

I've reached out to you a few times over the past week or so. I'm sorry we have not connected. By the way, congratulations on your recent acquisition!

I am an operations professional in the plastics industry. I managed four manufacturing facilities in four separate regions and exceeded production and profit goals for the last five consecutive years.

I am in a job search looking for a senior operations position in the plastics or rubber industries based in the South (Texas would be ideal).

Should you become aware of any positions that could be a match, feel free to pass along my information. My resume is attached.

Best Wishes,
Your Name

Let's examine this email in depth:

- It is short and to the point. This is important. Resist the temptation to provide too much information about your background and circumstances. You've already laid that groundwork with previous communications.

- It mentions a compliment, which could help get the rest of the email read. If you do mention a compliment, make sure it is sincere and substantive. If not, leave this part out.

- It identifies your role and an accomplishment.

- It clearly states that you are in a job search, what kind of position you're looking for, and where.

- It grants permission to the hiring authority to pass along your information, allowing them to help you should they become aware of an opening. The hiring authority does not need to reply to confirm that your information has been passed along.

As you use this technique, every once in a while you will get a reply email acknowledging your message or a job lead. As with all job leads, it can lead to further networking and possibly your next job!

Where to Spend Your Time and Effort

Now that you know the various avenues to locate open career opportunities, where do you distribute your time and effort? There is no definitive answer to this question. However, for most SEALs, the following breakdown is representative:

- Seventy to eighty percent or more on networking and proactively marketing your credentials.

- Ten to fifteen percent with recruiting firms (initial and follow-up contact).

- Ten percent (or less) on job boards or direct applications.

Networking and marketing your credentials lead to interviews (mentioned in the next section). Effective interviews lead to landing a job. And the key to an effective interview is to differentiate yourself from other job seekers by providing real-life examples of your skills and resulting accomplishments.

Part XI

Interviewing

To get something you never had, you have to do something you never did.

—Jose N. Harris[257]

How Much Are Interviews Worth?

Did you know that during an average round of golf, the actual amount of time the golf ball is in contact with the club face is a fraction of a second per swing?[258] Playing eighteen holes of golf results in a very short amount of ball contact overall. Remarkable! The same ratio of contact to length of an athletic contest likely holds true with other sports where there is an instrument striking an object (hockey, baseball, and tennis immediately come to mind). Now think of all the time these professional athletes spent over the course of their lives practicing, staying fit, being coached for hours, and so on to perfect, as much as possible, the technique and muscle memory to execute a swing that results in such a sliver of contact time. This analogy represents the small amount of time you spend interviewing relative to the total amount of work hours over the course of your career.

257 "Jose N. Harris Quotable Quote," Goodreads, http://www.goodreads.com/quotes/415120-to-get-something-you-never-had-you-have-to-do (accessed June 22, 2015).

258 "Ball at Impact," Golfswing.com, http://www.golfswing.com.au/139 (accessed February 15, 2016).

Let's do some math: Assume you work forty hours a week for fifty weeks a year (two weeks a year for vacation and personal time off). This totals two thousand hours of work time a year. Assume that you will work for fifty years—as a society we are choosing to work longer into our lives.[259] Therefore, your total number of career working hours is one hundred thousand hours. A little staggering when you think about it.

Statistically speaking, the average professional could have as many as ten jobs over the course of their career[260] (for some it could be more, or less, but ten is representative in today's free-agent market, and it makes the math easier). As a SEAL, you might already be thinking that you are not going to have ten more positions left in your career (hopefully). That's likely true, but this is all to illustrate a point. Back to the math . . . Assume that it takes twenty-five hours of total interview time to secure a new position. This includes the interview process for the job you're hired for, as well as all of the positions you interviewed for that did not work out. And, we know that interview processes have been lengthened for a variety of reasons.[261] So, ten jobs that took twenty-five hours of interviewing per job equals 250 hours of interview time over the course of your career. The ratio of 250 interview hours for one hundred thousand hours of career work time gets you .0025 percent. When viewed this way, those interview hours take on more importance. (And we're not done!)

Consider the financial impact an outstanding interview can have on your career and personal life. Assume that you were, *on average*, able to improve your compensation by $10,000 every time you changed jobs. (It is recognized that there is a plethora of circumstances that affect this generalization. There could be times when it is more or less, but on average, assume an improvement of $10,000 per job change. Play along here; it's to prove a point). So, ten jobs over the course of your career, with an increase of $10,000 per position, equals $100,000. Multiply that over a career of fifty years and that gets you $5,000,000.

Okay, if you find yourself thinking about these numbers, the analogy, and the way you could shoot more holes in it than a block of swiss cheese, you've missed the point! The numbers and the analogy are not perfect! In fact, you can say they are flawed. But, again, that's not the point. The point of the illustration is to impress upon you that interviews

---

259 Woods, Jennifer. "Working Longer—Whether You Want to or Not," CNBC.com, December 23, 2014, http://cached.newslookup.com/cached.php?ref_id=105&siteid=2098&id=10359558&t=1419339600 (accessed June 9, 2015).

260 Bureau of Labor Statistics, "Number of Jobs Held, Labor Market Activity, and Earnings Growth Among the Youngest Baby Boomers: Results from a Longitudinal Survey," news release, March 31, 2015, http://www.bls.gov/news.release/pdf/nlsoy.pdf (accessed May 29, 2015).

261 Susan P. Joyce, "After the Interview, What is Taking Them SO Long?" Work Coach Café (blog), September 17, 2012, http://www.workcoachcafe.com/2012/09/17/after-the-interview-what-is-taking-them-so-long/ (accessed February 15, 2016); "2015 Candidate Behavior Study," CareerBuilder, http://careerbuildercommunications.com/candidatebehavior/ (accessed February 15, 2016); Jena Mc-Gregor, "Interviewing for a Job is Taking Longer Than Ever," On Leadership (blog), Washington Post, June 18, 2015, http://www.washingtonpost.com/blogs/on-leadership/wp/2015/06/18/interviewing-for-a-job-is-taking-longer-than-ever/ (accessed February 15, 2016).

are critically important to your career enjoyment and financial well-being. Approaching interviews with a cavalier attitude or flying by the seat of your pants is professionally foolish. There's simply too much at stake. When it comes to interviewing for a job, take it seriously. Prepare! It's worth a lot of money, and it means a lot to your career and you.

Let's review for a moment. Remember from Understanding the Employer's Mindset, an employer hires with two main goals in mind: to make money or save money.[262] An interview is the platform that addresses those ultimate goals, through information exchange.

How an Employer Views an Interview

Employers want to answer five major questions as a result of the interview process:

1. Can you do the job? (skills and experience needed to perform the job)
2. Will you do the job? (motivation to actually perform the job functions)
3. Will your performance have a positive impact on company goals? (subjective prediction of future performance . . . will you be any good at it?)
4. Do you fit in? (cultural fit)

And, if those four questions are answered yes, then . . .

5. Are you affordable? (compensation)

When you answer all five of these questions affirmatively, you have a shot at the position. Other job seekers may pass the criteria, too. Failing to pass any one of these hurdles will result in the employer pursuing other job seekers for the opportunity. Let's look at how you can give yourself the best chance to win.

Can You Do the Job?

Questions in this portion of the interview will be about your technical skills, ability, and knowledge, as well as your transferable skills and professional qualities. The interviewer will be evaluating your qualifications for the job and determining whether you can actually perform the functions of the position. Emphasize your skills and abilities, and match the basic elements needed to perform the job functions.

---

262 Whitcomb, *Job Search Magic*, p. 274.

Will You Do the Job?

Motivation is pivotal to success in any job position (or job search), and is a professional quality all hiring executives want to see in any job seeker. The hiring executive needs to know whether you want to perform the job functions.

As a SEAL, you must convince the hiring executive that you have the required abilities and are motivated to use them! You must overcome any preconceived notion that you are interested in the job just to slide into retirement. This is achieved by educating the hiring executive about your passion for the job, work ethic, internal drive, and examples of taking the initiative and going the extra mile. Revealing that you have researched the company, position, and perhaps the hiring executive's background can also be a reflection of your motivation.

If the hiring decision comes down to two equally qualified candidates, the one who has demonstrated motivation and enthusiasm wins.[263] That's going to be you!

Will Your Performance Have a Positive Impact on Company Goals?

Here, the hiring executive will attempt to predict your future performance on the job and compare you to other job seekers. You may have the necessary skills and be willing to use them, but will your performance positively impact and significantly advance company goals, be an improvement from the previous person in the position, improve team performance, and so on? This is where competition for the position takes place in the mind of the hiring executive. It's about proving results and convincing the hiring executive that you can make things better. They want to hire the best!

It is imperative during the interview to stress your accomplishments, history of success, and work ethic. Ask about position goals, projects, and how you will be measured in the position. Then reference your accomplishments to match and exceed expectations.

Generally, in today's business environment, many employers are very sensitive about short-term goal achievement. They have a problem, and they need it solved yesterday. The lead-time to get quantifiable results in a position is getting shorter. Therefore, in interviews, focus your responses the best you can on providing value and results to the employer in a short period of time. (Just be careful not to over-promise and under-deliver.) Portray yourself as an expert who knows how to do a task and shorten the start-up time, leading to quicker ROI from hiring you. In other words, you can hit the ground running.

---

263 US Department of Labor, "Soft Skill #2: Enthusiasm and Attitude," Skills to Pay the Bills, http://www.dol.gov/odep/topics/youth/ softskills/Enthusiasm.pdf (accessed February 15, 2016); Adams, Susan. "How to Ace Your Job Interview," Forbes, March 1, 2013, http:// www.forbes.com/sites/susanadams/2013/03/01/how-to-ace-your-job-interview-2/ (accessed February 15, 2016).

Do You Fit In?

Cultural fit with the organization and personal chemistry with those you will work with is a big deal. Statistically, 60 percent of most hires are based on personal chemistry.[264] Employers tend to hire who they like even though more qualified candidates may be available.

Cultural and personal-chemistry questions explore likeability, connection, communication, values, interests outside of work, and dress/appearance. When the hiring executive shifts gears into more personal topics, they are assessing your cultural fit and personal chemistry.

Are You Affordable?

To land an offer, the compensation you will accept must generally fit within the hiring range for the position. That could be less than what you were previously earning. However, the more qualified you are, and the more they like you, the more justification exists to move you to the higher end of that salary range. Sometimes, if your qualifications and cultural fit are strong enough, employers will go beyond the original compensation range to capture extraordinary talent. It does happen, but don't bank on it as you pursue opportunities! All employers must be conscious of budgets and parity issues. There are limits to what they can or are willing to do.

Strategy for a Successful Interview

A successful interview involves four basic elements:[265]

1. **Uncovering the employer's need.** You achieve this through research, reading job descriptions, listening, and asking probing questions.

2. **Communicating to the employer that you can satisfy that need.** You achieve this by matching and relating skills and experience to what you've discovered the hiring executive wants.

3. **Persuading the employer to hire you.** You achieve this by emphasizing your past accomplishments and relating those accomplishments to the employer's need. Differentiate yourself.

4. **Showing enthusiasm for the position.** It has been repeatedly shown that top-

---

264 DiResta, interview by Canters, "How to Blitz."

265 Claycomb and Dinse, *Career Pathways*, Part 8.

qualified candidates who show enthusiasm for the position are more successful in receiving job offers.[266] Simply put, everyone wants to be wanted, and the more you convince an employer you want the job, the more likely you are to get it.

As you read through the rest of this chapter, keep these four strategies in mind, as their themes are woven into all of the substantive interview topics and techniques that follow. The concept behind this strategy is very similar to "Solution Selling," a sales methodology where the salesperson focuses on the customer's pain(s) and addresses those pains by introducing his or her product(s) and services.[267] As it applies to your job search, you must position yourself as the solution to the hiring need.

🐦 Keep in mind that most employers are looking for someone who can do the job, do it well, and not make waves. It's often not so much your chronological age but the perception of age-related issues regarding knowledge, skills, ability, and other age biases. Your goal in an interview is to have the hiring executive answer yes to the five questions and relieve him or her of any perceptions of age-related concerns.

Strategy for Opening the Interview

This is an interviewing strategy that can be very effective if the interview opens in a way that gives you the opportunity to use it. If the interview does not open in such a way to use this strategy, don't push it.

After pleasantries are exchanged, ask the hiring executive verbally describe what he or she is looking for. Listen very carefully. You are about to hear the answers to the test! Then, by reference to your background, accomplishments, and professional character traits (whatever might be the emphasis of the hiring executive's description), fulfill those needs or wants.

This proactive approach can put you in a strategic advantage. Whatever the hiring executive provides as what he or she is looking for (plus information you gathered from your research) are the "target" qualifications, professional character traits, needs and issues the executive wants or needs in the open position. You need to fulfill these targeted needs or wants by reference of your background, accomplishments, and past experiences. Successfully doing so can remove questions the hiring executive may have about your qualifications for the position. The tone of the interview may relax and take on an exchange of information rather than an examination and evaluation of qualifications.

---

266 US Department of Labor, "Soft Skill #2"; Adams, "How to Ace."

267 "What is Solution Selling?" Sales Performance International, http://solutionselling.learn.com/learncenter.asp?id=178455 (accessed February 19, 2016).

First Impressions

Research has repeatedly shown that hiring executives heavily base their evaluations on their initial impressions of a job seeker.[268] Therefore, the first thirty to sixty seconds of an interview are crucial to your success. The hiring executive creates first impressions of you, positive or negative, in that quick snippet of time.[269]

If the hiring executive draws a negative first impression, there is a tendency to ask tougher questions to validate that impression. Or, the hiring executive could elect to minimize the engagement and make the interview very short.

On the other hand, if the hiring executive has a positive first impression, there is a tendency to ask easier questions and even overlook deficiencies in qualifications.

🦶 Your appearance is very important in creating that positive impression. As a SEAL, this could involve some cosmetic adjustments. If you have too much gray hair, would dyeing your hair be advantageous? If you are a guy who wears a beard with gray whiskers, is it time to shave it off or dye it? If you are significantly balding, is shaving your head an option? What about your smile? Could it be time (perhaps) to invest in some cosmetic dentistry? Or professionally whiten your teeth? And, if you are carrying a few extra pounds, now might be as good a time as any to control your diet and step up your exercise—not only for your appearance, but your overall health as well!

Any improvement in your physical appearance can be a rejuvenating experience, which can increase your confidence and improve your attitude.

🦶 A small (but by no means insignificant) idea is to show up to interviews with a cell phone or tablet. Turn them off, but make them visible, sending the subtle message that you are in touch with technology.

Create an initial positive impression by dressing conservatively (over 50 percent of a person's impression of you is determined by physical appearance),[270] smiling, having a firm handshake, and by making opening remarks that demonstrate your sincere interest in meeting the hiring executive.

Be aware of your countenance (your facial expressions) during the interview. Try to appear positive even when you hear less-favorable information about the opportunity. Gather information and be slow to judge. The hiring executive will be watching, and your

---

268 Zolfagharifard, Ellie. "First Impressions Really DO Count: Employers Make Decisions About Job Applicants in Under Seven Minutes," Daily Mail, June 18, 2014, http://www.dailymail.co.uk/sciencetech/article-2661474/First-impressions-really-DO-count-Employers-make-decisions-job-applicants-seven-minutes.html (accessed June 5, 2015).

269 Regis University Career Services, "Interviewing Strategies for Non-Traditional Students and Alumni," Regis University, http://www.regis.edu/About-Regis-University/University-Offices-and-Services/Career-Services/Student-and-Alumni/Interviewing-Strategies.aspx (accessed June 19, 2015).

270 Jamal, Nina, and Judith Lindenberger. "How to Make a Great First Impression," Business Know-How, http://www.businessknow-how.com/growth/dress-impression.htm (accessed June 2, 2015).

unintended facial expressions could betray your negative thoughts (even though you may not yet have full information). This could have a bearing on the lasting impression the hiring executive has of you.

Creating an initial positive impression means you won't be playing catch-up during your interview.

One interview technique available to you that can help defuse the potential of a bad first impression and create a positive one is asking questions early in the interview about the job requirements or what the hiring executive wants. Use your qualifications, background, and accomplishments to match the needs of the position. This gets the conversation started on the right foot and is a fast way to help create a positive impression of you with the hiring executive.

If you believe that the hiring executive's first impression is not positive, you have some heavy lifting to do to recover, but it can be done.[271] Here are a couple of things you can do: First, ask questions about the job and answer using your success stories. By showcasing your past performance, you might be able to move the needle back in your direction. Second, name-drop if you can (capitalizing on the persuasion principle of liking and perhaps social proof). If you know that the hiring executive and you have someone in common, mention the name. That might be enough to redirect the dialogue into positive territory. Even if your performance is superior, you may not overcome an initial negative impression or rough interview start. Do the best you can to get off to a good start.

Interviews: Progression

Most interview processes have three distinct phases: Screening, Evaluation, and Consensus (Final Decision).

Screening. Frequently, screening interviews are conducted by phone with the primary focus of determining whether you have the requisite background, qualifications, and experience to do the job. Your goal for this interview is to make the cut and move forward in the interview process.

Evaluation. In this phase, the hiring executive(s) will dig deep into your background by asking specific and pointed questions about your technical knowledge and how you have performed in previous positions. You'll get into the nitty-gritty. Beyond your skills and capabilities, cultural fit and personal chemistry are also being evaluated. Occasionally,

---

271 "Cognitive scientists say it can take up to two hundred times the amount of information to undo a first impression as it takes to make one." Zack, Devora. "10 Tips for People Who Hate Networking," Careerealism, May 4, 2015, http://www.careerealism.com/hate-net-working-tips/ (accessed July 17, 2015).

a psychological profile or interview with an industrial psychologist may be a part of the process. Most organizations use the results as part of the hiring decision, not a litmus test whether to hire or not.

The last form of interview that can be a part of an evaluation process is an "approval" interview. It is with senior management (president, CEO, or someone else) and can either be traditional in length or very brief. This is an opportunity for the individual to meet you and give approval. With a certain degree of frequency, you may encounter one favorite interview question from this person, because many interviewers have one that they ask everybody. This is usually when the interview is going to be brief and the executive has limited time. Be on your "A" game here—it matters.

Consensus (Final Decision). This is when the decision about who to hire is made. This meeting may not happen for a few days or even a week after all the interviews are complete. It is a total assessment of your candidacy for the position, including overall qualifications and fit.

Interview Preparation

The interview process starts before you engage the employer in conversation. Here is a list of things you should do when preparing for an interview, regardless of format:

Research the company. Learn as much as you can. Get on the company's website and LinkedIn. At a minimum you must know:

1. The products and services offered by the company.
2. Who the buyers/consumers of these products and services are.
3. How these products and services are valued or needed by the buyer/consumer (the company's "value proposition").
4. Who a few of the company's market competitors are.
5. News, recent events, and any announcements regarding the company (often the website will have a "News" tab).

Check out the websites Glassdoor (www.glassdoor.com) and Vault (www.vault.com). These are websites where employees of companies can post comments about the company, both positive and negative.

If time permits, reach out to colleagues and ask what they know about the company. If you are interviewing with a publicly traded company, read the annual report, the CEO's letter to shareholders, and/or ask a financial planner or stockbroker for their assessment. Most job seekers won't do any of this. Referencing the most recent annual report will differentiate you from other job seekers, and your knowledge and insight will impress the employer.

Research the position. Read the job description, if there is one. Call colleagues who may have useful information, especially if a colleague works for the employer you are interviewing with.

Research the hiring executive(s). Get on LinkedIn and research the background of the hiring executive(s). Understand their career history and look for any common ground. Having something in common, either professionally or personally, creates personal chemistry—a principle of persuasion and an integral part of hiring. It's been shown that employers hire those they "most like being around," so establishing personal chemistry can significantly increase your odds of advancing in the interview process and getting hired.[272]

Research the industry. This is particularly important if you are changing industries. Research trends—these are the hot topics that are shaping and impacting the industry. What is the future outlook for the industry? Familiarize yourself with the companies in the industry. Do the best you can to determine who the industry leaders are and who are up-and-comers. Get educated.

Script answers. Take the time to script the answers to known or reasonably anticipated questions you will receive. Put yourself in the hiring executive's chair, think of the likely questions you would ask, and script your answers. Then, if those questions are asked, you will be prepared and will be able to provide a succinct response.

Prepare questions. Prepare questions to ask based on your research about the company, position, the hiring executive, and the executive's area of responsibility. Refer to your list of questions from your Target Opportunity Profile.

The interview is a two-way street. The hiring executive is evaluating you for the position, but you are evaluating the company, position, reporting structure, culture, and opportunity to figure out if this job at this company matches you.

Here are some powerful questions job seekers have asked that sparked engaging conversation:

- Why is this position available?
- What do you see as the most important task or challenge facing this position over the next six months?

---

272 Sutton, Robert I., PhD. *The No Asshole Rule: Building a Civilized Workplace and Surviving One That Isn't.* (New York: Warner Business Books, 2007), quoted in Kurtzberg and Naquin, *Essentials*, p. 18.

- Looking back on this job and how it's been done in the past, what would you change?

- Who would you point to as a top performer in this job? What traits made him/her so good?

- What actions made him/her successful?

- What obstacles do you foresee the selected candidate encountering that would hamper success in this position?

- What performance standards will define success in this position?

- What does success look like in the first ninety days?

- What stands between where the project/situation/company is today and where you want it to be?

- Why do you work for this company?

🔻 As a part of your overall research, explore job postings from age-friendly companies (especially for positions similar to those you are interested in). AARP and Retirementjobs. com have growing lists of companies that have either been certified as age friendly or have pledged to be.[273] Do these job postings reveal any insight that could lead to possible questions to ask in an interview? Are there any themes or company attributes contained in the postings that can help you evaluate your fit within a company or its culture?

Taking some time to do this research (you might only need to do it once) may help you in your evaluation of opportunities. An interview is an exploration of many things, but ultimately you (and the employer) are both looking for the best possible fit.

Interview Formats

The following types of interviews occur during the screening and evaluation stages of the interview process. As a SEAL, you have probably been through one or more of these. They are:

- Telephone (conducted either by the executive or human resources)

- One-on-One (just the hiring executive and you)

- Skype/Webcam (can be used at any stage, and allows the executive to see you)

- Succession (usually used as a second or home-office interview, this type is multiple

---

273 See also, Dugan, "10 Tips."

one-on-one interviews, typically with people from different departments—tailor your questions to the executive, such as asking an operations executive about efficiency and cost savings, and do your best to prepare questions for different departments)

- Group (either of your potential peers or of managers from different departments; direct your response to the person asking the question—bring up topics if you're in a peer group, but let superiors lead the conversation if in a manager group)

- Psychological (either in person, or over the phone; a psychologist is likely evaluating you to see if your personality lines up with the position you're pursuing—be yourself, don't overthink, and don't give answers you think the interviewer wants to hear)

- Stress (extremely rare, and designed to see how you react; you will not encounter this one, but if executives act angry, rude, or condescending to you or one another, it's likely an artificial scene—stay positive with your responses)

- Meal (can be over breakfast, lunch, or dinner)

- Behavioral and Performance-Based (questions here will focus on specific examples of your past behavior as indications of your future performance)

Practice Interviews

⬥ One of the best things you can do to prepare for interviews is to conduct practice or mock interviews. This is especially true for SEALs who have not interviewed for a job in several years. Interviews can be stressful, and practicing reduces that anxiety, boosts confidence, and leads to better performance. Prepare for all interviews thoroughly, so you won't treat the first real interview as your "practice interview." It's entirely possible you could get into that interview, realize the position is more intriguing than you thought, be unprepared, and regret your performance.

To conduct a practice interview, ask a trusted colleague for assistance. Explain the purpose of the role-play. It is not an exercise to "trip you up," but rather to prepare you. Use your resume to give your colleague a general outline to follow. Provide seven or eight likely questions you believe you may be asked, given your background and career history. To be truly effective, ask your colleague to research five or six interview questions from the Internet beyond those you provide.[274]

---

274 Smith, Jacquelyn. "How to Ace the 50 Most Common Interview Questions," Forbes, January 11, 2013, http://www.forbes.com/sites/jacquelynsmith/2013/01/11/how-to-ace-the-50-most-common-interview-questions/ (accessed February 19, 2016); Peterson, Thad. "100 Top Job Interview Questions—Be Prepared for the Interview," Monster, http://career-advice.monster.com/job-interview/interview-questions/100-potential-interview-questions/article.aspx (accessed February 19, 2016).

When conducting the mock interview, try to stay "in character" as much as possible. You can come out of character as you need to discuss responses, but just remember the more realistic you make it, the better prepared you will be.

Evaluate your performance and responses with your colleague. Be open-minded to their critique and suggestions. Make necessary adjustments. Having more than one practice interview (instituting any changes in approach and responses) is encouraged.

Answering Traditional Interview Questions: The UPAC Method

As you can well imagine, you will be asked many questions in the interview process. The UPAC Method is a very intuitive approach to answering these questions.[275] Its effectiveness comes from the accomplishment component. When possible, mention an accomplishment that supports your answer.

U **Understand** the question (ask for clarification if necessary).

P **Provide** the employer with your (concise) answer.

A Add an **Accomplishment** that supports your answer.

C **Confirm** that you answered the hiring executive's question satisfactorily, redirecting the question if needed.

🦅 Accomplishments are significant for any job seeker, but especially for a SEAL. During an interview, you need to emphasize recent accomplishments and not over-emphasize your years of experience. The concept is your recent accomplishments can make you come across younger. Overplaying your experience because you have experience dates you. Sell your accomplishments!

Here is an example of this technique:

Question: "We are looking for a product-training professional who can design and implement a training program for newly hired sales and account-management professionals. What has been your experience in that area?"

U You understand the question and what the employer is asking. Proceed with a response.

P *Over the last five years with Barlowe ASP, I designed and implemented two training programs for current and new employees, many of whom were sales and account managers.*

---

275 Adapted from Claycomb and Dinse, Career Pathways, Part 8.

A *The most recent was a custom-designed program that I worked on with a well-known technology-education consulting firm. We designed the content of the program incorporating both the technology elements of the products and sales approaches. We created a comprehensive manual and high-touch presentations using the most interactive touch-screen technology available. I then scheduled five half-day, in-house seminars. Each seminar was led by a consultant from the firm who was knowledgeable in that particular subject area. The seminars were a smashing success! The vice president told me that I had exceeded all expectations.*

C *Did I answer your question?*

Telephone Interview

Frequently, screening interviews are conducted over the phone. In this format, you must rely on verbal communication only. Slow your rate of speech and enunciate.

The advantage of a phone interview is the hiring executive can focus on the substance of your answers without distractions. SEALs can have information in front of them to refer to as needed. Taking notes is very useful during the interview and for follow-up communications.[276] Here are some tips to improve your odds of a superior performance during a telephone interview:

Prior to the Call

1. **Prepare.** Research the company and position with the same due diligence as you would for a face-to-face interview. This preparation will shine through to the hiring executive, especially if you're asked, "What do you know about our company?"[277]

2. **Phone Zone.** Create the same quiet place you did when you made your proactive marketing calls. Remove unnecessary paperwork and items from your work space and keep your resume, company information, job description (if you have one), success stories, questions to ask based on your research, water, pen, paper, and so on, nearby.[278]

---

276 Adams, Susan. "How to Ace a Job Interview on the Phone," *Forbes*, February 7, 2012, www.forbes.com/sites/susanadams/2012/02/07/how-to-ace-a-job-interview-on-the-phone/ (accessed November 4, 2015).

277 Llarena, Melissa. "What to Expect During an HR Interview?—Five Questions You'll Be Asked During a Screening Interview," *Forbes*, October 18, 2013, http://www.forbes.com/sites/85broads/2013/10/18/what-to-expect-during-an-hr-interview-five-questions-youll-be-asked-during-a-screening-interview/ (accessed November 4, 2015).

278 Adams, "How to Ace."

As a matter of human practicality, go to the bathroom before the call. Some telephone interviews are reasonably short (twenty to thirty minutes) while others can last over an hour.

If possible, use a landline. Cell-phone connections are less reliable and you risk dropping the call. If you do not have a landline, make sure your cell phone is fully charged and you take the call in a place where you know you have good reception.

Strategy during the Call

You have done your homework for the call and created your Phone Zone. Here are some strategic suggestions that will prove helpful during the call:

1. **After exchanging pleasantries, ask the hiring executive to explain what he or she wants in an ideal candidate.** Listen carefully. You are about to hear the answers to the test! Use your background, experiences, and successes to match the requirements and sell your accomplishments.

2. **Smile and stand up.** Doing both of these things will have a positive impact on your tone of voice and portray a positive attitude. Standing will improve energy during a longer call.

3. **Dress the part.** Consider dressing for the telephone interview as you would for a face-to-face interview. This will put you in an interview frame of mind.

4. **Remember your questions.** Use the ones you created during your interview preparation. Questions from you are a sign of interest.

5. Be careful not to over-answer. Most telephone interviews are screening calls. The hiring executive is frequently seeking information about qualifications. Answer questions completely, but avoid long-winded answers. This is an age-related bias you need to steer clear of. You want to be thorough, but know when to stop answering.

6. **Listen.** Don't formulate what to say next while you should be listening to the hiring executive. Be active and engaged. Take notes but do not worry about recording complete thoughts. Fill in the details after the call is complete.

7. **Ask for concerns.** Have the hiring executive let you know of pitfalls or issues he/she is aware of that may derail or sidetrack your success. Ask: "Do you have any reservations about me succeeding in this role?" Refer to your background to defeat any perceived obstacles or issues presented by the interviewer.

8. **Ask about the next steps.** Do this at the end of the call. Indicate interest in proceeding to the next step. Consider asking whether you will be advancing in the interview process, which appeals to the persuasion principle of consistency and commitment (provided you've had a successful interview thus far).

9. **Follow up.** You must send a follow-up thank-you communication. The most time-efficient way is through email. Refer to the Cover Letters and Other Written Communications portion of this book for examples.

The Unannounced Telephone Interview

There are occasions when a call will come unannounced. Although seldom the case, an employer may do this intentionally. But often the unannounced call is a result of a scheduling mix-up, perhaps due to time-zone differences. If this happens, simply tell the hiring executive that you are in the middle of something. You can reschedule the call or simply delay it by fifteen minutes. Give yourself time to gather your thoughts to make the call productive.[279]

Webcam or Skype Interviews

Many employers use these to help speed up the interview process. In fact, it has been referenced that as many as six out of ten companies use webcam or video interviews in their hiring process.[280] For some SEALs, this format for an interview is new and can be unnerving.

If you are unfamiliar with the use of Skype, relax. It's not as intimidating as it sounds. The first thing to do is get an account. Go to their website (www.skype.com) and sign up. It's free! Write down your "address"—it's your Skype phone number. Put it somewhere so you don't forget it. Get a camera from the computer store if your computer is not equipped with one. Cameras are reasonably inexpensive. Hook it up.

After you are set up, here are key strategies to help you succeed during a Skype interview:

1. Get comfortable with the technology. Be sure it's set up on your computer, and familiarize yourself with the basics. Adjust the webcam to pick up your face, shoulders, and maybe down to the middle of your torso. Practice with the webcam

---

279 Whitcomb, *Job Search Magic*, p. 348–349; Adams, "Interview on the Phone."

280 OfficeTeam, "Survey: Six in 10 Companies Conduct Video Job Interviews," news release, August 30, 2012, http://officeteam.rhi. mediaroom.com/videointerviews (accessed June 5, 2015).

and chat with friends or family prior to your interview. This will reduce anxiety. When the time comes to answer interview questions, look into the webcam's lens to give the impression of eye contact. Good posture is also important here. Do your best to remain still (on camera, movement can be delayed and therefore distracting). Be natural, and relax.[281] Technical issues may still come up. Take them in stride.

2. Control the scene. Similar in concept to the Phone Zone, set up a clean, professional background for the interview. Be aware of what is behind you.[282] Make sure any pets are out of earshot.

3. Wear professional attire. Dress like this is a face-to-face interview. There are a few special considerations. Don't wear clothes with busy patterns, as they tend to distract others. And dress completely, not just from the waist up.[283]

4. Have the hiring executive's telephone number. If the technology simply fails, you'll want to schedule a telephone interview as a fallback.

Screening Interview Conducted by a Human Resources Representative

These screening interviews (whether by telephone, webcam, or face-to-face) can pose a problem for some SEALs. Often the HR screener is a younger person in the HR department who is not far into their own career. They were in elementary school when you were already established in your career, and now you have to pass muster with them to move forward in the interview process. This type of interview can be hazardous because this individual likely has little or no influence on the ultimate decision to hire you, but has the power to eliminate you as a candidate for the job. Your goal for this interview is to put your ego aside, avoid being condescending, survive it, and move forward in the process.

Understand that HR professionals who conduct screening interviews are evaluated based on the number and quality of candidates they pass along to the hiring executive. The last thing they want to hear from the hiring executive is, "This candidate is weak." Or, worse yet, "What in heaven's name were you thinking? This candidate is not remotely qualified." So, study the job description and match your qualifications to it. Work to put the HR representative at ease that you are qualified and will make them look good.

Most times, interviews with human resources can be a bit scripted. The HR representative

---

281 Eric Bricker, "How to Ace Your Video Interview," *On Careers Blog, U.S. News & World Report*, July 11, 2013, http://money.usnews.com/money/careers/articles/2013/07/11/how-to-ace-your-video-interview (accessed December 1, 2015).

282 Ibid.

283 Ibid.

has a set number of questions or topics to cover with each candidate. The key, and the tricky part, is to provide the correct or acceptable answer. Too often, the HR representative looks for elimination factors rather than the totality of your qualifications.

With some limited exceptions, the questions you will likely encounter will be the general kinds of interview questions or statements, such as:

- "Tell me about yourself."[284]
- "What are your strengths?"
- "What are your professional weaknesses?"
- "Why are you interested in this position?"[285]
- "What do you know about our company?"[286]
- "Why are you interested in our company?"
- "Tell me why you decided to leave your previous job."[287]
- "Why are you looking?"
- And general questions evaluating your qualifications.

You will also encounter questions about your resume, why you made particular career moves, and your reasons for leaving or staying at particular positions. Do not show any resistance to the questions, regardless of your feelings about this type of interview.

Toward the end of the interview, you will undoubtedly hear, "Do you have any questions?"[288] Realize that this person will probably not know much about the actual functions of the job you are pursuing, other than to repeat what might be on the job description. Do not put this person on the spot by asking in-depth position questions. Instead, stay in the safe zone and ask a few general questions this person should be able to answer, such as:

- What do you like about the company?
- What has made the company successful?
- What are the company's future goals and vision?

Remember to be respectful, polite, and friendly. Endear yourself. The reality is that the HR representative holds the future of your candidacy in their hands.

---

284 Llarena, "What to Expect."

285 Ibid.

286 Ibid.

287 Adapted from ibid.

288 Ibid.

Meal Interview

This interview could be the most difficult type—it can happen at any step in the interview process, with any meal (breakfast, lunch, or dinner), and can trip up even the most confident of job seekers. Making this type of interview successful involves navigating a host of variables.

There are several reasons why employers conduct meal interviews:

1. Convenience. The hiring executive can multitask by conducting an interview during a meal.

2. Confidentiality. Other office personnel do not know that interviews are taking place for a particular position.

3. Information gathering. This includes your background and qualifications, just in a social setting.

4. Evaluation of personal factors. These would include social skills (useful for gauging how you would conduct yourself with clients, vendors, suppliers, key business partners, and so on) and your table manners.[289] If you are the leading candidate, an added bonus of a meal interview could be to impress you.

The reasons for a meal interview don't really matter. What does matter is that hiring executives believe they can tell a lot about you by the way you eat and interact in a social setting. Frequently, these interviews can go longer than traditional in-office interviews. Part of the key to success during a meal interview is not to be lulled into complacency. Make no mistake—this is an interview, not friends getting together just to catch up.

A meal interview is typically more conversational than a traditional face-to-face interview. It is fine if the conversation veers into personal topics. Remember, personal chemistry plays a significant role (up to 60 percent) in who the employer hires.[290] Follow the employer's lead. However, listen closely for when the conversation turns into questions or dialogue regarding your qualifications.

Here are some helpful things to remember about meal interviews:

1. Research the restaurant. Get the GPS out and know how to get there. Review the menu. Get some ideas on what to order.

---

289 Muse, The. "Let's Do Lunch: How to Prepare for a Job Interview Over a Meal," Forbes, November 12, 2012, http://www.forbes.com/sites/dailymuse/2012/11/20/lets-do-lunch-how-to-prepare-for-a-job-interview-over-a-meal/ (accessed November 4, 2015).

290 DiResta, interview by Canters, "How to Blitz."

2. Do not order messy foods like barbecue, pasta with lots of sauce, or any food that you would need to eat with your hands.

3. Order food that can be easily eaten with a fork and that can be cut into smaller pieces (that will help if you need to answer a question after taking a bite).

4. Do not order expensive entrées. Stay within the restaurant's mid-price range (you could make price part of your restaurant research).

5. Turn off your cell phone. Give the hiring executive your complete, undivided attention.

6. Be polite. Use "please" and "thank you." Be courteous to the servers.

7. Do not order alcohol, even if the hiring executive does. Being under the influence of alcohol during an interview shows poor judgment, impacts your answers, and takes you off your game.

8. Brush up on your etiquette and table manners! Know how and when to use the various utensils. Good table manners will give you an edge over other job seekers.

9. Allow the hiring executive to lead the conversation. The interview questions may not occur until the meal is finished.

10. After the meal, show your appreciation to the hiring executive. Remember, the restaurant was likely chosen because he/she likes it. Compliment the choice of restaurant.[291]

After the meal, do not worry about the check. The hiring executive will pay the tab. Make sure to ask about next steps. Write a thank-you note and send it within twenty-four hours of the meal interview. (Note: You should write a thank-you for every interview and especially meal interviews. The hiring executive did pay the tab.)[292]

If you handle it professionally, a meal interview can give you a distinct advantage over other job seekers. It is an opportunity to build personal chemistry, display your social skills and table manners, and convey your abilities and accomplishments in a social setting.

---

291 Muse, "Let's Do Lunch."

292 Ibid.

Behavioral Interview

🐦 Behavioral interviews are a very effective and common technique. As a SEAL, you must be prepared to answer these kinds of interview questions. If you have not interviewed in a while, the format could be unfamiliar to you. A behavioral interview question requires you to describe situations or past experiences where you have demonstrated certain skills or behaviors.[293] The idea here is past behavior is an outstanding benchmark of future performance.[294] These questions are designed so you have to describe a situation, what you did, and the results of your actions. How did you use your skills and professional qualities to achieve success in your past?

Most behavioral interview questions begin with "Tell me about a time when . . . " or "Describe a situation where . . . " Theoretically, behavior-based questions help hiring executives avoid making hiring decisions based on emotions or gut feelings. Instead, the hiring executive is able to gather objective information that assesses your job skills, abilities, experience, successes, and so on.

These questions can be unnerving. They require you to quickly think of specific situations in your past when you used specific skills. We generally don't remember things in this way . . . we just do the job using our skills. It is due to the unpredictable nature of these questions along with the nervousness associated with an interview that can stump any job seeker.

Although there is a myriad of topics or competencies an employer can inquire about, some of the most common are:

- Technical ability
- Analytical thinking
- Communication skills
- Time management, prioritizing
- Leadership
- Problem solving, innovation
- Collaboration
- Ability to learn, adapt

Notice that many of these competencies are the sought-after skills, transferable skills, and

---

293 Claycomb and Dinse, *Career Pathways*, Part 8.
294 Safani, "Tell a Story."

professional qualities previously listed in this book. There could be several behavior-based questions for the same competency.

Preparing for and Answering Behavioral Interview Questions

The first thing to do in preparation for these questions is to review (or write) your success stories. You should have five or six success stories describing your use of different skills and competencies. Reviewing or writing these success stories gets your mind thinking in terms of telling stories. It tends to awaken your memory about situations when you have used your various skills. As you remember situations, write a success story.

The next thing you can do to prepare for these questions is to "sit on the other side of the desk." Put yourself in the shoes of the hiring executive and think about behavior-based questions you might ask if you were hiring for the position you are pursuing. One technique that occasionally helps is to actually think or speak the beginning of a behavior-based question. That is, "Tell me about a time when . . . [then you finish the question]." This will occasionally make you think of questions that you had not previously thought of and you can now prepare for.

Read the job description. There are sometimes clues in a job description about the important skills or experience being sought. Those are often the areas that behavior-based questions will be directed toward.

Answering behavioral interview questions successfully involves being able to describe an experience directly related to the question (competency) being asked about. Use your success stories whenever possible. Here's how to answer effectively:

1. Understand the question. Listen very carefully and be sure you understand what is being asked. If you do not, ask the hiring executive for clarification. It is permissible for you to reframe the question and repeat it back to the employer.

2. Determine the professional competency being asked about. Then think of a situation in your professional experience that illustrates the competency being addressed. Thinking in terms of identifying the competency makes it easier to recall a situation when you used that competency. Take a moment. Don't panic if something doesn't come to mind right away. Ask the executive for more time if you need it.

3. Tell a brief success story that describes a situation illustrating your skill or competency. Highlight how your skill influenced the end result.

4. Confirm that your response answers the question. Responses such as "Does that answer your question?" or "Does that example give you the information you were asking about?" are good examples to start with here.

Remember this shorthand, five-prong formula for answering behavioral interview questions:

UNDERSTAND

DETERMINE THE COMPETENCY

THINK

TELL

CONFIRM

If the behavior-based question happens to be an experience you have dealt with, terrific! Tell your story using the C.A.R. approach (identify the Challenge or situation, your Action, then the Result).[295]

If the behavior-based question is not something you have dealt with directly, but you have an analogous situation, tell the hiring executive that you have not handled that situation directly, but you have handled a very similar situation and tell your story.

If the behavior-based question is not something you have dealt with directly and you do not have a similar situation, has a colleague handled that situation or one like it? If so, indicate to the hiring executive that you have not handled that situation but a colleague has. Tell the story, then indicate whether you agreed or disagreed with the way your colleague handled the situation. If you disagreed with the way it was handled, explain how you would have done things differently.

Finally, if the behavior-based question is not something you have dealt with directly, you do not have a similar situation, and you are unaware of whether a colleague has handled the situation, then indicate that you have not handled the situation described and offer to answer it in the hypothetical—describe what you would do. This form of an answer is not ideal, since the hiring executive believes it's an important question, but it is better than no answer at all.

🔪 It is inevitable that you will encounter behavioral interview questions. You will never be able to predict what behavioral questions you'll be asked, but you can prepare ahead of time with your prewritten success stories to defuse being put on the spot. This way, you will be able to answer smoothly when these types of questions come up. You can also ask for time to think of a response if you can't think of an answer right away—be sure to give an answer of some kind eventually, though. You don't want the employer thinking you only wanted to stall.

---

295 Safani, "Tell a Story."

Common Competencies Covered by Behavioral Interview Questions

Below are some competency topics with sample behavioral-based questions. The style of the questions should give you a good idea of what behavior-based questions sound like and how they may be asked in an interview.

Communication Skills

- Describe a time when you made formal recommendations or a formal presentation to senior management.

- It's difficult at times to get others to try new and innovative ideas. Tell me about a situation in which you persuaded others to explore something new.

- Tell me about a time when you dealt with the poor performance of a subordinate. How did you go about communicating this fact to the subordinate?

Time Management, Organization, and Planning

- Have you dealt with any simultaneous distractions, interruptions, or unanticipated events on the job? How did you resolve these situations when you found out about them?

- In the past, what types of far-reaching company goals have you set out to achieve? What has been your degree of success?

Management Skills

- Tell me about a situation in which you needed to raise the performance level of your group.

- Tell me about a time when you praised your group for a job well done. What did you do?

- Give me an example of a time when you dealt with an uncooperative subordinate who was disrupting your group. What did you do?

- Describe the last time you needed to terminate an employee. How did you go about that?

Problem-Solving

- Tell me about a serious on-the-job issue and how you worked through it.

- Think of a difficult decision you had to make. Explain what happened. If you could do it over, how would you do it differently?

- How would you describe your style or approach to solving problems? Give me an example.

Leadership

- Give examples that show how you influenced and led others.

- How do you delegate tasks at work right now?

- Describe a situation in which you assumed leadership duties and your method for doing so.

- What strengths of yours influence your leadership methods the most? Describe a situation in which you used them.

Your Interview Wardrobe

For SEALs, one word sums up your attire for an interview: conservative. Wearing traditional, professional business attire instantly communicates to the hiring executive that you are confident. It also gives you an advantage over other job seekers, using the persuasion principle of authority.

Looking sharp also has the added advantage of making you feel in control and sets the stage for a superior interview performance. As a result, the hiring executive and others will respond to your image of professionalism in a positive way.

When it comes to the specific dos and don'ts of what to wear, if you find yourself questioning whether or not to wear something to an interview . . . don't. Use conservative judgment and always err on the side of traditional, conservative corporate attire.

Interviews with Potential Peers or Subordinates

When interviewing with company employees who could be peers or potential subordinates, remember that they want to meet you and get to know you professionally. However, most likely they have two important hidden issues on their mind:

1. Do I like this person? Does he/she fit in? Can I see myself working with or for this person?

2. Friend or foe? Could this person represent a threat to my job or career at the company?

🦅 These are real issues for SEALs. You may have more experience and expertise than those you meet. Ingratiate yourself by asking questions of these people. Try to remove barriers by answering their questions and showing interest in them, both professionally and personally, if possible. It is not uncommon for the candidacy of a job seeker, SEAL or otherwise, to unravel as a result of internal political maneuvering by an employee who feels threatened.

Explaining a Job Termination in an Interview

The first thing to understand about a job termination is that it's not the end of your career or job search. Even if the termination was "for cause," it does not necessarily mean that landing a fulfilling career position is forever gone. A glitch in your employment history is something you can and will overcome. In fact, many hiring executives have had the very same experience at one time in their careers as well. They may be more empathetic and understanding than you think. The key is handling a past termination with professionalism and grace. Here are some tips to help you:

Get your facts straight. Set any emotions you may have about your termination aside, and communicate with your former employer. Come to an understanding on what the circumstances were and what public statements will be made, should a background check be performed. With that information, you must align your explanation with that of your former employer. Otherwise, you jeopardize landing future opportunities.

Be honest. Employers appreciate and value honesty. You are always safe if you tell the truth and provide the honest reason for your termination. Be positive about your former employer, as well (similar to concepts earlier in this book about explaining unemployment). Say only what's necessary (over-explaining is a common mistake). Answer any questions and focus on the position (without dodging the questions).

Script a response. Word choice matters. Don't use "fired" or "terminated." Instead, soften the language and use "let go," "released," and if applicable, "laid off" or "my position was eliminated." Phraseology can put a more positive spin on your job search. Reorganizations, corporate lay-offs, and downsizing are all accepted reasons for job terminations, and using those terms isn't as big of a negative as it was in the past.

Mention accomplishments in the position or since the termination. These can be ones you achieved in the position you were terminated from, or ones acquired since the termination. The key here is to match the needs of the open position. Moving the conversation toward those topics refocuses the discussion on how you can benefit the employer.

Know how to handle termination for cause. Explaining a job termination for cause involves many of the techniques already mentioned, plus a few others that can help overcome the concerns the hiring executive may have.

Be prepared to explain the circumstances. If applicable (and only if applicable), indicate that the company was right to terminate you. Indicate that you still respect your former employer as a company. Make it clear you have learned from the events that resulted in your termination. Accept your share of the responsibility and tell the hiring executive that it will not happen again. **This is important: This hiring executive must be convinced that the circumstances that led to your termination will not happen again.** The hiring executive does not want to knowingly hire a problem employee.

Put the employer at ease. A termination is a red flag that puts the hiring executive on alert to a potential hiring mistake. It is your goal to alleviate that concern the best you can through your honesty, accountability, and past accomplishments.

Explaining Employment Gaps or Long-Term Unemployment

If you have employment gaps in your job history or a long stretch of unemployed time, accept the reality that a hiring executive will ask about it. Many of the techniques from the previous section on handling job termination (never disparage a former employer, be honest, accept responsibility, acknowledge the circumstances and what you've learned) work here as well.[296]

As part of your explanation, inform the employer about what you have been doing during this gap time to stay current with your industry or to enhance your skills and knowledge. This can include activities previously mentioned, such as consulting, working toward an industry designation, and so on.[297]

Another approach is to mention you are being selective with your next career move and not looking for just any job.[298] With this approach, be able to list at least two or three criteria that you are looking for in your next position (to validate your selectivity claim). If you have turned down any offers, mention them (as further proof of selectivity). A severance

---

296 Pongo, "How to Explain Work History Gaps in the Interview," The Pongo Blog, https://www.pongoresume.com/blogPosts/372/how-to-explain-work-history-gaps-in-the-interview.cfm (accessed February 16, 2016).

297 Jill Kempka, "Resume FAQ: How Do I Handle Employment Gaps?" Career Coach (blog), Manpower, January 25, 2013, manpowergroupblogs.us/manpower/career-coach/2013/01/25/resume-faq-how-do-i-handle-employment-gaps/ (accessed February 16, 2016).

298 Biron, "How to Explain Employment Gaps in a Job Interview," Career Sidekick (blog), December 9, 2013, http://careersidekick.com/how-to-explain-employment-gaps-in-a-job-interview/ (accessed February 16, 2016).

package, if you received one in your last position, also supports the notion that you are looking for the right career fit.[299]

You can also mention that you underestimated the difficulty of finding a suitable position. But in response, you intensified your efforts and now have several opportunities "in play" (as long as it's true, of course). This approach may heighten the urgency to pursue you because the hiring executive knows you have increased your efforts and have other opportunities you are pursuing.

Finally, at the end of your explanation, ask a probing question about the position, preferably addressing an area where you possess a particular strength. This question directs the interview away from the gap and back to the position, where you can showcase your qualifications.

What if the employer does not ask about the employment gap? Do you proactively bring it up? Possibly. Doing so indicates you have nothing to hide, are willing to address concerns, and prepared for this situation. However, bringing up the gap may not be appropriate— use your judgment. If you do address it, simply asking if there are any concerns about your employment gaps is all that's needed to start this conversation.

When you do answer questions about gaps or extended unemployment, be confident. Part of the evaluation will be how you handle questions. And remember, employers today "are more understanding of employment gaps" than they once were.[300] Many job seekers with employment gaps have overcome employers' concerns and landed fulfilling career positions.

Explaining Job Hops in an Interview

As a general rule, employers begin to view a job seeker as a job hopper if they've held more than four to five jobs in ten years[301] or had a series of employments in a compressed period of time. Realizing that hiring is both time-consuming and expensive, employers view job hoppers as risky hires. In an employer's view, job hops reflect instability and give the impression of someone who gets easily dissatisfied or many other negative conclusions. If your work history has job hops, address them in an interview with the same formula as employment gaps (anticipate that employers will ask, explain the circumstances without

---

299 For Dummies, "Answering Interview Questions About Job History Gaps," Dummies.com, www.dummies.com/how-to/content/ answering-interview-questions-about-job-history-g0.html (accessed February 16, 2016).

300 CareerBuilder, "Employers Share Encouraging Perspectives."

301 Lisa Amstutz, "Survey of HR Managers: How Many Job Changes is Too Many?" (blog), Robert Half, January 17, 2014, http:// www.roberthalf.com/finance/blog/survey-of-hr-managers-how-many-job-changes-is-too-many?hsFormKey=06a77aee09a564e-ca4467cf5525e3c15 (accessed June 9, 2015).

giving extreme detail, and ask a probing question about the position to shift focus away from the moves and back to you and your qualifications).

There are also several explanations specific to job hops that you can use (if they apply to you). One is demonstrating a strategic plan for your job moves (even if they did not work out). Another explanation is that in order to be more rounded for executive positions you took a position with a higher level of responsibility or in a new area (for example, out of sales and into operations).

A third approach is to admit to the job hops, accept your share of responsibility, mention some lessons you learned, then emphasize that you are looking for stable long-term employment. You can't afford another short stint. Your plan is new employment that will last several years. Finally, you can inform the employer that you have reevaluated your career and focused your efforts toward a particular career path or position type(s). You must be logical and convincing if you choose this approach.

Job hops are not a death knell to a satisfying and fulfilling career. However, establishing tenure and a track record of success with a single employer is always the preferred goal.

Tough Questions Made Easy

"Isn't this a step back for you?"

As you interview, you may have a hiring executive ask: Isn't this a step back for you? (Or a similar question.) You *must* plan ahead and have a response. The hiring executive is concerned that you may leave when a higher-level position comes along. Recruiting, hiring, and interviewing are expensive, not only monetarily but in time and productivity. One of the gifts of being a SEAL is you now have perspective and are motivated by other things, or have a different view on life and your career. Perhaps gaining titles and climbing the corporate ladder don't mean as much to you as they did in your twenties, thirties, or forties. For some SEALs, they have moved from pursuing financial success to pursuing professional significance or professional contentment.

The most effective way to tackle this question is to respond that the position is not a step back. Rather, it's a step in the right direction. It is what you are looking for. But you have to explain why. The following are some conceptual responses, depending upon your circumstances:

- **Title.** "Titles are not that important to me. Just so long as the title is appropriate, which it is, I'm fine."

- **Management.** "I've been in management before, enjoyed it, and was successful at it. However, there's a lot to be said for just being responsible for yourself and not others."

- **Job function/role.** "I'm interested in the job, its challenges, and the contributions I can make to the team and the company. It's not a step back, but a step in the right direction."
- **Compensation.** "I know what the compensation range is for this position, and I'm comfortable with it."

You may find yourself in an interview where your professional judgment tells you that you need to proactively bring up this topic. A good segue could be, "Let me put your mind at ease . . . " Or, "If you have thoughts that this position is a step back for me, let me address that possible concern."

"Aren't you overqualified for this job?"

The hiring executive is concerned you will become bored and disinterested in the position and become a distraction to the team. Or they may suspect you of taking the position until something better comes along. These are legitimate concerns.

The answer to the question is "Actually, I'm perfectly qualified for this position." Now, proceed to tell the hiring executive why by explaining your achievements and skills in light of what the executive wants in a candidate. Then emphasize that you are passionate and interested about the position, the work involved, and the challenges it will give you. Express your desire to stay for an extended period of time.

Depending upon the circumstances and how you feel about this next idea (or how the hiring executive might receive it), you could propose that you will commit to stay with the company for a minimum period of time. You could offer to pay back a sum of money if you should leave early. If you pursue this angle, as part of your commitment consider asking for some additional training in areas where you might feel deficient. This idea would enhance your skills if the hiring executive agrees to it.

The goal is to put the hiring executive at ease that you can find professional contentment in the position you are interviewing for. You can achieve this with preplanned responses or by taking the initiative of addressing the topic if your professional judgment indicates that you should.

Handling the Money Question

Never bring up the topic of compensation during screening interviews. You want to establish that you're a match for the position and build rapport with the employer. Bringing up the topic too soon sends the wrong message.

However, there is a growing trend among employers to inquire about compensation early in the interview process. CareerBuilder found out nearly half (48 percent) of employers now ask about compensation in their first talk with a job seeker.[302]

What if the employer asks you about compensation? The question can be viewed two ways: it could be a standard question asked of all candidates, so the employer can look for the price tag; or, it could be an expression of interest, and a classic buying sign. The problem is there is no way to know for sure, unless you ask the hiring executive(s), which could create an awkward moment in your interview. Try to avoid that.

If the subject of money comes up, a response like this can help:

> *"Right now, I earn $_____. But I know any offer from you would be fair, given my previous achievements and potential with (the company). Based on this position's requirements, I think my talents can serve your organization's goals well by (list how you intend to bring value)."*

This response handles the question and maximizes it by giving you an opening to sell yourself.

If you are uncomfortable disclosing your compensation, this response can work well also:

> *"I appreciate that you mentioned it. All I'm requesting here is that the compensation for this position be fair and competitive, and I'm sure we will arrive at a fair number once we have thoroughly discussed the position and my qualifications."*

This response puts the hiring executive at ease about compensation and invites further discussion about the position and your qualifications.

---

302 CareerBuilder, "Forty-Nine Percent of Workers Do Not Negotiate Job Offers, Finds CareerBuilder Compensation Survey," news release, August 21, 2013, http://www.careerbuilder.com/share/aboutus/pressreleasesdetail.aspx?sd=8/21/2013&id=pr777&ed=12/31/2013 (accessed June 2, 2015).

Closing the Interview

Closing an interview persuasively can be amongst the most important moments in an interview. It can differentiate you from other candidates. If done well, you can move closer to a job offer.

Provide a Summary Statement of your Qualification.

Analogous to the closing argument of an attorney to a judge or jury, try to close the interview with a brief summary of how your skills and background match the position and how being hired will benefit the company. This is a great technique to remind the hiring executive of your qualifications for the job.

Ask to Proceed or Ask for the Job.

If you have a sincere and earnest interest in the position and the company, make sure to express your interest in the proceeding in the interviewing process.

Should your interview be the final step in the process, and you want the job, ask for the job! Doing so removes the mystery for the hiring executive and could be exactly what he or she wants to hear. Don't be coy. If you want the job, say so!

Ask about Timing

Make sure you get some commitment on the timing of a decision (Persuasion Principle of Consistency and Commitment). This could be a decision for the next step or the final hiring decision. Then, to control your own expectations, add one week. Discussions like these just seem to take longer than anticipated.

General Interview Tips

Some general suggestions to remember about interviews:[303]

- Arrive ten to fifteen minutes early. Being late is never excusable. If you are going to be late, call the hiring executive.

- Smile. Maintain good eye contact with the hiring executive. If you don't, the hiring executive may draw a conclusion that you are being dishonest or have something to hide.

- Get the hiring executive to describe on-the-job responsibilities early so you're able to match your qualities, achievements, and experience to those requirements. This is an effective interview tactic.

---

303 Portions adapted from Claycomb and Dinse, *Career Pathways*, Part 8.

- Try to avoid answering questions with a simple yes or no. Whenever possible, mention an accomplishment or success story.

- Stick to the facts and be genuine when discussing personal strengths or achievements with the hiring executive. Remember: Only you are responsible for "selling" yourself to the hiring executive. Make the hiring executive realize the company needs you in the organization.

- Take extra copies of your resume. You may meet with others you did not know about. Don't be caught unprepared.

- Do not exaggerate (or lie). Answer questions truthfully.

- Never be negative regarding current or past employers. If you are, it conveys to the employer that you hold a grudge or may have an attitude problem.

- ✒ Do not over-answer or give long-winded responses. Give appropriate and responsive answers, but keep them brief. There is anecdotal evidence that more job seekers advance in the interview process and receive more offers when the hiring executive talks more in the interview than the job seeker.[304] Answer questions, but be sure to listen.

- Do not ask about "perks" (paid time off, compensation, performance increases, and so on) in any first interview(s) unless the hiring executive does first. If he or she requests a salary figure, refer to the script from Handling the Money Question.

- Behave as if you want to be hired for the position you're interviewing for, but be open to different opportunities. Being able to choose from multiple offers is more advantageous than having just one.

- Ask questions throughout the interview—without interrupting the hiring executive—not just when the hiring executive is finished. An interview should be a mutual exchange of information, not a one-sided conversation. Frequently, you will be evaluated based on the questions you ask.

- If you feel the interview is going badly or realize you've been passed over, do not let your discouragement show.

---

304 "Understanding the Employer's Perspective," Internships.com, http://www.internships.com/student/resources/interview/prep/getting-ready/understand-employer (accessed July 10, 2015).

Debrief Yourself

After every interview, take a few minutes to reflect upon how it went. This self-debriefing is designed to help you collect your thoughts on what *you* liked or disliked about the company, opportunity, people, office environment, products, services, and so on. It is also an opportunity for you to reflect upon your interview performance and make necessary changes.

Ask yourself these questions:

1. *How long did the interview last?* As a general rule, the longer an interview lasts, the better. Remember that approximately 60 percent of all successful hires are based on personal chemistry.[305] The longer the interview, the more rapport is built.

2. *What things did I do well?* Praise yourself for those things you did well in the interview(s). Write them down.

3. *Was I unprepared for any questions?* Write them down and craft an answer. There's always the chance you'll be asked that question again.

4. *What important issues were mentioned in the interview?* Use these items as part of your thank-you letter.

5. *What did I learn during my research and interview that appeals to me?* List the positive things about the company, opportunity, people, and so on.

6. *Identify any concerns and negatives.* This is different from identifying unanswered questions. Items that go here are red flag areas (e.g., the company is about to file for bankruptcy).

7. *Rate the opportunity on a scale of one to ten.* This is an emotional, gut feeling. How do you feel about it? You are looking for an opportunity that not only seems right, but feels right, too.

8. *Was compensation discussed?* You will not bring up the topic of compensation, especially during initial interviews. However, if the hiring authority broaches the topic, it could be a sign of interest. Write down what was said.

9. *How was it left?* Were the parting comments simply a description of the interview process or was there a definite indication that you would be asked back for more interviews? Obviously, you want an expression of continued interest.

10. *How do I rank this opportunity against others I am pursuing?* Keep track of the

---

305 DiResta, interview by Canters, "How to Blitz."

opportunities and how they compare to each other. If an opportunity is not for you, notify the hiring executive and release yourself from the interview process.

11. *Was there anything I could have done better or differently?* Honestly assess your performance. Make note of those things you would do differently or better.

Write a Thank-You Letter

You need to thank the hiring executive for their time. See Cover Letters and Other Written Communications.

- Immediately following the interview, write down key issues discussed. Think of the qualifications and perhaps professional traits the employer is looking for and match your strengths to those.

- Send the letter (email or U.S. Mail) no later than twenty-four hours following the interview.

- If there's no communication in one week's time, call to let the employer know you are still interested and want to move forward in the process.

Second and Home-Office Interview Strategies

Second interviews (as well as home-office interviews) are conducted to clarify information; dig more deeply into your background, skills, and experience; secure additional input from others; and ensure you are a fit with company culture and personality. Planning and preparation are keys to a successful second interview.

The following tactics will help you achieve success at a second interview—hopefully leading to a job offer:

1. **Get an agenda that identifies your interviewer(s).** Once you have it, research their backgrounds, tenure with the company, promotions, previous employers, schools, and so on.[306] Look for something you share in common with them, and before the interview mention that you've read about them. Most executives will be impressed you took the time to research them (especially if you offer a sincere compliment). All of this taps into the persuasion principle of liking and personal chemistry.

2. **Review your notes from the first interview.** Try to decipher what about your

---

306 Hansen, Katharine, PhD. "Do's and Don'ts for Second (and Subsequent) Job Interviews," Quintessential Careers, http://www.quintcareers.com/second-interviewing-dos-donts/ (accessed February 16, 2016).

qualifications, professional skills, and qualities scored enough points to earn you a second interview. Also, determine where you might be weak. Emphasize your strengths, and compensate with assets to offset weaknesses.[307]

3. **Prepare questions.** Focus on the company, position, and each of the hiring executives you will meet. Make sure your questions are focused on their area of responsibility. A good general question is, "What is the number one issue or challenge you are facing in the (Name of Department)?"

4. **Be ready for in-depth conversations.** Fully engage every hiring executive in deep discussions about your skills. Remember the UPAC formula for answering general interview questions and showcasing yourself. In-depth interviews are normally where behavioral questions come up. Remember the process of handling those kinds of questions. Keep in mind you are being evaluated on your overall fit within the company as well as your ability and skillset.[308]

5. **Ask for concerns.** This is the same tactic as with screening interview(s). Try to defeat the concern and emphasize a compensating asset.

6. **Close (and, when appropriate, ask for the job).** As the second round of interviews winds down, close by telling the hiring executives that you *want the job, and ask for an offer*. This is especially true if this is a final home-office visit. Be ready to discuss compensation should the employer bring it up.

7. **One final thought: Get a good night's sleep.** Second or home-office interviews can be long, especially if your day is comprised of a series of interviews.[309]

Common Interview Mistakes

There are a plethora of mistakes that can be made during an interview. Many are common sense, such as don't chew gum in an interview. However, lesser known are the verbal and nonverbal mistakes that job seekers make.

This is a big deal. Research indicates that over 98 percent of hiring executives base much of their hiring decisions on both verbal and nonverbal communication skills.[310] Below is a list of the most notable verbal and nonverbal communication mistakes job seekers make:

---

307 Ibid.

308 Ibid.

309 Ibid.

310 Peterson, Marshalita Sims. "Personnel Interviewers' Perceptions of the Importance and Adequacy of Applicants' Communication Skills," Communication Education 46, no. 4 (1997): 287–291, quoted in Kurtzberg and Naquin, Essentials, p. 31.

- Not listening.[311] This includes interrupting the hiring executive.

- Not making eye contact.[312]

- Being careless about appearance and hygiene. Wearing unprofessional attire (including accessories). Wearing too much perfume or cologne. Having bad breath.

- Failure to provide a coherent and organized response to the question asked.[313] Failing to articulate.

- Giving rambling responses. Providing needless information. Boring the hiring executive. Not staying on topic.[314] Being long-winded.

- Lacking enthusiasm about the position or company.

Game-Day Tactics

Thus far we have covered several topics about interviewing. It is a lot of information, a lot to remember and at first glance and it can seem overwhelming. Review the information occasionally to stay sharp— especially for screening interviews.

The purpose of this topic is to give you game day prep that you can briefly read and review before going into interviews. Interviews can create anxiety, so this brief tactics section will focus your mind before going into interviews. And remember, if you feel you have achieved the goals of the four-prong interview strategy (below), to the best of your ability, your interview was a success regardless of the end result. Focus on successfully executing these strategic goals during an interview and you will eventually have a job offer.

These are thoughts, ideas, and strategies that can be used during interviews. These concepts work; however, every interview has its own personality. If it doesn't feel right to use as an approach, don't force it.

Strategy for a Successful Interview

Remember that an employer hires to make or save the company money. **An employer looks to answer five questions in an interview:**

- Can you do the job?

---

311 Kurtzberg and Naquin, Essentials, p. 31.

312 Ibid.

313 Ibid.

314 Ibid.

- Will you do the job?
- Will your performance have a positive impact on company goals?
- Do you fit in?
- Are you affordable?

Opening the interview

If appropriate and after pleasantries are exchanged, ask the hiring executive verbally describe what he or she is looking for.

Remember the four-prong strategy for an interview:

1. Uncover the employer's need. Achieve this through research, listening, and by asking probing questions.

2. Communicate to the employer that you can satisfy that need. Achieve this by clearly communicating your overall qualifications.

3. Persuade the employer with accomplishments. Achieve this by emphasizing your past accomplishments and relating them to the employer's need. Differentiate yourself.

4. Show enthusiasm. Achieve this by showing sincere interest in the position and the company.

Answering normal or traditional interview questions:

U—**Understand** the question

P—**Provide** an answer

A—Include an **Accomplishment** as part of your answer

C—**Confirm** that you have responded to the question.

Answering behavioral/performance-based questions:

UNDERSTAND—listen very carefully to the question to ensure you understand what is being asked.

DETERMINE the **COMPETENCY** or **FUNCTION**—that the employer is asking about.

THINK—of a situation or major accomplishment that exemplifies the competency or function in question.

TELL—a story that illustrates your competency, ability, or skill. Draw the comparison of an accomplishment to the function in question.

CONFIRM—that your story is responsive by asking a question to make sure you responded correctly.

Be Prepared to Answer these Common Questions:

1. **Tell me about yourself?**

2. **Why are you looking?**

3. **Why are you interested in our company? What do you know about the company?**

4. **What job did you like best? Why?**

5. **What are your strengths?**

6. **What are your weaknesses?**

7. **What was your biggest failure?**

8. **Could you explain your professional goals?**

9. **Why do you believe you would do well in this position? Why should we hire you?**

10. **What would you do in the first XX days in this position?**

11. **Tell me about your greatest professional achievement? What professional achievement are you most proud?**

12. **How would your boss and co-workers describe you?**

13. **The Money Question**

14. **Prepare responses to questions you know will be asked of you that are unique to your circumstances.**

15. **Do you have any questions?**

Have Questions Prepared to Ask The Hiring Executive

Have prepared questions about:

The company—what is its history, what is its current position, what are its future plans, what type(s) of products, services, and projects does it have, and so forth.

The position—specifically the position's duties, responsibilities, and expectations.

The hiring executive—ask questions and engage the hiring executive in conversation to establish rapport, since a high percentage of hires are made on the basis of personal chemistry.[315]

Closing the Interview

As the interview is winding down, consider closing the interview with a brief summary of how your skills match the company's needs and how your accomplishments benefit the company.

And, by all means, if you know you want to work for this company, or be considered for the next step(s), ask! A lot of times, the hiring executive could be waiting for that type of response.

Not Getting the Job: Handling the Rejection

Accept this fact: You will experience rejection. For some SEALs, this can be one of the most emotionally difficult things to endure. It can come verbally, by email, or by written letter. It can be disheartening . . . all of your time and effort for nothing. Well, not exactly. As a SEAL and a mature adult, you are compelled to review and analyze (generally). After you receive the news, decompress for a while, and then evaluate the entire interview experience you had with the employer. Think through it step by step. What did you do well that got you into the process? What did you do well during the process? What did you learn? Now, what could you have done better? Take it apart and perhaps write down your observations. Reinforce deep inside yourself what you do well and keep doing that. Learn from any mistakes and make adjustments. You don't want to make the same mistake(s) again. Ask the hiring executive (or someone in the process) for candid feedback. Many employers resist doing this for fear of possible litigation—some even have company policies prohibiting the giving of feedback. If you get feedback, learn from it.

Finally, after sending a thank-you letter, move on. Your future (today) is not with that company, but it will be with some other employer. It's up to you to persevere and move forward. Your next career position is out there waiting for you!

---

315 DiResta, interview by Canters, "How to Blitz."

Hiring Timeline: A Longer Process

Hiring practices have changed over the last several years. Most notably, the interview process for many professional-level positions has gotten longer.[316] There are a multitude of reasons for this. Here are some common ones:

1. The business climate or priorities have changed. Slowed sales, legislative threats, financing, product and service issues, or any one of a number of other business issues may take a higher priority than filling the position.[317]

2. A change or review of company strategy. A senior-management or board of directors can change or review the business necessity for the position. These high-level meetings can also bring into review the hiring profile or job description of the professional background needed to fill the position. If these meetings get scheduled or are in the near future, the hiring process will wait until decisions are made.[318]

3. Economic fear. Delay in hiring can be an indication of lack of confidence in economic conditions, because a slow economy and hesitation about hiring reinforce each other.[319]

4. Scheduling issues of the hiring executive or someone necessary to the process. Business trips, client meetings, off-site strategy meetings/retreats, vacations, illness, family issues, and so on can prolong the process. Until schedules can be reconciled, the process stalls.[320]

5. Scheduling issues of other job seekers. Employers will accommodate the scheduling needs of well-qualified job seekers. While these schedules are worked out, you wait.[321]

6. Courting passive candidates. When employers recruit currently employed candidates, this can often extend the hiring process. Courting employed candidates can take longer than hiring those who are actively seeking new employment.[322]

---

316 Weber, Lauren, and Rachel Feintzeig. "Why Companies Are Taking Longer to Hire," Wall Street Journal, September 1, 2014, http://www.wsj.com/article_email/companies-are-taking-longer-to-hire-1409612937-lMyQjAxMTA1MDIwMjEyNDIyWj (accessed February 16, 2016).

317 Joyce, "After the Interview."

318 Ibid.

319 Weber and Feintzeig, "Why Companies Are Taking Longer."

320 Joyce, "After the Interview."

321 Ibid.

322 Weber and Feintzeig, "Why Companies Are Taking Longer."

7. Fear of making a hiring mistake. According to a CareerBuilder study, "The vast majority of employers admit that making a bad hire is far more costly than leaving a position open."[323] A mistake can also blemish the hiring executive's track record with the company, which scares the executive.

As a defense mechanism against making a hiring mistake, many employers have elevated the requirements for a qualified candidate and put elaborate interview processes in place. This includes adding several other executives into the process, using personality profiles and other tests more often,[324] and employing industrial psychologists, among other mechanisms (hence creating perceived safeguards against a bad hire and shared risk if the hire does not work out). As a result, you will interview with more people and "jump through more hoops" as you go through the interview process.

You need to accept the reality that many interview processes will take longer than you expect. Accepting this fact will help you control your expectations and make it emotionally easier to deal with.

There are a couple of things you can do to avoid getting frustrated about these elongated interview processes. First and foremost, continue your job-search efforts unabated! Don't stop. Find new opportunities with other employers.[325]

Stay in routine contact with the hiring executive. Put the hiring executive at ease that you are a good hire (and not a hiring mistake waiting to happen). Through your communications, continue to match your background to the needs of the company. Stress your accomplishments. Use your best judgment on what other kinds of information to provide (see the list in the Drip Marketing section).

Another way is to inform the hiring executive of another pending offer. Only use this tactic if the other offer is real. Sometimes this can motivate an employer to move forward. With others, it won't.

There are a couple of hiring "excuses" you may hear that you should be aware of:

"We want to make sure we hire the 'right' person for the job."

If this were true about you (from their perspective), you would be progressing in their interview process.

"We've decided to put the position on hold."

---

323 CareerBuilder, "2015 Candidate Behavior Study."

324 Jena McGregor, "Interviewing for a Job."

325 Joyce, "After the Interview."

Seldom does an "on hold" position resurface anytime soon.

If you should hear these phrases, take those opportunities off your active list. It is highly improbable they will result in further interviews and a job offer.

Eventually these long interview processes will shorten once employers begin to lose out on enough desirable candidates. Forward-thinking companies that are more aware of the hiring market will catch on quicker and change, as opposed to those companies that seek the perceived comfort of process and time. Until that happens, you will have to contend with longer interview processes.

Part XII

Unique Tactics That Create Differentiation

Gather in your resources, rally all your faculties, marshal all your energies, focus all your capacities upon mastery of at least one field of endeavor.

—John Haggai[326]

Differentiation has been mentioned numerous times in this book. It is pivotal to your job search to persuade the hiring executive (especially during the interview process) that you are special. Creating differentiation in the mind of the employer is powerful because it taps into the persuasion principle of scarcity.

The following four interview techniques will help further differentiate you from other job seekers. Each requires time, effort, and thoughtful preparation. To be effective, each tactic must be a substantive, impactful, and well-presented package or document. Otherwise, they distract from your candidacy. Weigh how these tactics would be received by the hiring executive when deciding to use them or not. Well-timed and properly used, these tactics can catapult your candidacy to top-contender status for the open position.

Brag Book

One of the more impactful strategies to create differentiation is a brag book. It is a collection of bound documents supporting (and showcasing) the qualifications and accomplishments referenced in your resume. In a business context, think of a brag book as your marketing packet. It contains important information about your candidacy for the job. The brag book also differentiates you from other job seekers by demonstrating your initiative. And after you leave the interview, the brag book stays as a visual reminder of your qualifications and accomplishments.

---

326 Tracy, Brian. Eat That Frog! 21 Great Ways to Stop Procrastinating and Get More Done in Less Time, 2nd ed. (Buchanan, NY: ReadHowYouWant, 2008), p. 84.

While it takes some effort, creating a brag book also builds your confidence. There's something gratifying about seeing your accomplishments in print; it's a surefire way to boost your self-esteem.

The brag book should be bound in a presentation binder and can be discussed during an interview, left with the hiring executive to review afterward, or both. The brag book's length is up to you, but keep it to a maximum of fifteen pages as a general rule.

Here are some suggested key documents to include in your brag book: Cover Page—Include your name (in large print), the position you are interviewing for, and the name of the company giving the interview.

1. **Table of Contents**—There will be groupings of documents. You can either number each page in the book or delineate by sections (for example, Resume, Letters of Recommendation, and so on).[327]

2. **Resume**—When possible, customize the resume to the job you are pursuing.[328]

3. **Awards**—These demonstrate that you have been recognized for your ability and expertise.[329]

4. **Press Releases**—Press releases regarding any project or achievement that you were involved with or named in.[330]

5. **White Paper**—Portions of any significant business analysis or white paper you wrote.

6. **Graphs or charts**—Graphs or charts that demonstrate your performance.[331]

7. **Job Performance Reviews/Summary**—Positive comments from job-performance reviews (be careful not to include references that could be considered confidential or proprietary).[332]

8. **Personality Profile Results**—Summary page or selected pages from a personality profile that you believe enhances your candidacy.

9. **Articles**—Articles written about you, especially from industry or trade publications. Articles (or portions thereof) that you have authored.

---

327 Matt. "Brag Book."

328 Ibid.

329 Ibid.

330 Hallowell, Million Dollar Race, p. 184.

331 Ibid.

332 Ibid.

10. **Letters of Recommendation**—Letters from clients, former bosses, colleagues, and so on.[333]

11. **Endorsements and Testimonials**—Get together every positive thing anyone has ever said or written about you, such as emails with professional compliments or LinkedIn recommendations.[334]

12. **Professional Organizations**—A list of these demonstrates that you are involved in your industry.

13. **Civic Involvement**—Any documentation regarding your civic and philanthropic involvement.[335]

14. **References**—Provide a list of references who will attest to your ability, professional qualities, and personal character.[336]

🔖 When you consider the contents of your brag book, think on two different levels. First, be sensitive to biases. You may choose to omit dates on some of the documents. You will want to include information that would help defeat or minimize perceived biases, such as any letters or emails that say anything about your dedication, hard work, problem-solving skills, or willingness to put in extra effort, for example. Secondly, consider what types of documents would impress the hiring executive.

A brag book is a great topic of discussion during interviews. It focuses the hiring executive's attention on skills, abilities, and accomplishments and not age-related issues. As a leave-behind, it reminds the hiring executive of your abilities and accomplishments.

When to Present the Brag Book

There is no right or wrong time, just perhaps a good or better time, to present the brag book. It is a matter of reading the situation and choosing the moment that feels best. However, it is normally best to introduce the book early in the interview so the hiring executive can be impressed (the majority will be), and possibly talk about its contents during the course of the conversation.

A brag book's primary function is to showcase your credentials and demonstrate your

---

333 Matt, "Brag Book."

334 Ibid.

335 Neely, "How to Develop a 'Brag Book' for Job Interviews," Splash Resumes, July 25, 2013, http://www.splashresumes.com/2013/07/25/how-to-develop-a-brag-book-for-job-interviews/ (accessed February 16, 2016).

336 Hallowell, Million Dollar Race, p. 184.

interest in the position and company. It will also assure the employer that you have tangible proof of your abilities and accomplishments. Few people take the time to provide any sort of validation or proof of their abilities. A brag book shows potential employers you are serious—a high achiever who will put in extra effort now and on the job, which gives you a competitive advantage over other job seekers.[337]

Career Summary Sheet

A Career Summary Sheet is usually a one-page document designed to intrigue, inform, and impress an employer. It summarizes your career experiences and focuses them specifically on an employer's particular need. When properly written and presented, the Career Summary Sheet can be a notable differentiator and possible conversation starter. Use this as part of an interview where you want to make a brief presentation about your qualifications and understanding of the industry, as a leave-behind, or in various other ways.

The most important consideration when contemplating whether or not to prepare a Career Summary Sheet is the employer's receptivity.

A Career Summary Sheet is not a restatement of your resume, although there could be information common to both. Unlike a resume that has standard sections (Professional Summary, Core Skills, Employment History, and so on), or a cover letter that has rules for proper formatting, a Career Summary Sheet allows you to sell yourself in a persuasive (and therefore impactful) manner. It is about you. Because of these unique characteristics, creating a Career Summary Sheet can be difficult on the one hand, yet creative on the other.

In deciding whether to prepare a Career Summary Sheet, first determine whether you can create an impactful, unique document. If you're unsure, don't pursue a summary sheet. If you do create a Career Summary Sheet and objective observers don't give you positive responses, reevaluate whether a summary sheet is right for you. If a Career Summary Sheet isn't customized or unique to the employer and their needs, it's just another distracting piece of paper.

Some ideas for an impactful Career Summary Sheet include:

• Ask a question (to create intrigue); then answer it.

• Address a market trend.

• Use recommendations creatively.

• Reveal a professional insight using the first person ("I").

---

337 Strankowski, Donald J. "Your License to Brag: The Brag Book," Ascend Career and Life Strategies, LLC, April 2005, http://www.ascendcareers.net/newsletters/April2005.html (accessed February 17, 2016).

- Use your professional profile—similar to your resume's summary, but written differently.
- Emphasize an achievement with bar graphs.
- Reference any online information.
- Write a personal note at the bottom.
- Sign the document.

Finally, format and present the Career Summary Sheet professionally. Make it consistent with your resume's formatting style, fonts, and so on.

A Career Summary Sheet is a blank canvas. Properly created, it can showcase your abilities, skills, and professional qualities; be a platform to provide information; and attack age-related biases with recommendations. As with the brag book, think on two levels—provide information and sell capabilities—but also think of information to include to help defeat any age-related biases.

In the following example, the job seeker knows the employer needs a senior-level sales professional with a demonstrable track record of success. He also learned that senior management had concerns about market shifts. He specifically targeted those issues in the Career Summary Sheet.

Career Summary Sheet—Example

Jeff Holmes
123-456-7890
jeffxyz@yahoo.com
www.linkedin.com/in/jeffxyz

Do you need a proven sales and marketing professional on your team?
"Watching Jeff work with clients, media, markets, and more is a delight. His effectiveness in understanding and delivering the key messages to support our business goals is of the highest caliber. His work ethic is unmatched."
—Peter Pumlin, Vice President of Worldwide Sales, Big, Inc.

Are shifts in market trends impacting your business?
Having thrived through two major technology changes in two different industries, I have extensive experience with the effect of market shifts on organizations and business

conditions. Throughout the economic slowdown and dozens of corporate downsizings, I have continued to exceed expectations. Regardless of the industry or the company maturity, I want to help a business maximize its results by leveraging my experience and marketing capabilities with my successful selling skills.

Notable accomplishments

- First sales executive to ever negotiate an exclusive five-year single-supplier contract.
- Maintained 82 percent of sales revenue in single-supplier relationships.
- Mentored China sales team to achieve a 300 percent increase in sales for 20XX.
- Consistently overachieved sales goals from 20XX–20XX with 105 percent to 200 percent performance.
- Managed a project in excess of $3 million with global operations and teams spanning three continents.
- Grew segment customer base by 100 percent and capacity by 300 percent.
- Positioned flagship product to be chosen by 74 percent of professionals, marking a 34 percent increase.
- Increased attach ratio of segment-related products from 8 percent to 30 percent of divisional transactions.
- Improved Go-to-Market Plan to reduce start-up time by two years and save $500,000.

Does your business need a results-oriented sales professional?

"Jeff is a dynamic business-to-business sales and marketing professional who leverages technology to deliver bottom-line results."

—Cindy Frene, CEO, Frene Consulting Group

Profile

I am a visionary sales and marketing executive with over fifteen years' experience in corporate and private business. In my career, I have worked with businesses of all sizes and scopes, from start-ups to international conglomerates. I have also sold and marketed everything from a $30 consumable to capital equipment in the $500,000 to $1 million range.

I have worked in both B2C and B2B environments, and I have recently been developing business models in the evolving B2B2C markets. I have a track record of simultaneously exceeding sales goals and delivering customer satisfaction.

Capabilities

- Plans multimillion-dollar, capital-equipment sales campaigns.
- Delivers compelling sales presentations.
- Develops business and market concerns.
- Assesses landscape for competition.
- Exceeds sales and budget goals.
- Possesses local, national, and worldwide sales experience.
- Communicates comfortably with operational staff to C-level.

Videos

- Jeff Holmes sales presentation—YouTube
- Jeff Holmes interview 20XX—YouTube

Testimonial Sheet

A testimonial sheet is normally a one- to two-page document containing testimonial statements about you from former bosses, executives, and colleagues.

The document's persuasive powers (and potential for differentiation) come from the notion that others promoting you is more persuasive than you promoting yourself (the persuasion principle of social proof).[338] Therefore, the testimonial sheet must contain truly stellar statements—and enough of them—to convince the hiring executive that the statements are a true reflection of your performance and professional character.

There are a variety of sources for testimonials, including letters of recommendation; LinkedIn profile recommendations; statements contained in a job-performance review; complimentary emails from clients and colleagues; responses from quality-assurance questionnaires from clients; and even excerpts from speakers' notes from an awards banquet. Regardless of the source, the key is the testimonial or recommendation must be significant enough to impress the employer.

Identify the source of the testimonial by name, title, and company whenever possible, to ensure credibility. Inform your source that you are identifying them on the testimonial

---

338 Matt, "Brag Book."

sheet. This is unnecessary with testimonials or recommendations from your LinkedIn profile, since that information is already in the public domain.

When to provide the testimonial sheet is a matter of professional judgment. Timing is important to ensure maximum impact. Other documents you plan to provide to employers could influence when you provide the testimonial sheet. It can become a matter of "which document when" during the interview process.

Consider withholding the testimonial sheet until mutual interest has been established in the interview and you sense the time is right to provide unique information that differentiates you from other candidates. Trust your professional judgment.

🐦 Consistent with the theme of these unique tactics, try to include recommendations and testimonials that attack age-related biases. You may want to approach former bosses, colleagues, or vendor partners and ask if they feel comfortable giving you a recommendation that includes certain statements that attack certain biases (they must be true, of course). Statements about your commitment, work ethic, and use of technology combat biases well. Also, showcase statements in areas where younger job seekers sometimes struggle . . . problem-solving and communication skills—notably written communication skills.[339] These types of statements could be helpful as well.

Here is an example of a testimonial sheet:

Tamara B. Mersmann, RN

84 Mashapaug Avenue ~ Boston, MA 01566

Home: 123-856-8990 ~ Cell: 123-893-6861 ~ tmersmann@charter.net

Colleague Testimonials 20XX–20XX

I have greatly enjoyed working alongside you. I also have the greatest confidence in you and would hire you in a flash for any other sales role. I told Michael (CEO) that you have the purest motives/no agenda (i.e., get the job done) of anyone on his team. He agreed. As a person, you are the best! Great values, great faith, and great humanity all rolled into one.

Patrick Kahler

Senior Advisor, Strategy and Development

Acme Co.

---

339 Adams, "Older Workers, There's Hope"; Wilson, "Why Millennials Are Often Poor Writers."

I have had the privilege to work both as a management counterpart and direct report to Tammy. During both experiences, I was very impressed with Tammy's abilities. Tammy's style is very conversational with a get-it-done mentality. I would describe Tammy's management style as one that allows individuals to be empowered. Tammy is a listener not a teller. She does not try to mold you into her shadow, but wants you to bring forward new ideas and ways to be successful. Tammy sees the value in success for all, not just herself as a manager, which is why I believe she is such a strong leader. Her view of a team, not a group with a leader, allows all to flourish and goals to be attained.

Stephan Wilkinson
Former Sales Executive
Fusion, LLC

Tammy is an asset to our company. She is a gifted individual who is able to blend her knowledge of operational and sales process to improve revenue trend and team performance. She has turned a sub-performing infusion branch into a revenue leader.

Robert Enright
Chief Executive Officer
Fusion, LLC

An "energizing individual," a "power professional," "possessing a clear presence of mind in the face of difficult situations."

All of these and more are what is routinely spoken when one attempts to describe Tamara's work ethic, effectiveness, and true business savvy. I have personally witnessed Tammy emerge from some of the most challenging scenarios that one might meet in business today! Incredible!

Andrew Piper
Former Regional Sales Director
Hope Hospice

Tammy is truly a gifted sales professional, and I am fortunate to have worked alongside her. She is knowledgeable about the industry, works diligently, and focuses on tailoring solutions to meet customers' needs. In short order, Tammy was able to penetrate a new market, leverage existing products and services, and create market demand. As a result of Tammy's efforts, TopInsurer was able to add new clients to its roster and generate revenue from nontraditional sources. Tammy is a great sales executive, and I am happy to recommend her.

Jayson Andrewjeski
Former Vice President, Operations
TopInsurer, Inc.

I worked with Tammy at TopInsurer when she was the national sales director leading the implementation of a new market for the organization. Tammy is an extremely professional, results-oriented leader. She has an ability to work across strategic and tactical levels based upon the situation, issue, or project. In all situations, I found Tammy very easy to work with and a respected leader of the executive team within the organization.

Jason Tobias
Director of Operations
TopInsurer, Inc.

Tammy's enthusiasm is wonderful. She has great initiative. She has hit the ground running, and we are happy to have her as an employee.

Mischelle Murphy RN, MS
Vice President and Chief Operating Officer
Medical Management, Inc.
(excerpt taken from performance review)

One of the bright spots in today's board meeting was the progress on the commercial market. I went over the pipeline with the board, as well as the contracts that we are in the final stages of negotiating/signing, and there was general agreement that this activity on the assessment side represents a real positive for TopInsurer. I want you to know that I am very upbeat about the progress you are making and the impact for us.

Laura Thompson
Former President
TopInsurer, Inc.

I have worked as Tammy's peer for over a year now. In my role as AVP of Client Management at TopInsurer Inc., I have found Tammy to be an excellent clinician, sales person, and team player. Tammy and I needed to work very closely, as I became the client manager of Tammy's (non-long-term care) clients. Tammy's role at TopInsurer was a challenging one, as TopInsurer had never "branched" out into the non-long-term care arena. However, that did not deter her in any way, and she was able to bring in four new accounts in six months—an achievement her predecessor had not been able to accomplish in a span of three years.

Tammy has outstanding verbal, written, and presentation skills. Her clinical knowledge, in particular Medicare/Medicaid, is extensive. The fact that she presents herself as a nurse first and a salesperson second provides the customer a comfort level that makes working with her easy. Whether you are her peer or her client, Tammy treats every individual with respect, support, and confidence. She will deliver on what she says.

Tammy's comprehensive approach to researching clients, understanding their needs, and calibrating their requests with our company's expertise allowed a seamless transition from negotiation to process rollout. I would not be able to do my job, or do it well, without the groundwork that Tammy laid.

Shannon Kearney, RN, BSN
Former Assistant Vice President, Operations
Client Benefit Manager
TopInsurer, Inc.

This person wore many hats in 20XX, with responsibilities for her own sales territory as well as managing the territories of several other account executives. She grew her own territory over $1 million from the year prior, representing an increase of 28 percent—truly a great accomplishment when you consider she has the company's third-largest territory for an account executive while juggling sales-management responsibilities, including helping with many company-wide sales-training and marketing initiatives.

Peter Deirks
Former President and Chief Executive Officer
House Calls, Inc.
(quote taken from the 20XX National Sales Awards Banquet)

Action Plan

Another way to impress the employer and differentiate yourself from the competition is with an action plan, or a mini-business plan written specifically for the position you are pursuing. This is a tactic normally reserved for when you are advancing in the interview process with an employer.

From the first interview and your independent research, you should have a good idea about the job and the challenges facing the position or company. With this information in mind, write an action plan (thirty, sixty, or ninety days). You can go even further out if you want. The point is to demonstrate to the hiring executive you took the time to contemplate how you would begin performing the position's duties and responsibilities.

Consider some of these topics when formulating your action plan:

- Analysis of current market conditions
- Analysis of top competitors—strengths, weaknesses
- Analysis of products and services.
- Any issues on distribution.
- Analysis of any noteworthy regulatory compliance issues.
- Any issue on delivery, implementation, client retention, technology, operations, and so on.
- Any and all relevant topics related to your particular industry or position function.

With an analysis of the topic (potential challenge), provide your proposed action steps followed by a reasonable prediction of positive outcome (result). Think as if you are writing a success story using the CAR (Challenge, Action, Result) formula mentioned earlier.[340] Overall considerations for the action plan include:

- Identifying needed or potential resources for your plan
- Identifying priorities and timing
- Determining how your plan would achieve the organization's potential goals
- Identifying which functional areas or company departments would need to be changed or engaged to achieve success
- Calculating how to measure success

---

340 Safani, "Tell a Story."

There are a myriad of topics that could be addressed. Once you tap into your experience and critical-thinking abilities, the ideas and words will follow.

The action plan should be at least five pages in length, but no more than ten. Consider emailing the document to the hiring executive twenty-four to thirty-six hours prior to your interview so the document is read before you arrive. Be prepared to talk in-depth about its contents.

The action plan can also be in the form of a PowerPoint presentation. If you can borrow the design of the company's website as the background, do it. Keep the presentation reasonably short and focused on relevant topics.

For both written or PowerPoint action plans, don't get too detailed. Stay within your comfort zone of information. And make sure you make a statement early on that you are working from the limited information that has been shared in the interview process so far.

If it comes down to you and another candidate, your action plan differentiates you by offering the hiring executive insight into how you will provide results.

Advanced Techniques to Create Differentiation

The next three techniques will significantly differentiate you from other job seekers. They require additional time and commitment to be executed successfully, but can be well worth it.

Personal Website

There are several benefits of having a personal website when conducting a job search. First, and perhaps foremost, having a personal website is a clear differentiator. According to Workfolio, an application development firm, just 7 percent of people looking for a job have their own website.[341] That means that 93 percent don't! By having a well-designed and informative personal website, you differentiate yourself from over 90 percent of all job seekers, regardless of age. In addition, creating a personal website demonstrates initiative. You took the time and effort to do something unique.

A personal website can create a very positive first impression of you in a hiring executive's mind, often before your first face-to-face meeting. This is important, as "56

---

341 Smith, Jacquelyn. "Why Every Job Seeker Should Have a Personal Website, and What It Should Include," Forbes, April 26, 2013, http://www.forbes.com/sites/jacquelynsmith/2013/04/26/why-every-job-seeker-should-have-a-personal-website-and-what-it-should-include/#73ae8b8a902e (accessed February 17, 2016).

percent of all hiring managers are more impressed by a candidate's personal website than any other personal branding tool."[342] Starting the hiring process on that note is a significant advantage.

⚓ A personal website tells an executive you are tech savvy, attacking the bias that SEALs are just the opposite, or behind the times. It's nice that most webpage-builder sites are designed to be reasonably simple to navigate and understand, with templates, drop-down menus, and drag-and-drop functions. These services try to make it a very easy, step-by-step process to build your own site.

If you are uncomfortable venturing into this, don't abandon the idea! Find a friend or a younger person and do it together. Don't shy away because of the technology. Once you start the building process, most people find it fun! Besides, when it's done, you can mention your site in an interview as a reflection that you are not afraid to learn new things, especially when it comes to technology.

A personal website increases your "findability" and presence. Recruiters, HR, and hiring executives can find you online and view your site.

Naturally, a personal website is a great platform for job-search content. There is a lot of job-search information you can put on your website. This includes your resume, contact information (make sure it appears in several places or is easily found), a personal bio, awards, recommendations, and so on (review the lists in the Brag Book and Drip Marketing sections for ideas). It is also a way to give a hiring executive insight into your personal life in addition to your professional experience (which is how younger bosses often prefer to get to know you). Just use good professional judgment on what information you disclose. And make sure that your resume, LinkedIn profile, and website information line up (employers, dates of employment, and so on).

Finally, a personal website is a great platform to communicate and advance your brand. Who you are and how you promote yourself is very important. When your branding message comes together with color and design on a website, you've created a message that can emotionally appeal to a hiring executive.

Before you start building your personal website, take some time and think through what kind of content you want to include, how you can differentiate yourself, and how you would like it to appear, among other considerations. This is a cool thing you are going to create, and it can be exhilarating! Take some time and do it right the first time. And remember, it doesn't have to be built in a day.

As for platforms and service providers, there are quite a few available. If you search for "The Top 10 Website Builders" on the Internet, you will get a list to choose from.[343]

---

342 Ibid.

343 See also, "The Best Website Builders 2016," Top10WebsiteBuilders, http://www.top10webbuilders.com/?s1-google/s2-us-search/s3-website-builder-p (accessed February 17, 2016).

A Blog

A blog is a website where you can write about your experiences, display your expertise on a topic, express opinions, comment on trends, and more. Frequently, your personal website will have a blogging feature. Blogging can help your job search in several ways.

Starting a blog is a clear differentiator. How many of your colleagues have a blog, especially for the purposes of a job search? Most likely not very many. Having a blog will certainly catch the attention of a younger hiring executive.

A blog will attack several age biases, including that you're technologically behind the times or not "with it" in general.

When it comes to posting content to your blog, you can write on industry topics or your expertise to show you are current with your industry and trends. This defeats the age bias that you are intellectually stale (and can help build your professional brand as well).

Tips on content: Write on topics you are comfortable with. Research and read up on pertinent issues. Now, what's your opinion or insight on those topics and trends? Reading about industry topics and trends keeps you mentally engaged in your industry and might even move you forward. It's fine to write a lengthy piece, but break it down into small posts. Make it an eight-part series, for example. This way, you are not constantly creating content. Try to be routine when posting—once a week on Tuesdays, for example.

Your network will expand with a blog. It will start very slowly, but as you post interesting information, the word spreads, both verbally and electronically. Put a link to your LinkedIn page on your blog, and vice versa. This can eventually lead to referrals, introductions, conversations, and job leads. But it takes time.

A blog can be an extension of an interview. Imagine this: In the course of an interview, a topic comes up that you have written about on your blog. If the conversation aligns with what you wrote, tell the hiring executive about your blog entry. That's not something a hiring executive hears often. Or, once the interview is almost over, suggest to the hiring executive that he or she check out your blog (and personal website) for more in-depth information on you. If the hiring executive does, that amount of time spent on your blog is actually an extension of your interview.

As with personal websites (most are blogs), there are several service providers you can choose from. Wordpress is often mentioned, but look at the list referenced in the personal website section.

A word of caution: Remember that blogging is a job-search tool. For some, it can become addictive. However, networking and marketing your credentials will advance your job search much more than creating blog entries. Don't fool yourself into believing that posting entries on your blog is significantly advancing your job search. It is clearly a differentiator, but it's not likely to be the driving force for job leads.

Infographic Resume

An infographic resume is a colorful, high-resolution document that visually presents your background and accomplishments by using pie charts, bar graphs, and timelines in creative ways. They can be particularly impactful when displaying notable achievements, high-level recommendations, and patterns of success, among other things.

The impact of an infographic resume comes from the fact that readers are drawn to colorful images. That attention can set you apart in today's crowded job market.[344] There's a tendency to remember things better when they are presented with images.

An infographic resume can, in limited circumstances, replace the traditional resume. This is most often the case in the creative fields like design, marketing, advertising, digital media, and so on.

However, for most, an infographic resume should be used as a supplement or differentiation tactic in conjunction with a traditional resume. Even then, its use is better suited for some positions (sales, for example) than others.[345] An infographic resume can be very effective where your job search is concerned; just keep in mind these caveats.

There are advantages, disadvantages, and considerations for using an infographic resume in a job search. Let's start with a few advantages:

It differentiates you. An infographic resume is clearly a differentiation tactic. Although the idea of an infographic resume has been around for a while, they are not widely used and therefore seldom seen by hiring executives in most industries. A well-thought-out, well-prepared, and well-presented infographic resume can make you stand out compared to other job seekers.[346]

It works well as a networking tool. You can use an infographic resume alongside (or instead of) your traditional resume and business cards when you network at an event or industry function.

One unique approach would be selecting your most persuasive achievements and creating an infographic "handbill." Create a four-inch-by-six-inch infographic handbill and

---

344 Pamela Skillings, "The Ultimate Infographic Resume Guide," Big Interview (blog), June 18, 2013, http://biginterview.com/blog/2013/06/infographic-resumes.html (accessed February 17, 2016).

345 See also, ibid.

346 Ibid.

put it on thicker paper or use it as a large business card. This is truly unique and seldom seen; it's guaranteed to create conversation.[347]

It provides insight into your thinking and presentation skills. One interesting advantage to an infographic resume is it opens the door of insight into how you think and creatively present ideas and concepts. This can be very persuasive if the position(s) you are pursuing require presentation skills.[348]

It vividly presents your professional background. Infographic resumes are colorful, high-resolution documents. Unlike your LinkedIn profile (which is an online template) and your resume (which has expected and accepted sections), an infographic resume is a blank canvas (similar to a Career Summary Sheet, but different). It is a platform to creatively present your professional background and accomplishments any way you choose, using color and graphics.

Although the advantages of an infographic resume are attractive, there are considerations that may turn into a disadvantage if not handled properly. These include:

How will it be received by hiring executives? This is a serious consideration. An infographic resume is a neat idea and can be very intriguing. It can open your mind to all sorts of creative thoughts on how to present your information. This is especially true once you start viewing examples. However, it may not be the best or most impactful strategy for every industry or position.[349] Only you can gauge the receptiveness and persuasive influence an infographic resume would have on hiring executives in your job search.

It must contain impactful information. If an infographic resume is not persuasive or is poorly constructed, it will hurt your job search. It can be a distraction, reflect negatively on your candidacy for the job, or eliminate you as a contender for the position.

It must look great! Not just good. Your final product must have a "holy cow this is really cool" factor. Otherwise, it will not have the persuasive and differentiating effect you are looking for. One interesting concept you could explore is creating an infographic section to your traditional resume. This would be a form of a showcase resume using color and graphics as your showcase section. Then, resume information would follow in the usual style.[350]

---

347 See also, ibid.

348 Ibid.

349 Ibid.

350 See also, ibid.

A Few Final Thoughts about Infographic Resumes

It is highly recommended that you speak to professionals who create these documents. Seek their opinion as to whether you have the caliber of career information and accomplishments to have an impactful infographic resume (with the understanding that they will have the incentive to persuade you to buy their services). Set aside any negative thoughts about the infographic resume as an idea, and objectively seek out and evaluate examples of other infographic resumes from people with similar backgrounds to yours (if possible). Since creating the document on your own can take countless hours, hire a professional to do it for you. The time required to create an infographic resume is better spent pursuing other job-search activities—networking, marketing your professional credentials, and so on.

If you create an infographic resume (or have one created for you), get it out there! One easy thing to do is attach it to your LinkedIn profile. Obviously you want to have it to hand out during networking events and as a supplement to interviews. Since you put the time, effort, thought, and money into this tactic, look for ways to leverage it in your job-search activities.

Caution: Creating an infographic resume can be a distraction or become busywork stopping you from moving your job search forward. Be aware of your time and use it wisely. An infographic resume is a differentiator, but it will not get you a job all by itself.

Discovering examples of infographic resumes and professionals (vendors) who create them is as simple as conducting a Google search for "infographic resumes."

Part XIII

References

The key to your universe is that you can choose.

—Carl Frederick[351]

References often receive insufficient attention. They become an afterthought of the job-search process until suddenly they are needed.

References can have a significant influence on the hiring decision. Depending upon who you provide as a reference, the reference can appeal to the persuasion principles of authority, liking, and/or social proof.

Many employers never ask for references. They often rely on written recommendations on your LinkedIn profile. Yet another good reason to have a robust profile with recommendations! Then there are others who ask only to look at the list and decide whether they appear credible. And some call. Regardless, you must always be prepared to provide references. Put into a business context, references are your client testimonials.

As you think about your references, think about people who can attest to different aspects of your professional experience, professional skills (hard and soft), and professional

351 "Carl Frederick Quotes," World of Quotes, http://www.worldofquotes.com/author/Carl+Frederick/1/index.html (accessed June 10, 2015).

qualities. This can save you time when it comes to providing references. For example, let's say one of the themes of the interview process was technical skills and the professional quality of integrity. Who do you know who could speak to your technical skills from their own experience? Who could attest to your professional integrity? It could be two different people.

References can play a vital role in who gets a job, especially if the decision to hire comes down to two or three candidates. The recommendation from a solid reference can move the decision in your favor.

Choose Your References Wisely

A good reference is someone with firsthand knowledge of your ability, track record, and character. They can persuasively articulate your qualifications, experience, strengths, and results to the employer. Choose someone you feel good about, who believes in you, wants you to succeed, and has your best interests at heart. Be sure to ask for permission to use them as a reference (as a professional courtesy), and ensure they will be positive about you. Also, touch base with your references regarding your job search, and notify them when you know (or have reason to believe) references will be checked. Prepare them with key information (details of the position, challenges the employer told you about, and so on), so your reference can showcase you to the employer.[352]

🪝 When choosing references, consider asking people who could provide information that defeats age biases. References who can speak to your positive attitude, intellectual curiosity, energy, technology awareness, and so on would be good people to ask. As appropriate, you can alert references to make statements that work to defeat those biases as well as provide information that differentiates you from younger job seekers—statements about your problem-solving skills, for example.

References and a Secret Job Search

This can be tricky. You do not want the word getting out that you are exploring a career move because that could have negative ramifications. But you still need references. The key is approaching people you can trust.[353] You may have to inform the hiring executive of

---

352 Hering, Beth Braccio. "How to Choose Good Job References," Newsday, July 11, 2012, http://www.newsday.com/classifieds/cars/how-to-choose-good-job-references-1.3430287 (accessed February 17, 2016).

353 Ibid.

your situation and indicate the sensitivity of your references. Most hiring executives will completely understand.

Unsolicited Third-Party Affirmation

This technique, if properly used, can be extremely persuasive. It can be used any time during the interview process, but can be most persuasive when a final hiring decision is about to be made. Here is how it works:

Ask one of your references, or someone who can vouch for you, to call the hiring executive unannounced (it must be a phone call, not an email). The purpose is to speak with the hiring executive and provide persuasive information about you and your fit for the job (attempting to capitalize on the persuasion principle of social proof).

This technique works best when your reference does not mention that you asked them to make the call (leave that decision up to your reference). This technique's impact is further enhanced if the reference happens to know the hiring executive *and* that relationship is positive. Imagine the scenario: The hiring executive is at his desk. Hiring for that open position is in the back of his mind. His receptionist pages him and says there is a person on the line who would like to speak with him about you. Curious. If he has a moment, he will take the call. Then, out of the blue comes this glowing recommendation. Calls like this do not happen every day. That call and the contents of the conversation will linger in the mind of the hiring executive and differentiate you, which is the desired effect. You may or may not get the job, but you can feel good that you gave one last shot at persuading the hiring executive in your favor.

Part XIV

Evaluating and Negotiating a Job Offer

By fighting you never get enough, but by yielding you get more than you expected.

—Dale Carnegie[354]

One of the most important steps in your job search is navigating all the stages of a job offer, once one is received.[355] According to a nationwide survey conducted by CareerBuilder, nearly half (45 percent) of hiring executives wish to be flexible on a first offer. Negotiations are almost always an expected part of the process of receiving an offer, especially for "professional and business services workers."[356]

In employment negotiations, it is imperative that you be sensitive to your emotions as well as the employer's. Both parties must treat negotiations with respect and dignity so everyone feels good at the conclusion of the process.

In this chapter, we will discuss basic steps involved in successful negotiations so you can approach this process with knowledge, insight, and confidence. What follows are the top-tier guidelines of the art form that is negotiation.

---

354 Carnegie, Dale. How to Win Friends and Influence People. (New York: Simon and Schuster, 2010), p. 134.

355 Portions of this chapter adapted from Claycomb and Dinse, Career Pathways, Part 9.

356 CareerBuilder, "Forty-Nine Percent of Workers Do Not Negotiate."

Never Play Hardball

Never play hardball when negotiating a job offer. If you do this, one of two things will happen. One, the employer withdraws the offer. Two, the employer may take some form of reprisal later. Hardball simply has no place in employment negotiations. For example, many home buyers and sellers use these types of tactics when they negotiate.[357] It is a one-time transaction. This is why home buying has the potential to be such a confrontational and unpleasant experience. Do you want to start your new employment relationship under a dark cloud? Enough said.

Ten Steps for Evaluating and Negotiating an Offer: The WITS Approach

Throughout the interview process, the employer has made a series of judgments as to whether you can make or save the company money;[358] whether you can do the job and do it well; and whether you are motivated to do the job and fit in culturally. All of this also influences your perceived value and return on investment (ROI) in the mind of the executive.

The results of interviewing ultimately determine the decision to hire and any offer's monetary amount.

When an employer extends an offer of employment to you, it is easy to allow your excitement, emotions, or nerves to cloud your thinking. When that happens, you can make mistakes in judgment that may potentially be costly. According to a survey conducted by LinkedIn, 60 percent of job seekers rely on their own subjective judgment when negotiating compensation.[359] Relying on purely cosmetic factors to judge a job offer can cost you. That is not to say you shouldn't be excited—you should be. In fact, be ecstatic! An offer is the positive result of your hard work. However, this is the time to finish strong and make sure you evaluate the terms of the offer objectively and handle negotiations professionally.

The following ten-step methodology provides structure around evaluating, negotiating, and closing an offer of employment. You can call it the WITS approach: *Wait* before negotiating. *Investigate* the offer's terms. *Tally* and assess the terms both objectively and emotionally. *Settle* the negotiations. With these broad themes in mind, below are the intuitive

---

357 Lisa Earle McLeod, "The Big Mistake People Make When They Negotiate," Life on Purpose (blog), McLeod & More, Inc., March 26, 2014, http://www.mcleodandmore.com/2014/03/26/the-big-mistake-people-make-when-they-negotiate-2/ (accessed June 19, 2015).

358 Whitcomb, Job Search Magic, p. 274.

359 LinkedIn Talent Solutions, "2015 Talent Trends," p. 30.

steps for evaluating and logically negotiating a job offer:

1. Research
2. Preparation
3. Receiving the offer
4. Gathering all information
5. Evaluating
6. Negotiating (if necessary)
7. Reevaluating modified terms
8. Closing the negotiation and reaching an agreement
9. Accepting the offer
10. Getting the final offer in writing

And always remember: In a negotiation, keep your WITS about you.

Step One: Research, Research, Research

Before you can successfully evaluate and negotiate an offer of employment, it may be necessary to research the marketplace to discover how people with similar positions are compensated. Many SEALs may already know this information using their skillset and experience as guidelines.

Sources

There are several websites that provide information on compensation for a variety of positions within an industry (www.salary.com, www.rileyguide.com). Another interesting site is www.jobstar.org, which is promoted as a reliable aggregator of salary and compensation.

Unfortunately, some information can be dated and is not an accurate reflection of current compensation. However, the published information will give you some benchmarks to guide your thinking.

The best method for determining a position's fair compensation is to contact colleagues with the same or similar positions. Presumably they will help you determine what is competitive in the market.

Another method to determine competitive compensation is to contact people in similar positions from companies in your industry. This takes the form of a research interview, previously discussed in this book. There is a strong chance that your target can be identified and contacted via LinkedIn.

If you adopt this approach, introduce yourself to the contact and be transparent about what you are doing—conducting market research on compensation parameters for the position type you are interviewing for. When you make contact, offer general information about the job duties and responsibilities and a brief history of your background and experience level. Ask the individual what they feel would be fair compensation based on the position and your experience and qualifications.

Take this one step further and contact executives responsible for hiring. These people could be the same hiring executives you established a relationship with in your marketing efforts. Simply reintroduce yourself, explain what you are doing, and ask about general compensation parameters for the position you are anticipating an offer on.

The major benefit of this proactive approach is the possibility of uncovering additional job opportunities (Hidden Job Market) and generating further job leads. For a fair indication of compensation, contact a minimum of two to three companies. Remember, packages may differ based on specific benefits offered by each company.

The final research method is to contact recruiters with whom you've already made contact. Who knows better than a recruiter about compensation being paid for various positions? Again, this method might uncover an additional interview opportunity with a recruiter's client looking for someone with your background and qualifications.

After you have researched the marketplace, document your findings, as you may want to refer to this research when negotiating your compensation. Record the company name, the person you talked to and their title, the date of your conversation, and the compensation information provided.

Step Two: Preparation

This is an area most SEALs either fall short in or neglect altogether.

Preparation brings together the information you have learned and received during your interview(s), and the research information you have discovered, and aligns it with your Target Opportunity Profile. Preparation also includes your assessment and insights on what you know and believe are the hiring executive's needs and wants in the open position. It is this insight—how the employer views his/her needs—that too often gets forgotten by SEALs and other job seekers at this stage of the process (review Understanding the Employer's Mindset).

Thinking about, assessing, and understanding the hiring executive's point of view is critical when you are evaluating and negotiating a job offer. Any insight on how the hiring executive sees things or calculates the company's needs, wants, goals, and limitations is powerful, regardless of how imperfect your information is.

After you write down how the opportunity fits your Target Opportunity Profile, write down how you fulfill the needs and wants of the employer. Make note of any information you may want to mention or emphasize.

This preparation process will bring everything together, spark your thinking, and prepare you mentally to evaluate, engage, and negotiate a job offer.

Step Three: Receiving the Offer

Offers can be extended over the phone, by email, or face to face. Always express your appreciation and interest, but ask the hiring executive for some time to evaluate the offer.

It is not uncommon for an offer to have a deadline. However, most companies will give you at least twenty-four to forty-eight hours, and perhaps more, if necessary. The key at this juncture in the process is to make a well-informed decision. If you feel the need to buy time, this is when you can request more information, especially concerning benefits.

Resist the impulse to negotiate at this time. Wait. You may not have all the information you need to evaluate the offer and make an informed decision.

Step Four: Collect Additional/Missing Information

Review the information about the offer and its terms. Remember to ask for and collect any missing information necessary to help you evaluate the offer fairly. Below is a non-exhaustive list of job-offer components:

- Salary
- Insurance—health, life, disability, dental
- 401(k)—retirement plan
- Bonus pay, structure, factors regarding how to earn bonuses
- Salary adjustments—timing of performance reviews and percentage
- Relocation expenses
- Tuition assistance
- Vacation or Personal Time Off (PTO)
- Commission structure
- Equipment: car, cell phone, computer, office equipment for home office, and so on
- Professional organization membership dues
- Stock options/stock grants
- Memberships (country club or fitness)
- Severance package

Step Five: Evaluate the Offer

When evaluating the offer, try to determine its total value in terms of compensation and benefits. Are there any tradeoffs? Is there intangible value (less travel, shorter commute time)? If you are relocating, is there a cost-of-living adjustment that could positively or negatively affect the offer's value?

Judge the offer on professional and emotional terms. What are your feelings about working for the company? Or the hiring executive? Are there other emotional or logistical considerations?

How does this career opportunity line up with your Target Opportunity Profile?

Speak with a trusted, uninvolved friend or colleague—their objective insight may help clarify matters or bring up advantages or concerns you hadn't considered.

🦭 Determine your walk-away point on monetary compensation. For some SEALs this number could be lower than their previous salary. It has been referenced that SEALs may need to take as much as 20 percent less in salary.[360] The concept behind this ugly truth is "take less on salary and have a job, or remain unemployed and have no salary at all." This can be a lousy situation to be in, but for many it is a reality. This is one reason why having complete information regarding all components of the offer is important. You can evaluate the total value of the offer. When all the components are valued, it might not be as bad as you think.

Although you may not know exactly what your bottom-line amount is, you should have a good initial feeling of it. Negotiations have not begun, but have a sense of when to walk away. When it comes to negotiations, only you can assess the offer's terms to determine whether it will work for you. Assess whether you might be willing to negotiate away something in exchange for something else you want.

And there is always a chance that the offer is acceptable just as it is. If so, accept it—congratulations, you've landed a job!

Step Six: Negotiation: Establish a Tone of Cooperation and Justify Your Requests

Establish a Tone of Cooperation

If negotiations are necessary, call the hiring executive again and express your interest and enthusiasm about the opportunity. This next point is important: Hopefully you have established good rapport with the hiring executive. Set the tone for the negotiations by indicating that you want the job, and by working together you should be able to reach a mutually beneficial agreement for the company, the hiring executive, and you. This step

---

360 Career-Intelligence, "Think Over 50"; Eisenberg, "Older Job Seekers."

is important because it establishes the environment of cooperation. Inform the hiring executive that there are a few topics that need to be discussed, and once they are resolved, you would be in a position to accept the offer.

Justify Your Requests

Employers do not mind negotiating job-offer terms as long as the requests are reasonable and the negotiating process is done quickly. One of the most powerful negotiating techniques is providing logical and reasonable justification for a request. Research indicates that people have a deep sense of fairness.[361] Justification appeals to the hiring executive's sense of fairness. It doesn't always work, but it can help.

Begin the conversation on a positive note with those major items you agree upon. Then discuss points of negotiation, beginning with the most important. Frequently this will be compensation, although there can obviously be others such as benefits, PTO, and more.

If the point of negotiation is compensation and the salary is not high enough, ask whether it can be increased; state a specific number. Justify the increase based on your past earnings, qualifications, accomplishments, and so on.

As a SEAL, your experience tells you that there could be several reasons for a significant difference between what you are seeking and what the company is offering. The company may not have the budget for the difference between what you want and what they can offer. Another explanation is perhaps the company has a parity issue—in other words, there are other employees with the same position getting paid less. Hiring executives must be sensitive to these and other issues.

One way to handle this issue is to explore a title change that could put you in a different pay range or a customized title that justifies the compensation difference.

Another approach to increased compensation is to ask for a sign-on bonus or to have a job-performance review in three to six months. Perhaps you can negotiate higher incentive compensation based on agreed-upon performance. These techniques can increase your total annual compensation.

However, another concept is to leave some money on the table! The idea here is this: If you negotiate higher compensation, the hiring executive may hire you, but since you were so expensive their expectations are heightened. The timeline for a return-on-investment for hiring you may get shorter.

Silence Is Golden

One of the most difficult things to learn in negotiations is silence. Silence in negotiations is not a bad thing; in fact, it can be golden (literally).

---

361 Honck, Alan, with Gordon Orians. "Are We Born With a Sense of Fairness?" Pacific Standard, December 26, 2012, https://psmag.com/are-we-born-with-a-sense-of-fairness-edd2d2680c10#.ce304fxbb (accessed April 18, 2016).

⬩ For some SEALs, enduring silence can be hard, especially when you really want the job. You don't want to make the hiring executive uncomfortable or risk having the executive pull the offer altogether. That is very unlikely to happen. Just make your request and resist any urge you have to speak—bite your lip if you have to; it'll heal. The employer has the ball in his court. Do not interpret any silence as a rejection from the hiring executive. Give the hiring executive the time necessary to process your request. If you speak and break the silence, there is a high probability that you will not get your request (at least in the form you requested). The end result is you may have just negotiated against yourself!

Step Seven: Reevaluate Modified Terms

As negotiations proceed and terms are modified, reevaluate how you feel about the job, the offer's terms, and the opportunity. Remain aware of how the modified terms fit into your Target Opportunity Profile. Are the modified terms moving you closer to what you feel comfortable accepting?

Step Eight: Close Negotiations and Reach an Agreement

Sometimes during negotiations, proposals and counter proposals will be exchanged between you and the hiring executive. New terms may be offered and other considerations may come into play. But when terms seem to be reaching a point of agreement, you need to close the negotiations by telling the hiring executive that if he/she can meet the points of negotiation, you will:

- Accept
- Resign from your current position (as applicable)
- Refuse a current employer's counter offer (if offered)
- Discontinue discussion with other companies
- Start on an agreed-upon date

These closing statements finalize the negotiations. If the hiring executive accepts your requests, there are no more negotiations and you must follow through and accept.

Step Nine: Accepting the Offer—Be Timely

Always show appreciation for an offer of employment. Accept an offer immediately (or as timely as possible), especially if the terms have been negotiated and mutually agreed on. Doing so starts the employment relationship on the right foot, with optimism. Your excitement about the company and opportunity will also be communicated to the employer.

Step Ten: Obtain Final Offer in Writing

Ask for the final offer in writing and establish a start date. Start dates are generally negotiable if you have special circumstances that prevent you from starting when the hiring executive wants.

If Negotiations Fail

If negotiations cannot resolve the differences, close the negotiations professionally. Never burn bridges! You never know when you will encounter or interact with the hiring executive again under different circumstances.

It is not uncommon for a hiring executive to approach you later with different terms. Things can change in a company to open the door for an opportunity. Closing negotiations professionally keeps that door open for the future. More on turning down an offer in the next section.

Declining an Offer of Employment

The key to declining an offer is to do so professionally and gracefully. The employer has put in hours of time and effort and concluded that you can add value to the company. However, for any one of a hundred reasons, the job is just not right for you.

Your decision to turn down the offer must be prompt. The employer has a position to fill, and your decision allows them to move forward with their process. Delaying your decision and notification is not fair to the employer.

It is always best to verbally tell the employer of your decision. It's the mature and professional way to handle the situation. Also, follow up your call and conversation with a brief email declining the offer.

In your communications, always show your appreciation for the hiring executive's time and interest. Pay a sincere compliment to the hiring executive, the company, its future, and so on.

Provide a reason for your decision. It can be general or reasonably specific depending upon the circumstances. Never state a negative reason for your decision.

If you are not already connected to the hiring executive on LinkedIn, extend a customized invitation. This creates a line of communication for future employment opportunities.

Below is a letter that contains the important points mentioned above, which can function as an outline for your call to the hiring executive as well:

"Thank you so much for the offer of the assistant manager position. I am flattered to be chosen. I do appreciate your time and consideration. ABC Company is a dynamic organization with innovative products and services. Its future is bright!

However, after careful consideration, I have decided to pursue another opportunity that I believe is a better fit for me at this stage of my career.

It has been a true pleasure getting to know you and the other members of your team!

Sincerely,
Your Name

Although the hiring executive will likely be disappointed, you want the hiring executive to come away from the engagement with good feelings about you, as a candidate and a professional.

Negotiation Mistakes

In addition to failing to establish a tone of cooperation, not justifying requests, and negotiating against yourself by speaking when you should be silent, here are other common negotiating mistakes:

1. **Not preparing for job-offer negotiations.** Compile all the information you have about the company and opportunity, how it fits your needs, and—most importantly— how you solve the employer's hiring need.

2. **Misrepresenting yourself or any of the facts involved in the negotiations in any way.** If you lie and get caught, you lose big. The offer will go away and your reputation will be tarnished.

3. **Overemphasizing salary.** Avoid doing that. Compensation is important, but it should not be the sole determining factor in negotiations. Instead, evaluate the total offer inclusive of benefits and the non-tangibles (living in Charlotte, shorter commute, and so on). It is also important to evaluate the opportunity and how it can benefit your career path.

4. **Over-negotiating.** Use your discretion and professional judgment. Pick the item(s) of most importance and negotiate on those topics, falling back on less important topics if needed. It is one thing to be respected for your good, professional negotiation ability. Being viewed by the hiring executive as "gimme, gimme, gimme," is entirely different. That raises doubts in the employer's mind about whether you'll fit into the company culture.

Final Thoughts on Successful Negotiation

Negotiation measures both your and the hiring executive's views, with an acceptable outcome for both parties being the preferred goal.

Ideally, both you and the executive will be willing to accept what the other is willing to give.

Remember, the ultimate goal is for both you and the hiring executive to feel comfortable with the offer's final terms.

Part XV

Resignation and Counter Offers

If you're brave enough to say goodbye, life will reward you with a new hello.

—Paulo Coelho[362]

Resignation

Resigning from a position must always be done with the utmost professionalism. Avoid resigning and departing on bad terms or under a cloud of misgivings.[363] The world is small, and how you handle your resignation and departure could impact your future, especially for those in a niche industry or smaller market. Although resigning is always awkward, if you use the following recommendations, your resignation will be smoother.

First and foremost, do not resign until you have an acceptable and unconditional offer of employment from your new employer. Although you may have (and signed) a written offer letter, that offer might depend on background or drug checks, and/or reference verification.

362 "Paulo Coelho Quotable Quote," Goodreads, https://www.goodreads.com/quotes/599176-if-you-re-brave-enough-to-say-good-bye-life-will-reward (accessed April 12, 2016).

363 Alison Green, "How to Resign Your Job Gracefully," On Careers Blog, U.S. News & World Report, July 28, 2008, money.usnews.com/money/blogs/outside-voices-careers/2008/07/28/how-to-resign-your-job-gracefully. (accessed February 17, 2016).

After all that, then the offer is "live," not before. Check with your new employer's HR department to confirm that contingencies are satisfied and you are cleared to resign.

Check the employment documents and policy and procedures manual of your current employer, understand the requirements, and tender your resignation to comply with them. Normally, two weeks' notice is standard, but some employers require more.[364] Don't risk losing pay or benefits by not following procedure.

If possible (and frequently it is not possible), wait to resign so there's no issue about retaining any pensions or other time-dependent bonuses you're entitled to.

The actual act of resignation can be awkward and tense. You are about to deliver unexpected news. Script or list talking points and practice them before meeting with your boss.

Realize the act of resigning is the culmination of a negotiation—one your boss did not know he was in. Your resignation could reflect poorly upon him. To gain an understanding of what has just happened, your boss may seek a time-out, usually by asking you not to make any rash or final decisions. Your boss is buying time to figure out what to do. This might be followed by an invitation to discuss company problems, your career path, or any one of a number of topics to sway your decision, including a counter offer.

Be prepared. Your boss will likely ask why you are leaving. There are choices to make. Your professional judgment and discretion will guide your decision. Provide an honest answer and reason(s) for your decision. Occasionally, providing your reasoning could be giving your current employer information and insight your own boss may not be aware of. It can be valuable to the employer. However, if your honest answer would create turmoil, burn a bridge, or simply be inappropriate, opt for a generic reason ("a better opportunity," "a different direction I want to go in my career," "a different role," and so on).[365]

It is not uncommon for a boss to inquire about the new employer. Revealing the name of your new employer may depend on the kind of relationship you have with your boss. It is entirely your decision whether or not to release this information, and there are reasons to withhold it. For example, your boss (and others at your current employer) could use the information to tell you about all the bad things they've ever heard about the new company. In fairness, however, you should inform your employer of the nature of your new employer's business. If your new employer is a competitor, your employer should know this. Some companies have policies of immediate discharge when an employee accepts employment with a competitor.

Assume that, upon resignation, you will be asked to leave immediately. This may or may not happen, but be emotionally prepared either way. Consider taking steps to remove

---

364 Ibid.

365 Ibid.

your personal property from your office before officially resigning—and only your own property. Be absolutely certain you don't take any private or patented company items with you.[366]

Prepare mentally for some emotion, including your boss's reaction. He or she will probably be surprised, disappointed, and maybe even angry. Make your resignation clean and professional.

Don't procrastinate or make things take longer than needed. And don't entertain a conversation about circumstances that would change your mind. If your boss asks that you not announce your resignation to your coworkers, comply with that request, as they likely need to make adjustments and business arrangements before formally announcing your resignation. Once the resignation meeting is complete, professionally end the conversation and walk away. Removing yourself from your boss's office (or from the call, depending on the circumstances) ends the engagement and allows you to breathe a sigh of relief. It's over, and you can move forward.

Always resign in writing and, whenever possible, in person. If you happen to be an off-premises or remote employee, a telephone call is fine. Do not just send your resignation by email. If resigning by phone, speak with your boss first and tell him you will send a formal resignation letter.

Offer to assist in any transition of projects and work to others. This is a professional gesture and will leave your employer with a favorable last impression of you. Stay engaged in your job if your employer asks you to work out your resignation period. Come in on time, do your job, and don't leave early. Finish strong and be professional to the end.[367]

Some odds and ends to consider:

- Inform important contacts both inside and outside your organization of your resignation.[368]

- Confer with your boss about when it would be appropriate to inform others.

- Ask your boss about changing your voicemail greeting or creating an email auto-response regarding your departure (if appropriate).[369]

- Provide your employer with all passwords.[370]

---

366 Calvin Sun, "10+ Things You Should Do When You Resign," 10 Things
(blog), TechRepublic, March 17, 2008, www.techrepublic.com/blog/10-things/10-plus-things-you-should-do-when-you-resign/ (accessed February 17, 2016).

367 Green, "How to Resign."

368 Sun, "10 Things."

369 Ibid.

370 Green, "How to Resign."

Finally, consider sending a thank-you note to your boss about a week after you leave the company. Express your appreciation for the opportunity, experience, and so on. Express your best wishes for their continued success. Send a similar note of appreciation to appropriate contacts higher on the organizational chart. This classy move can pay real career dividends later.

Writing a thank-you note is a differentiator for you as a professional. You are building bridges for the future and enhancing your professional reputation. This is especially true for niche-industry workers, or those in a small city. Your former boss and other people from your former employer could become:

- A future employee of your new employer (future colleague).
- A customer of your new employer.
- An advocate for you and your new employer.
- A referral source.

Below is a resignation letter that is simple and direct:

Name
Address
City, State ZIP

Subject: Voluntary Resignation of   (Your Name)

Dear   (Superior)   :

This letter constitutes notification of my resignation from   (Former Employer)   . My last day of employment will be   (Date/notice required by former employer)   .

Please accept my sincere gratitude for the opportunities extended to me during my time with the company. My decision to resign was reached after careful consideration. I have accepted a position with another company that I believe allows me to make positive steps both personally and professionally.

Please understand that my decision to resign is final.

Sincerely,

(Your Name)

Counter Offers

The longer I live, the more I am certain that the great difference between men—between the feeble and the powerful, the great and the insignificant—is energy, invincible determination—a purpose once fixed, and then—death or victory!

—Sir Thomas Fowell Buxton[371]

A counter offer is any effort designed to entice you to ultimately withdraw your resignation and continue employment.[372] There are four types of counter offers:

1. Financial
2. Promotional
3. Emotional
4. Preemptive

Financial

This is the most common form of counter offer. It is normally an increase in your compensation through salary, bonus rate (or potential), commission structure, stock options or grants, and so on.

---

371 "Thomas Fowell Buxton Quotable Quote," Goodreads, http://www.goodreads.com/quotes/891186-the-longer-i-live-the-more-i-am-certain-that (accessed June 10, 2015).

372 Love, Scott. "Counter offer—Should I Entertain a Counter offer?" The Vet Recruiter, http://thevetrecruiter.com/important-information-about-recruiters-for-job-seekers/counter offer-should-i-entertain-a-counter offer/ (accessed June 11, 2015).

Promotional

This form of counter offer could be a change in title (sometimes with a modest increase in salary), change in duties and/or responsibilities, or a move to a different department. Too frequently this kind of counter offer ends up having less substance than represented.

Emotional

This form of counter offer borders on dirty pool. It is delivered to appeal to your loyalty. Statements like "It just won't be the same around here without you" are standard fare. Promises of improvements, promotions, or any other sentiment designed to invoke a feeling that "you'll really miss out if you leave now" is an emotional counter offer. So is any statement designed to elicit guilt or play on your emotions, such as "How will Ben ever finish that project with you gone?" Beware.

Preemptive

This type does not fit the definition of the previously discussed counter offers because it occurs prior to your resignation. It is an improvement in your employment situation that miraculously happens, unexpectedly, while you are exploring and interviewing for a new position. How lucky can you get, right? If any bells of suspicion start ringing in your head due to this timing, trust your instincts. Something is up.

Here's how a preemptive counter offer comes about: While you are interviewing, on the premises of a potential employer, or offsite at a coffee shop, someone recognizes you with an executive of another company. That person tells someone else, and the news gets repeated until your boss finds out. Not to be outflanked, your boss improves your employment situation with the desired effect of having you discontinue your job-search activities. It's sneaky and it can work. You are left guessing whether the improvements are a sincere gesture from your employer or a counter offer tactic.

Career Hazards of Accepting a Counter Offer

Receiving a counter offer can be flattering and a boost to your professional ego. However, virtually all career experts agree that you should not accept one.[373] Understand this next point very clearly: The time, cost, and effort in recruiting and training a new employee are

---

373 Love, "Should I Entertain"; Lankford, Kim. "Should You Take That Counter offer?" Monster, http://career-advice.monster.com/in-the-office/leaving-a-job/should-you-take-that-counter offer/article.aspx (accessed June 11, 2015); Alison Green, "Why You Shouldn't Take a Counter offer," On Careers Blog, U.S. News & World Report, March 26, 2012, http://money.usnews.com/money/blogs/outside-voices-careers/2012/03/26/why-you-shouldnt-take-a-counter offer (accessed June 11, 2015).

substantial for any employer and far outweigh the cost of offering you a counter offer.[374] A counter offer is a business decision (a cost calculation) and seldom a sudden awakening to your worth or company issues.

Realize that your current employer has an investment in you through your training, experience, and expertise. They do not want to lose that investment to another company (especially to a competitor). Again, the extension of a counter offer is a business calculation.

When you prepare to resign, realize that a counter offer may come, and remember the reasons why you wanted to make a job change in the first place. Think about the excitement of going to your new employer. Company culture, practices, policies, and a host of other factors seldom change, and if they do, it's gradual. The events that inspired you to move on from this employer will likely happen again.

If you accepted the new offer to pursue an entirely different avenue in your career, a new challenge, or a passion, accepting a counter offer will delay or prevent you from accomplishing those goals.

When you accept a counter offer, you burn bridges with the prospective employer who offered you a new job.[375] They most likely won't consider hiring you again. Accepting a counter offer also calls into question your loyalty and motives with your current employer, and you will be scrutinized. Internal relationships that you have with your boss, other managers, peers, and subordinates could change.[376]

Accepting a counter offer can slow your career growth and advancement. Once your loyalty and motives are brought into question, promotions will be much more difficult to come by (if ever). You may be passed over for advanced training. Your employer will hesitate to invest in you.

All companies face difficult times that could require cutbacks and staff reductions. When that happens, your boss may choose to honor your resignation after the fact by laying you off.

Where is the money for a financial counter offer coming from? Has your next raise merely been moved up?[377] Is it coming from another department's budget (if so, have you raised the angst of another department head)? All companies have wage and salary guidelines that create strained budgets and parity issues with others. This could backfire and create animosity toward you.

For all of these reasons (and others unique to the company and circumstances), accepting

---

374 Love, "Should I Entertain."

375 Green, "Counter offer."

376 Love, "Should I Entertain."

377 Ibid.

a counter offer creates a high probability you will leave or get fired within one year.[378] Some career experts say that "statistically, four out of five employees who accept a company's counter offer end up leaving that company within 6 to 9 months anyway."[379] Accepting a counter offer is not a good long-term career strategy—it's a short-term fix.

Detachment: A Technique to Defuse the Emotions of Resignation

When you resign, wisely assume you will receive a counter offer, either immediately or shortly after the resignation conversation. Here is an excellent technique that has helped others in this situation: Mentally detach yourself and become a student of your boss's reaction. Is it surprise (likely), disappointment, or anger? Does he call time-out and ask you to delay your decision? Does she extend a financial, emotional, or promotional counter offer? Or nothing at all? This detachment technique significantly reduces the situation's inevitable emotional charge. You will see the situation from an objective (or perhaps academic) perspective. The resignation and counter offer are easier if you employ this approach.

Can accepting a counter offer ever be a good career move? Yes. However, it is very . . . very . . . very (catching the emphasis here?) . . . very rare.

Aside from very limited circumstances, the ultimate truth about counter offers is they don't work. Accepting one is more of a quick fix, and you will be conducting a job search sooner than you think.

---

378 Green, "Counter offer."

379 "Counter Offers," Cybercoders, http://www.cybercoders.com/home/counter offer/ (accessed June 11, 2015).

Part XVI

Covenants-Not-To-Compete and Non-Solicitation Agreements

Disclaimer: *The contents of this chapter are not legal advice. They are for educational purposes only. None of the information provided should be construed, interpreted, or acted upon in any way in determining a course of action. If you have or believe you may have a legal restriction on your employment, seek legal counsel. Do not rely on the information contained in this chapter or book.*

Our doubts are traitors, and make us lose the good we oft might win, by fearing to attempt.
—William Shakespeare, Act I, Scene IV, *Measure for Measure*[380]

Covenants-not-to-compete and non-solicitation agreements can have a significant impact on your job search. In some industries, they are deemed unnecessary and therefore seldom used. In others, they are an ingrained business practice.

The purpose of this chapter is to give you a general understanding of these agreements and the potential effects they can have on your job search.

---

380 "William Shakespeare Quotes Measure for Measure," http://www.william-shakespeare.info/quotes-quotations-play-measure-for-measure.htm (accessed June 11, 2015).

Definitions of a Covenant-Not-to-Compete and a Non-Solicitation Agreement

Setting aside true legal definitions, the following definitions will guide our discussion:

- Covenant-Not-to-Compete: A contractual agreement forbidding a job seeker from obtaining employment with a competitor of a former employer.
- Non-Solicitation Agreement: A contractual agreement forbidding a job seeker from soliciting business from a client (vendor, supplier, and so on) of the job seeker's former employer.

A covenant-not-to-compete has significantly more impact on a job seeker's search. Depending upon the terms, this can be an inconvenience (a short and mild restriction) or a career-changing event (lengthy and highly restrictive). These agreements hamper your ability to obtain employment in the field or industry of your former employer.

A non-solicitation agreement can be less problematic, allowing you to work in the field of your choice with a competitor, with the understanding that you will not approach or solicit the clients (vendors, suppliers, and so forth) of your former employer.

Where They Appear

These agreements generally appear in three places:

1. As part of a written offer of employment
2. A separate agreement, normally supplied with the offer letter
3. Employer handbook

Determining Which Kind of Agreement You Have

As you read the appropriate documents, look for this kind of language (or similar):

Covenant-Not-to-Compete

"During the period of time that the Employee is employed by the Company and for a period of two (2) years after the termination or cessation of such employment for any reason (both periods of time, taken together, being referred to hereinafter as the "RESTRICTED PERIOD"), the Employee shall not, anywhere in the United States, directly or indirectly, whether individually or as an officer, director, employee, consultant, partner, stockholder (other than as the holder of not more than one percent (1%) of a publicly held corporation), individual proprietor, joint venturer, investor, lender, consultant or in any other capacity whatsoever, develop, design, produce, market, sell or render (or assist any other person in developing, designing, producing, marketing, selling or rendering) products or services competitive with those developed, designed, produced, marketed, sold or rendered by the Company at any time during the Restricted Period."[381]

Non-Solicitation Agreement

"During the Restricted Period, the Employee shall not, directly or indirectly, whether individually or as an officer, director, employee, consultant, partner, stockholder, individual proprietor, joint venturer, investor, lender, consultant or any other capacity whatsoever: (a) solicit, divert or take away, or attempt to solicit, divert or take away, the business or patronage of any clients, customers or accounts, or prospective clients, customers or accounts, of the Company or (b) hire, retain (including as a consultant) or encourage to leave the employment of the Company any employee of the Company, or hire or retain (including as a consultant) any former employee of the Company who has left the employment of the Company within one (1) year prior to such hiring or retention."[382]

Enforceability

You must understand that these agreements are enforceable. Only by application of law do they become unenforceable.

These agreements are interpreted by state law. Each state handles these agreements its own way. California has outlawed covenants-not-to-compete as a legislative concern.[383] There are a few other states that have as well. You will need to determine whether your state of residence enforces such agreements (most states will).

Reasonable in Scope, Space, and Time

For a covenant-not-to-compete to be enforceable it must be reasonable—an issue to be

---

381 Non-Compete Agreement—Art Technology Group Inc. and Joseph Chung, http://contracts.onecle.com/art/chung.non-comp.1998.08.18.shtml (accessed March 16, 2016).

382 Ibid.

383 Izzi, Matthew. "California Ban on Covenants Not to Compete," LegalMatch, http://www.legalmatch.com/law-library/article/california-ban-on-covenants-not-to-compete.html (accessed June 11, 2015).

determined by the facts and the courts. Generally speaking, a covenant-not-to-compete must be reasonable in scope, space, and time, which usually breaks down this way:

Scope: What you are forbidden from doing.

Space: Where you cannot do it, geographically.

Time: How long you cannot do it.

There are a myriad of factors that influence what is reasonable in scope, space, and time that will be tied directly to your specific situation.

For a covenant-not-to-compete to be unenforceable, it must be unreasonable (in scope, space, or time). Generally, if a covenant is deemed unreasonable in any of the three criteria, the whole agreement fails. There are exceptions to this generalization. The most notable is some courts will rewrite unreasonable provisions to make them reasonable under the circumstances. This practice is called "blue lining."[384] In essence, the court takes a blue pen and will rewrite the provision. However, many courts will stick to the facts to determine enforceability.

Employer's Reactions to Breaches of Agreement

Employers respond differently to violations of these agreements. They can do or have done the following:

- Nothing

- Send a threatening letter, normally by certified mail

- Have a lawyer send a threatening letter, normally by certified mail

- Send a copy of your agreement to your new employer (yes some have done this!)

- Seek a preliminary injunction—this is a legal maneuver preventing you from working for about ten days

- Seek a permanent injunction, which would stop you from working completely until the issue is resolved

- Seek active litigation—file a lawsuit

Sometimes employers will growl and bark but not bite, stopping short of legal action.

---

384 Broadcasting and the Law, Inc. "Employment contracts—'blue line' rule." Abstract. Broadcasting and the Law (1997). http://www.readabstracts.com/Mass-communications/Employment-contracts-blue-line-rule-Noncommercial-stations-underwriting-announcements.html (accessed June 11, 2015).

Do not assume this is true for every employer. If they have the grounds to pursue you for breach of the agreement, they have the right to do so. Sometimes it's a matter of how much of a threat you are to their business.

Right-to-Work States

Some job seekers believe that restrictive agreements are not enforceable because they live in a right-to-work state. This is generally not true. The right-to-work statutes of a particular state seldom have any bearing on the legal enforcement of these agreements (unless some language relevant to these agreements is buried within the statute).

Practical Application—Effects of These Agreements on Your Job Search

As a practical matter, non-solicitation agreements are less concerning than covenants-not-to-compete. You simply need to avoid the prohibited clients (vendors, suppliers, and so on) for the restricted period of time. You are permitted to obtain employment in your field of choice and with a competitor if you choose.

Covenants-not-to-compete, on the other hand, can significantly impact your job search by restricting your field of options. This bears repeating because many do not take these implications seriously enough. Careful consideration must be made regarding how you choose to proceed, and you should prepare yourself for the possibility that you may not be able to find work in your industry for months or years, depending on the terms of your agreement.

Always advise a potential employer that you have a restrictive agreement. Failure to do so raises fidelity issues in the employer's mind, such as, "What else didn't he (or she) tell us?"

One workaround to consider is to obtain a waiver from your employer, which protects you from legal action if you accept employment that could violate your agreement. This is a very good tactic if the new employer's products and services are less important or not as widely known as your current employer's products are. Generally, a waiver will be a written letter from an executive with the authority to waive a potential violation. It is a way to sleep at night if you wish to eliminate concerns you may have.

Part XVII

Working Successfully for a Younger Boss

*The apprenticeship of difficulty is one which the greatest of men have
had to serve.*
—*Samuel Smiles*[385]

As you conduct your job search, it is likely, if not inevitable, that you will interview with a company where you will report to a younger boss. This could be someone your son's or daughter's age, which could stir some uncomfortable feelings. That's perfectly normal; it's different and it's a change. However, there are some very practical perspectives to adopt and steps you can take that can make reporting to a younger boss not only workable, but actually enjoyable. These include:

Improve your attitude. Start from the point of view that the reporting structure and relationship will be a positive one. You're not there to "see if it will work," but rather to "see that this *does* work." Discard any feelings of superiority. Fully appreciate the fact that your younger boss is in that position because he or she earned it. You need to be respectful at all times.

Change how you view your experience. Don't assume your experience and tenure grant you respect from your boss (or others for that matter). In today's business environment, only performance and value (useful business knowledge and innovation) earn you that. Set out to prove yourself.

Learn your boss's communication channels. This is a big deal and an area where you may need to show adaptability. Perhaps you will need to learn new things, including how your boss communicates. The days of face-to-face conversations have eroded to emails, text messages, instant messaging, and video chats. If your younger boss communicates through these mediums, learn which one(s) and adapt, even if it means learning new technology. Grow comfortable, if you have not already, with the fact that you are reachable almost

---

385 Smiles, Samuel. Character, new ed. (London: John Murray, 1876), p. 350.

every minute of every day. It's likely that you will need to sync your smartphone to your business email account. Generally, at the professional level, the days of going off the grid when you go home are fading.

Respond as promptly as you can to electronic messages. Understand that a missed call from your boss (without him or her leaving a message on your cell phone) is still a message to call back.

All of this might be uncomfortable at first. You're learning new things, and once you get the hang of it, you'll probably like it! The trick is discovering how to use new technology, so don't be afraid to ask.

Identify your boss's strengths. Your younger boss is in that role for a reason. Identify his or her strengths and expertise. Learn what he or she achieved to earn that position. Keep your mind open to new ideas. Learn. Don't show resistance or make any reference to "the way we did things in the past."

Make your boss look good. Find out how your boss is being measured and evaluated. Adopt those goals as a part of your own. Strive to make him/her look good.

Get a clear understanding of job-performance expectations. Like any new job, get a clear understanding of what is expected of you. Find out what superior job performance is and strive to achieve it. At some point in the course of events, (and it could come during interviews), state to your boss that you expect to be treated fairly and evaluated objectively like anyone else, whether you're twenty-five or fifty-five. This statement puts the topic on the table and your younger boss will agree.

Don't mentor. And avoid giving unsolicited advice. Your younger boss may resent it. Even though your experience would likely help the situation, it's not your place. Like you in your past, your younger boss may need to learn through mistakes. That is his or her growing experience. However, if your insight is requested, by all means offer it!

Don't ever make reference to your boss's age. Avoid referencing your boss's age or level of experience to anyone at the office, including your boss. Never refer to your boss as reminiscent of your son or daughter (or granddaughter). Age was not a factor when you were hired, and neither is your younger boss's now that you are employed.

Avoid giving history lessons. If you start telling war stories, you'll bore your boss and others to death. Regardless of how interesting you find (or fondly remember) your story, they likely won't feel the same. Only reference the past if your point has significant relevance to the business issues of the present.

Don't complain up the ladder. Your younger boss's boss might be more your tenure.

Surely he'll understand, right? Wrong. If you ever complain to your boss's boss, you risk significant reprisals. You could eventually get fired and have to start a job search again (now that's a pleasant thought, eh?). If there are issues, address them with your boss directly or go to HR with your concerns.

Although your younger boss and you are separated by years, it doesn't mean you can't have a successful, and frankly enjoyable, professional relationship.

Part XVIII

How to Relaunch a Stagnant Job Search

Every champion was once a contender that refused to give up.
—Rocky Balboa[386]

You're engaged in a job search and things have slowed to a crawl. You've done everything you know to do, and still have no results. Don't panic. There are practical steps you can take to get back on track. These are:

Learn something new. This may not sound like a tactic to reignite a job search, but it is . . . and it's a big one. You need to stimulate your mind with new information. Identify a professional designation and start the work to achieve it. If you need to improve your technology skills, now is the time to do it. Whatever you learn stimulates the mind and when completed, can differentiate you from other job seekers.

Many job seekers find they feel renewed and have a more optimistic outlook on a stale search when they begin learning new things. You feel better knowing you are doing something to move your job search forward.

Another approach to learning something new is to seek out information about job searching. This could be LinkedIn groups, podcasts, or blogs that focus on job searching as an idea in itself. Accessing this information may give you nuggets of information that you had not thought of that could improve the effectiveness of your job search.

Help someone. This will improve your attitude and help shake off the disappointments of the past. As you go about your day, look for opportunities to help others. This could be passing along a job lead to another job seeker or simply holding the door open for someone. Becoming others-focused shifts your mind and gets you out of yourself and focused on service. This can give you a daily dose of purpose, value, and accomplishment. Becoming

386 "Rocky Balboa Quotable Quote," Goodreads, http://www.goodreads.com/quotes/3228059-every-champion-was-once-a-contender-that-refused-to-give (accessed April 12, 2016).

service oriented will improve your attitude and make you feel better about everything. Today is a new day! You're going to change your activities and be more productive.

If your circumstances permit, consider volunteering. Depending upon the organization, it could present networking opportunities. According to LinkedIn, many employers consider volunteering equivalent to employment.[387] In addition to the job-search advantages, there are a host of positive emotional and physical benefits to volunteering as well.[388]

Revamp your resume. Does it present "you" persuasively? Be honest. If you wrote your resume yourself, seriously consider contacting a professional resume writer and have it evaluated. Could improvements in content and formatting be worth the cost to have it redone? Having a new resume is a change that can improve your confidence during your search. (Don't forget, any changes to your resume should also be reflected on your LinkedIn profile.)

Refresh your LinkedIn profile. Like your resume, critically evaluate your LinkedIn profile. Is it as complete as it could be? Is it optimized for maximum exposure when a hiring executive or recruiter searches for a person like you? Are your keywords placed in the optimal sections of your profile (headline, summary, career experience, interests, and so on)?[389] Is it compelling (using accomplishments)? As a general rule, are you getting at least twenty profile views a week?

Improve your attitude. You have reason to be optimistic! Things are about to change because you are going to use new strategies to create job-search activities. It will be work, but the results will be different. And it all starts with your attitude. Get positive. Be positive. Do what needs to be done (with a smile, despite momentary setbacks) and you will experience positive results!

Increase your networking activities. You've likely networked as a part of your search. To reignite your networking efforts, start making new connections, especially on LinkedIn. Focus on new connections who you believe may be able to help or hire you. For every two new connections (or LinkedIn invitations extended), reach out to an existing networking contact and bring them up to speed on your job search (or any other relevant topic). For all new connections, wait a few days and then communicate with them. Going through this process will expand your network and lead to new conversations with new contacts while touching base with your existing network. Are you on the telephone, reaching out to

---

387 Dougherty, "16 Tips to Optimize."

388 "Volunteering and its Surprising Benefits," HelpGuide.org, http://www.helpguide.org/articles/work-career/volunteering-and-its-surprising-benefits.htm (accessed February 17, 2016).

389 See also, Frasco, "11 Tips."

people voice to voice? And making a minimum of twenty outbound calls a day to current, but more importantly, *new* contacts? If you can get on a roll making calls, that's great! This requires planning and some research for telephone numbers. Do that later in your day and use the morning to generate calls. The more calls you make, the quicker your job search will end successfully. Remember to network face to face as well. Don't curl up in a ball—get out and meet people. Attend industry gatherings, whether local or national, or get together with friends and neighbors. This can be a bonanza of networking opportunities. People will help you if they can and if you give them the opportunity to do so.

Use job alerts more strategically. If you have not been using job alerts, do so now (Indeed.com, SimplyHired.com, LinkedIn, or job boards). If you have been using them, review them and include other jobs you are interested in and qualified for. Get a new flow of information on opportunities in the market.

Proactively market your professional credentials. The mantra here is: Don't think in terms of a job—look for a company you'd like to work for.[390] Once you identify companies that are (or could be) interesting to you, hunt in the Hidden Job Market by reaching out directly to the likely hiring executive and presenting your professional credentials. This technique requires effort, but you will find jobs and job leads that you otherwise would not find.

Exercise. There are two reasons why exercise is a technique to reignite your job search. The first is it's healthy. As a SEAL, perhaps you have a few pounds you could live without. It can improve your appearance. Secondly, exercising routinely gives you a sense of accomplishment. When tough days happen, at least you got your exercise in.

Focus on differentiation. What in your background and accomplishments makes you different, unique, and/or valuable to an employer? Think hard about this. Are you making these factors apparent to employers? If not, showcase them. Now is not the time to be humble!

Seek out a career-transition coach. A coach is an objective source who can help you in many ways—to empathize with you, as well as challenge, educate, counsel, and encourage you. Simply having a professional to talk to (and be accountable to) who is experienced in career transition can open your mind intellectually, help you deal with the many emotions that accompany a job search, and more. If you choose to go down this path, evaluate a coach to ensure they have the insight necessary to benefit and guide you.

Think through these techniques. Find the ones that apply to you, then implement them!

---

390 Whitcomb, Job Search Magic, p. 273–274.

All it takes is one of these techniques (but more likely the combination of several) to reignite your search and land job offers.

Part XIX

Hire Yourself—Becoming a Consultant or Opening a Franchise

You shouldn't focus on why you can't do something, which is what most people do. You should focus on why perhaps you can, and be one of the exceptions.

—Steve Case[391]

Opening a consulting practice or franchise is a career path many SEALs consider when going through a career transition. For some, it can lead to a new, exciting, and very fulfilling experience. For others, it can lead to disastrous results, both personally and financially.

In this section, we will take a high-level view of what you should think about before you venture too far down this path. If you choose to explore either consulting or franchising as a career path, it is highly recommended that you seek out the professional advice of a business attorney, accountant, and/or possibly a "business advisor" (anyone who can provide sound business advice based on experience). These professionals will undoubtedly tell you things you did not know or consider.

The first thing to be cautious about is your current employment situation and its effect on your reasoning and critical thinking. You may be bored (if unemployed), worried about doing "something" (if your current position is vulnerable to elimination), ready to just quit (if you are unhappy in your present position), or any number of other things, depending upon your situation. Keep all of your emotions in check, don't do anything rash, and keep a level head.

Be careful about indulging visions of grandeur. It's easy, fun, and perfectly natural for your mind to venture off into what could be . . . what it might be like to be a consultant or business owner. That's dreaming and it's a great thing! Allow yourself to do this. However (you knew the other shoe would drop), fully comprehend that most of your thoughts will

391 Rampton, John. "50 Inspirational Entrepreneurial Quotes," Entrepreneur.com, December 9, 2014, https://www.entrepreneur.com/article/240047 (accessed April 12, 2016).

be about the end result—not so much about the work, the hours, and the drudgery of getting to your dreamy end result. Don't get caught living in your visions of grandeur.

Another caution is especially applicable to opening a franchise. Be careful about "buying a job." All businesses (with very limited exceptions) have start-up costs. These costs can be significant (over $100,000 or more) in some cases. Do you have the financial resources to open your franchise (the right way) and sustain your standard of living during the ramp-up period? Think long and hard about this. Be especially cautious about cashing in your savings, 401(k), stock certificates—any money earmarked for retirement. Understand the financial risks.

This next statistic is intended to keep you sober in your thoughts about opening a business. It has been a consistent statistic that somewhere around 50 percent of start-up businesses fail sometime during the first five years.[392] Even fewer make it longer than that.[393]

Now that we have covered a couple cautionary notes, let's move into some of the more practical considerations for opening a consulting practice or franchise.

Opening a Consulting Practice

Simply put, a consultant advises and shares expertise with a company for a fee. Sounds simple enough, right? Well, yes and no. The following is a list of things to consider before becoming a professional consultant:

What do you have to offer? This is a big question. What is your value proposition? This is directly aligned to your value proposition for your job search. Is your expertise unique in some way? This is all about your experience and your credentials (including professional designations). Can your advice anticipate, divert, or solve a problem?[394] Can you move a company forward based on your expertise? All of these questions are identical to those in your job search.

Will companies pay for your expertise? Having a "value proposition" is one thing. But is what you have to offer significant, different, or unique enough that a company will pay you for it? Is there a market demand for what you do or what you know?[395] In simple terms, this goes to your "target market." For example, larger companies may have no need

392 Sangeeta Badal, PhD, interview by Jennifer Robison, "Why So Many New Companies Fail During Their First Five Years," Gallup Business Journal, October 23, 2014, http://www.gallup.com/businessjournal/178787/why-new-companies-fail-during-first-five-years.aspx (accessed February 17, 2016).

393 See also, Patel, "90% of Startups."

394 See also, Whitcomb, *Job Search Magic*, p. 289.

395 See also, Patel, "90% of Startups."

for your expertise, while small to midsize employers might. Again, this issue of market demand and target market aligns directly to those considerations in your job search.

What are the initial business costs of becoming a consultant? Not many. In some cases, you may need to register with a government agency depending upon your industry. This could involve a fee. You will need business cards and perhaps some print materials (brochure, marketing packet, or something else), and a website. But, all things considered, one of the positives about becoming a consultant is it generally doesn't cost much to get started.

Do you have the energy, work ethic, and passion to get your consulting practice off the ground and make it sustainable? This is where the rubber meets the road and where most SEALs fail. Declaring yourself a consultant (after due consideration) is the easy part. Now, do you have the energy (beyond your initial excitement), work ethic (needed to attract paying clients and sustain your practice), and passion (love of your area of interest) to make your practice successful? Many SEALs fancy the idea of being a consultant but don't have many of the skills necessary to make their practice thrive. The difficult part is normally the marketing for new clients. It's easy to call those you know, but that list gets exhausted quickly. It's far more challenging to identify new companies, find the correct contact person, and make a persuasive pitch about your services. Marketing your services aligns directly with networking and proactively marketing your professional credentials in your job search. If you hesitate about networking or proactively marketing your credentials, you will likely struggle to market yourself as a consultant, and your practice will eventually fail.

Job-Search Strategy: Offering Yourself as a Consultant

As mentioned, there are several elements of opening a consulting practice that are virtually identical to your job search. In fact, offering yourself (your services) in a consulting capacity is a very good job-search strategy. For example, if a company shows interest in you but hesitates to hire you, offer the idea of hiring you temporarily as a consultant. For the company, consulting fees could be a different line item in their budget than the salary of a full-time employee. This approach has several advantages. It provides you with employment while you continue your job search. You get to experience working for the company to see how you might fit in . . . this goes for the company also. It's a "try it before you buy it" concept. It'll give you firsthand knowledge of what it's like to be an independent consultant.

It is not at all uncommon for consultants to be offered full-time employment with clients. Much of that decision turns on the value of your work, just as if you were a full-time employee.

Opening a Franchise

Opening a franchise is for those SEALs who truly have an entrepreneurial spirit. They want to run a business, be the decision maker, and commit to the work (and headaches, both physical and emotional) that go into running a small business. Pursuing a franchise opportunity demands thorough research and the willingness to ask lots of questions.

Before getting into some of the practical considerations, let's discuss some of the emotional ones first.

It's already been briefly touched upon, but well worth emphasizing: To be a successful franchisee, you must have the entrepreneurial spirit, drive, and work ethic to make it succeed. Having the passion to run a business is a non-negotiable requirement.

Running a franchise takes energy . . . and a lot of it! This is always true, but especially so during the start-up period. Your franchise will require long hours. Even when you're not physically present, your franchise business lives and draws both emotional and physical energy from you. Your business becomes almost like another member of your family.

To make a franchise successful, you should believe in, or have a sincere interest in, the products and/or services you're selling. You can get dazzled with the money potential of a successful franchise, but if you don't really have your heart in it, your franchise can become drudgery and, in some cases, the worst job you ever had. Only pursue those franchise opportunities where the products and services honestly appeal to you.

Now, let's move the discussion to more practical considerations. Remember, this is designed to spark your thinking and is by no means an exhaustive list. Here are some things you need to be sure of:

Is the business model proven? One of the big advantages of a franchise is that it's a proven business system. Make sure the system works and that operational training is included (how to actually run a business—from administration and bookkeeping, to marketing, legal issues, and more).

Who will you be dealing with? Is the franchisor financially stable? What level of ongoing support is given? Do they help with advertising? How do they treat franchisees? Research these aspects of the business.

Who has worked in this business before? This is likely one of the most important questions you'll ask as you research a franchise. It is highly recommended that you speak with other franchisees—beyond those whose names were provided by the franchisor. Get the real scoop. Ask a lot of questions. Get opinions and dig for how franchisees really feel about their experience with the franchisor.

What costs are involved? Thoroughly understand the true costs of buying and operating the franchise. Ask other franchisees. Don't get blindsided with unexpected costs and expenses.

Do you have the resources? Once you know the costs, do you have the capital (or access to resources) to start and run the franchise? This could involve a loan of some kind. Are you prepared to take on debt at this time in your life?

How does your family feel? Is your spouse supportive? Does your family believe it's a good idea? Will they help or chip in somehow? Don't go into a franchise unless you have unwavering emotional support from your loved ones. Don't do it to "prove them wrong."

How much can you earn? Is it worth it? Will the earnings of your successful franchise generate the income you desire? And how much work will that require? Some franchises need multiple locations to generate enough profit to fulfill financial goals. Are expansion opportunities available to you—and are you up for that?

How strong is the franchise's brand? Name recognition is a big help toward success when your consumers know what to expect from your product or service.

Is your territory exclusive? Depending upon the product or service, having geographical exclusivity is vital. Having competitors is one thing, but having competitors who are your fellow franchisees can cause trouble. Make sure the territory is big enough to succeed and lock out future franchisees.

Who is your competition in the industry? What are their strengths? Can you exploit weaknesses? What's your franchise's competitive advantage? Is it product, service, price . . . where can you win on the competitive landscape? Running a successful franchise requires a competitive advantage.

What's the endgame? As you venture down this path, pause and think about your endgame. Assume the franchise succeeds. What happens to the franchise when you do want to slow down or retire? Would your kids (or grandkids) want to take over? How about other family members? Is there a market to sell your franchise? Will the franchisor help in that regard? Do you just want to close shop? You don't have to know the answers. Just know that at some point in the future, there will be a decision to make regarding what to do with your franchise business.

As a SEAL, you should well understand many of the real-world factors, implications, and ramifications that are involved in opening a franchise business. Not everyone has what it takes to successfully run a franchise. However, for those SEALs who do have what it takes and have done their homework, owning a franchise can open a career path, new life experiences, and a world of opportunity that you would not have contemplated otherwise. It can be an exciting career adventure!

Part XX

A Personal Letter to You about Career Management

A bold heart is half the battle.
—Dwight D. Eisenhower[396]

Being a SEAL engaged in a job search is not a lot of fun. As we have discussed, there are age-related biases that could be stacked against you. The best way to avoid this entirely is not to be in a position where you need to conduct a job search in the first place.

In this final section, I want to offer advice so you will never again be unemployed or, if you do find yourself without a job, to ensure your unemployment period is as brief as possible.

Do you remember when I listed six career tenets that will add clarity, understanding, and perspective to your career? Whether you intend to work five more years or twenty, it is worth repeating the list again:

1. I am solely responsible for my career success.

2. It is my responsibility to enhance my value proposition. To achieve this, I must find opportunities to learn, improve, and expand upon my skills.

3. I must deliver an ROI to my employer through the value my function brings to the company.[397]

4. I am responsible for my work-life balance. Wherever I determine to spend my time and place my priorities, they are ultimately in my control.[398]

5. It is my responsibility to stay informed about the financial health and well-being of my employer and the industry in which I work.

---

396 Maxwell, John C. The Maxwell Daily Reader: 365 Days of Insight to Develop the Leader Within You and Influence Those Around You. (Nashville, TN: Thomas Nelson, 2011), p. 227.

397 Whitcomb, Job Search Magic, p. 12–13.

398 Yate, Social Networking, p. 246.

6. Change is inevitable in my career. How I respond to change is completely within my control. Change often creates opportunities that can be capitalized upon given perspective, knowledge, a positive attitude, and focused effort.

If you'll notice, each tenet has its own message but at the foundation of each is personal responsibility. The success of your career is your personal responsibility . . . and no one else's.

I want to give you twelve tips—pieces of advice, really—that will not only prepare you for new career opportunities, but also help you rebound more quickly from an unexpected job loss.

1. Create a rainy-day fund.

In my opinion, this first point doesn't seem like it has much to do with career management at all. But it does. As a SEAL, job searches can take you six months, sometimes longer. Save your money to cover living expenses for at least six months.

With this strategy, if you lose your job unexpectedly, you won't panic. You can engage in a self-motivated job search with purpose and strategy and find the right career opportunity, not just a job to pay the bills.

The rainy-day fund also gives you resources to invest in job-search tools and services. This could include a resume-writing service, business cards, wardrobe necessities, a career coach, or other services. The rainy-day fund has emotional benefits as well, allowing you to pay the bills, prevent feelings of desperation, and keep fear at bay.

2. Keep your resume current.

It is easy to let your resume grow stale. That's understandable—you are busy doing your job. But you're not managing your career. It takes precious little time to keep your resume up-to-date. Whenever something positive happens in your career or at least once a year—use your annual job-performance review as a reminder—update your resume. Or, at minimum, put a note at the end of the resume and handle it later. The point is to jot it down, with a date, so you don't lose track.

3. Keep your LinkedIn profile current, too.

The same line of thinking applies to your LinkedIn profile (and any other professional online profiles). Keep it as vibrant as possible. As you know, your LinkedIn profile is pivotal to a job search and equally important for career management. Your LinkedIn profile is how opportunities will often find you. It is imperative that your online presence is up-to-date.

4. Stay informed and in tune with your employer, industry, and the value of your job.

There is a lot to talk about here. When I speak with candidates who have lost their jobs, a sizeable number had warning signs of trouble. Either they ignored the red flags and hoped they would be saved from any layoffs or thought the situation would blow over. As you now know, you are personally responsible for your career. There are a few times when a candidate lost their job without warning. People do get blindsided, but frequently there are warning signs.

Be aware of how your employer is doing financially. Is there talk about mergers, acquisitions, or IPOs? Significant governmental or regulatory threats? Ask yourself: How does this information positively or negatively affect my career? Evaluate the information, assess the situation, do research, communicate with others, make a determination, and judge timing. Use your business knowledge and trust your business instincts. Then act if needed.

The same kind of analysis applies to your industry as well. It is important to be knowledgeable and aware of its overall health. Industry shrinkage by market forces or government intervention should cause a moment of pause and reflection regarding career choice. It is always better to move away from an industry in decline to one that is growing and expanding, if in fact your transferable job skills permit.

Finally, stay acutely aware of the value of your role in a company. Do you, in your job and function, make or save the company money?[399] If the value of your job is fading, seriously consider making a proactive career move.

5. Plan your career path.

Regardless of where you are in your career, allow yourself to dream and explore what you want to do and where you want to take your career (even post-retirement). Where do you want to go?[400]

For any plan to be effective, you must write it down. It is remarkable how writing solidifies a plan and creates a sense of self-accountability. Start with one-, three-, and five-year plans. In my experience, going much further is not realistic. Too many things can change—interests, opportunities, setbacks. In other words, life happens.

Write down the specific actions and steps to move you forward. Add timelines. It's been said that "a goal is a dream with a deadline."[401] This exercise is very similar to Profiling

---

399 Whitcomb, *Job Search Magic*, p. 274.

400 Yate, *Social Networking*, p. 247.

401 "Napoleon Hill Quotable Quote," Goodreads, http://www.goodreads.com/quotes/244859-a-goal-is-a-dream-with-a-deadline (accessed June 11, 2015).

Your Next Career Opportunity, with a broader scope and longer timeline. You might want to review that part of this book and its concepts with a self-motivated, career-management point of view.

6. Network.

Network actively. Build contacts inside and outside your company. Review the Networking section and focus on strategies most impactful to you. Ask yourself this question: If I lost my job today, do I have a Cabinet and a Sales Company I could reach out to that would help me? This should be the minimum amount of "go-to" networking contacts you have.

The power that professional networking can have on your career is remarkable. Remember that in networking, "those who give, get."[402] When the time is right (whenever that time might be), networking can propel your career to heights and a level of professional satisfaction that you might not have thought possible,[403] regardless of age.

7. Stay sharp and develop new skills.

One of the keys to employment and career management is to become indispensable. I don't think this can be completely achieved in most companies, but you want to get as close to it as you can. At a minimum, you want your employer to see that it will hurt the company if they should ever lose you.

One way of achieving this is by enhancing your current skillset and developing new skills. Attend workshops, seminars, and conventions. Stay informed about emerging trends and technologies or products.

I highly recommend that you earn an industry designation, regardless of your age. This adds credibility to your name and your brand (more on that in a moment). Getting a "certificate of completion" from a one-day seminar is okay, but it's not really what I mean. Rather, pursue those industry designations that take effort and have substantive meaning, both in content and with your peers. It may take time and effort, but the knowledge and differentiation you gain with your current employer and for future employment opportunities make it well worth it.

Many SEALs have told me that pursuing an industry designation rejuvenated them.

---

402 Vlooten, "The Seven Laws."

403 Yate, Social Networking, p. 246.

8. Nurture your brand.

Good career management encompasses brand management. Review this book's Branding section. Stay aware of your value proposition, ROI, and differentiation factors. These and other factors create your brand, which must be nurtured and guarded, like your professional reputation.[404]

To nurture your brand, ask yourself a two-part question: What am I known for? And is that getting communicated to those who matter? Assess, evaluate, and make adjustments if you don't like the answer.

9. Ensure your visibility at work and in your industry.

Closely tied to branding is the concept of visibility. Work to get known within your company and your industry in ways that support your brand. Becoming known in a positive way within your employer's company can help make you indispensable (to the extent that's possible). It could be as simple as some internal networking—but don't become a politician. You can be subtle to get your work noticed.[405] Or, you could speak at an industry conference. It's easier to gain visibility via LinkedIn and its Groups feature, by starting discussions or contributing insightfully to existing ones. If you are not sure, don't post it. Ask a colleague to double-check the idea. Visibility can work for you, but if mishandled, it can work against you.

Regardless of your tenure in an industry, I suggest finding a dynamic professional association that piques your interest. Find a way to get involved. Your involvement does not have to be time consuming. The point is to contribute and become known. It will enhance your networking efforts.

10. Be aware of opportunities in the market.

Although you may be content, challenged, and fulfilled in your current position, it is incumbent upon you to be aware of new opportunities that can enhance your overall lifetime career experience. LinkedIn has ways for you to be alerted about opportunities that would interest you. Use it.

Return calls and emails from recruiters and others; listen to opportunities they present. The bottom line is this: Whether you stay with your current position or pursue a new opportunity—it is ultimately your choice. You are proactively managing your career. What a great position to be in!

---

404 Ibid., p. 244–245.
405 Ibid., p. 245–246.

11. Consider getting a mentor/confidant.

As a SEAL, this might seem odd. At your stage of life and career you should be the mentor. This is true. Nonetheless, consider finding a confidant. A good choice would be a professional colleague you can trust and talk to about career issues (perhaps from your Cabinet). It does not need to be a formalized relationship. The most important thing for you to remember about this kind of relationship is to engage in conversation while also being able to listen and learn. Frequently, you will receive not only valuable insight and knowledge, but also wisdom. This information can have a profound impact.

12. It's a matter of attitude, introspection, and perspective.

Over the course of my career, I have reviewed the career paths of thousands of people. One frequent theme is common to most: Your career will be an unpredictable journey.

Regardless of the twists and turns, I highly encourage you to always maintain a positive outlook and attitude. Consider it an invaluable career-management strategy. Want proof? "Nearly 88 percent of the 3,785 senior-level executives surveyed by ExecuNet said they would rather enhance their team with that individual who possesses a good attitude, even if he or she does not perform to the highest level or have top qualifications."[406] This statistic applies to internal promotions as well as external job opportunities. Having a positive attitude will enhance your career opportunities.

Another related career-management concept is introspection. I have spoken to professionals who have developed in their careers and woke up one morning regretting the ways their career reshaped them. I remember one candidate shared he had become irritable, impatient, and overly consumed with thoughts about money, among other things. He wanted a change from the demands of his current job so he could return to a less stressful career existence and get back to the person he truly was.

Career management means remaining true to who you are and being comfortable with the fit between your personal needs and the demands of your job. When they do not match closely enough, you—and your family—will likely experience outward signs of the internal friction (irritability, reclusiveness, impatience, and so on). Good career management requires times of introspection to examine yourself for who you are (or are becoming) as a result of your career. The outcome of that introspection may be motivation to make job or career adjustments.

Tied to introspection is the concept of perspective. Introspection is an internal evaluation

---

406 Hr.comt, "Senior-Level Business Leaders Say Positive Attitude is the Key to Getting the Job," news release, March 25, 2013, http://www.hr.com/en/communities/senior-level-business-leaders-say-positive-attitud_hesqvt4k.html (accessed April 14, 2016).

while perspective is an external evaluation. Perspective, as I am using the word, frequently comes to the surface with SEALs. They begin to ask themselves these kinds of questions:

"What is the purpose of what I do?"

"Am I helping anyone?"

"Do I provide any value?"

Or, in a grander sense . . .

"Why am I on this earth?"

These are deep questions and ones that are perfectly normal to ask. From my experience, the key is to discover *and name* at least one, and hopefully more, redeeming qualities of your work that others value, whether directly or in conjunction with coworkers or others.

The naming process identifies and solidifies the value of your work in your mind (intellectually) and your heart (emotionally). What your heart and mind hold on to will bring feelings of professional worth. It's a great feeling that your heart and mind know your work matters and has purpose.

Let's tie this all together: attitude, introspection, and perspective. Working backward, when you genuinely feel your work matters, you have professional self-worth. When your job is consistent with who you are as a person, there is internal peace and a match with you and your career. Both affect your attitude in a very significant and positive way. Having a positive attitude is a career strategy and leads to more career opportunities, which is a component of proactive career management. I love it when it all comes together!

I hope these twelve tips, based on my personal experience and professional experience with others, impart valuable insight on proactively managing your career.

It is my heartfelt and sincerest hope that you experience the most successful and emotionally fulfilling career you possibly can!

Best Wishes Always,
Brian E. Howard

Appendix A

Success Story Worksheet and Samples

Employer:

Your Position:

When:

Skill/Competency:

Challenge (Situation/Task):

Action:

Result:

Success Story—Example

Employer: XYZ Insurance Company

Position: Vice President of Product Development and Contracting

When: 20XX

Skill/Competency: Creativity, Critical Thinking, and Analysis

Challenge: While I was working at a large national insurance carrier [you would use the actual name in your story], their workers' compensation product portfolio was missing an ancillary product line/division. This was causing us to miss out on a potential revenue stream and the opportunity to compete against those companies providing these products as a standalone service.

The theory was that by adding ancillary services, we would add revenue, increase customer retention, and promote long-term loyalty from our existing client base.

Action: We developed a new line of contracts for ancillary providers. We established a list of providers in multiple fields (i.e., DME,[407] O and P, home health, and so on). With these providers, we contracted and negotiated pricing. Once we had 80 percent of the contracts signed, we began marketing the new product offerings through conferences, seminars, and email blasts to existing and potential clients. At the same time, we developed a fully insured product that provided us with a one-stop-shop ability to service existing and potential clients.

Result: The end result of this effort was our ability to grow the bottom-line revenue by 27 percent in the first year after the network was up and running. This product division stands today and continues to grow.

---

407 "Durable medical equipment"; see "Durable Medical Equipment (DME) Center," Centers for Medicare & Medicaid Services, http://www.cms.gov/Center/Provider-Type/Durable-Medical-Equipment-DME-Center.html (accessed July 13, 2015).

Appendix B

Sample Resumes

The following resumes are examples of the three most common resume formats. Some follow the advice of the resume section, and some do not. They are for illustrative purposes only.

Example 1:   Traditional Reverse Chronological Resume

Example 2:   Functional Resume

Examples 3 and 4:   Showcase Resumes

Example 1—Traditional Reverse Chronological Resume

Jack Johanson
1234 State St. Kansas City, MO 64066
816-555-4444 • jjohan@ymail.com

PROFESSIONAL PROFILE

A results-oriented and driven insurance sales, marketing, and business-development executive with a distinguished reputation for profitable new business growth, prospect identification, pipeline development, product promotion, and creative sales and marketing strategies. Extensive expertise in customer-needs analysis with a consultative approach to C-level insurance products, services sales, and account retention. Repeated success guiding sizeable, cross-functional teams in the design, development, and roll out of innovative solutions driving record-setting sales. Expert presenter, negotiator, closer, and businessperson able to forge solid relationships and build partnerships across multiple organizational levels.

National Sales Strategy — Technology-Driven Solutions — Key Performance Indicators

Branding and Market Positioning — Data Analytics/Predictive Modeling

Market-Share Analysis — Product-Line Growth and Profitability

Client/Account Development — Home-Office Coordination — Team Building/Coaching Claims-Cost Reduction — Customer Service

PROFESSIONAL EMPLOYMENT HISTORY

20XX–Present   **THERAPY AND REHAB, CO.**

Vice President National Accounts—Wausau, WI

Business-development executive in charge of identification and development of new markets and innovative insurance products to increase revenue and open new channels to expand market presence.

- Successfully implemented nationwide new-markets strategy and action plan for developing new sources of business including brokers, reinsurers, captives, self-insured associations, assigned risk plans, guarantee funds, and managing general agencies.

20XX–Present   **THERAPY AND REHAB, CO.**

Vice President National Accounts—Wausau, WI

Business-development executive in charge of identification and development of new markets and innovative insurance products to increase revenue and open new channels to expand market presence.

- Successfully implemented nationwide new-markets strategy and action plan for developing new sources of business including brokers, reinsurers, captives, self-insured associations, assigned risk plans, guarantee funds, and managing general agencies.

- Created and led development, design, and roll out of nationwide, regional sales-expansion plan.

- Earned top salesman status by bringing on eight national accounts and increasing revenue by 33 percent.

20XX–20XX   **LIABILITY INSURANCE COMPANY**

Sales Executive—Chicago, IL

Regional manager leading company's Midwest expansion into a retail agency distribution model for selling property and casualty products and services.

- Grew premium and expanded customer base by 40 percent.

- Appointed forty-five new agencies.

- Introduced Agency Growth Action Plan and reporting tools.

20XX–20XX   **MEDICARE COMPLIANCE CORPORATION**

Director Sales and Marketing—Minneapolis, MN

Director of Sales and Marketing for nationwide insurance consulting operations, including managing all aspects of the $30 million, five-region, twenty-five-member sales and marketing organization, and the growth and development of its 550 carrier, third-party administration, self-insured, state-funded, and broker clients.

- Top architect of nationwide sales and marketing expansion plan leading to the increase in overall revenue to $30 million from $1.5 million and market position to #2 from #31.

- Top salesman for both 20XX and 20XX. Increased Midwest region revenue by 875 percent (from twenty clients and $400,000 to 180 clients and $3.5 million) during that period.

- Introduced web-based claims-auditing program to show clients extra cost-saving opportunities.

19XX–20XX	**ALL RISKS INSURANCE CO.**

Vice President—New York, NY

Vice President in charge of twenty-five-employee, $40 million property and casualty (excess and surplus lines) wholesale brokerage and managing general agency operation. Worked with over two hundred retail agents.

- Redesigned sales and brokerage units leading to revenue growth of 22 percent.
- Successfully negotiated three new carrier contracts for new program opportunities.
- Introduced agency-automation training program.

19XX–19XX	**REECE INSURANCE GROUP, INC.**

Chief Operating Officer—Atlanta, GA

Executive in charge of four-office, fifty-employee, $42 million multistate property and casualty (excess and surplus lines) wholesale brokerage and managing general agency operations. Sold services nationally to over 250 retail agencies and brokers.

- Led merger of two newly acquired operations, resulting in 30 percent expense reduction.
- Expanded agency base by 30 percent and successfully negotiated five new carrier contracts for new program opportunities.

19XX–19XX	**NICHOLS HOLDINGS, LLC**

Manager, Product Development—Baton Rouge, LA

Director of new product development initiatives for the national rating organization's seven hundred insurance carrier affiliates. Consultant in charge of emerging issues and trends practice.

- Led the design and development of online Underwriting Workstation, Pricing Analysis Tool, and PricePoint projects.
- Heavy emphasis on e-commerce strategic planning, claims benchmarking, and actuarial analysis.

Education   Top Flight University

BSBA, Management and Marketing

Example 2—Functional Resume

Kelsey Owen
890 Cedar Street • Sunset, NM 12345 • H: 123-456-7890 • C: 861-123-4567
kowen@nomail.com

Specialty Pharmaceutical Sales
Energetic professional dedicated to developing business relationships for revenue growth.

Driven health-care professional with entrepreneurial experience developing business referrals through hard work and relationships. Transitioning to sales career to deliver sales results through business development, marketing, and strategic planning. Successfully leverages core strengths and connections across the region to develop new business.

Core Strengths

√ Cold Calling	√ Sales Presentations	√ Networking
√ Negotiation	√ Relationship Cultivation	√ Marketing Tactics
√ Business Retention	√ Operations Management	√ P and L Experience
√ Vendor Relations	√ Compliance	√ Employee Relations

Career Skills

- **Sales**—Utilized a solution-based sales approach to successfully gain an audience, assess needs, recommend solutions, negotiate terms, and close sales.

- **Networking**—Established a referral network and created a steady stream of clients.

- **Consultation**—Educated client-patients on the validity and effectiveness of physical therapy, which resulted in a profitable business enterprise.

- **Product Development**—Created new services in response to market demand and patient needs.

- **Operations/Entrepreneurship**—Took start-up of a rehab and physical therapy health-care clinic to profitability in just three years.

Professional Experience

Co-Owner/Sports Therapist, The Sports Rehab Center, Sunset, NM, 20XX–20XX:
Built a start-up rehab clinic; established and maintained a profitable business for eight years.
Rehabilitation Director, Pinnacle Therapy, Sunset, NM, 20XX–20XX
Rehabilitation Therapist, Ferguson Chiropractic Center, Sunset, NM, 19XX–20XX

Education, Licenses, and Certifications

BS, Kinesiology, Stretch University, Muscle, AZ
New Mexico Board Certified Rehabilitation Specialist • Certified Sports Therapist

Example 3—Showcase Resume Focused on Business Relations and Product Knowledge

Dan Evans

Contact Information:

danevans@nomail.com
8526 Glenwood Street
Somewhere, OR XXXXX
Cell: (503) 123-4567

Professional Positions Held:

Independent Consultant
(Current) SNL (20XX–20XX):
VP of Sales

HMO Consulting Inc.
(20XX—20XX): President

D&E Corporation
(20XX–20XX): Director
of Operations, Sales, and
Marketing

Big 6 Consulting (20XX–
20XX): Senior Manager

Hooligan Consulting (19XX–
20XX): Senior Manager

A+ Consulting (19XX–19XX):
Project Manager

GPS (19XX–19XX):
Client Manager

Summary:

Currently an independent consultant serving the payer and provider health-care community. Business-development, marketing, operations, and product executive with over twenty years of experience in leading consulting, cost-containment, and technology organizations in the health-care industry, focusing on various payer and provider clients. Successful track record working with leading health-care executives to help reduce costs, increase revenue, implement technology, and create efficiencies to improve overall organizational growth. Over the past eight years, major focus has been on business development, leading two separate organizations to over 30 percent annual growth in overall revenue.

Industry Experience:

SNL: A national leader in cost management for out-of-network claims reimbursement. Products were rolled out as revolutionary in 20XX as a cost-based data and transparent solution to determine a rational reimbursement of claims for payers, providers, and consumers. General responsibilities and accomplishments include:

- Leading business development for the innovative repricing methodology to the market. The product is transforming the industry for reimbursement of out-of-network claims, determining a rational reimbursement to providers based on actual cost plus a fair margin, as opposed to a discount off an inflated billed charge. Impactful outcomes include:
  - New sales efforts helped lead the company to revenue growth in excess of 30 percent for each of the past two calendar years, virtually doubling the overall company revenue

Products:

- Claims Repricing
- Claims Audit
- Bill Review
- Claims Adjudication
- Claims Clearinghouse

Sample Clients:

- BCBS Western Pennsylvania
- BCBS Florida
- BCBS Michigan
- BCBS Massachusetts
- BCBS Louisiana
- Blue Cross of California
- Capital Blue Cross
- Empire BCBS
- HCSC (BCBS IL, OK, TX, NM)
- WellMark
- Various Other Blues Plans
- Aetna
- CIGNA
- Coventry
- UnitedHealthcare
- Mutual of Omaha
- Fortis Health / Fortis Benefits
- Over Twenty Various Health Plans
- Over Fifty Various TPAs

- Increasing the overall group health payer client base by over 25 percent, which included third-party administrators, as well as large insurers Cigna and Coventry

- Entering the organization into two new sales markets— workers comp and the government health sector

- Delivering hundreds of sales presentations to clients, prospects, payers, employer groups, industry leaders/ think tanks, associations, health-care conferences, and government officials

HMO Consulting: Incorporated independent consulting firm to conduct several initiatives within health care, including:

- Leading a tactical strategy within Blue Cross Blue Shield of Florida to boost the EDI rates within the Florida Provider Network

- Acting as a liaison between Blue Cross Blue Shield of Florida and the Florida provider community to implement a successful conversion to the National Provider Identifier, as legislated by the HIPAA mandates

- Working with the product-development team to develop and roll out innovative cost-based methodology to payers

D&E Corporation: A health-care-transaction clearinghouse and professional-services organization that provides technology and services to payer, provider, and employer organizations to transmit and process claims and other health-care transactions. General responsibilities and accomplishments included:

- Leading the business development, operations, IT, and product development of all clearinghouse activities, which included over 80 percent of the corporation's overall revenue

- Growing the revenue base by 30 percent in the first calendar year of the leading product, Medicare Claims Crossover, that sent claims from CMS to secondary payer organizations for supplemental coverage and interfaced with over seventy payer clients, including twenty different Blue Cross Blue Shield organizations

- Increasing the revenue of the EDI Clearinghouse for providers in the Midwestern states for all HIPAA-related transactions

Education:

Bachelor of Science

Minnesota State University

Continuing Education at the School of Computer Technology

Pittsburgh, PA

Other Areas of Interest:

Director of Basketball Operations: St. Michael Parochial School

Prior President of the Total Board of Education—St. Michael School

Leader of various charitable organizations including United Way, Urban Education Service,

Athletic coach for Elementary School, Junior High, and YMCA

Former Board Member of St. Michael Parish Council

Big 6 Consulting: Provides strategic advisory and technology experts to help deliver integrated solutions to optimize business performance. General responsibilities and accomplishments included:

- Identifying all record-retention requirements—legal and business—for large payer organizations
- Conducting an assessment of a hospital's strategic initiative to outsource their supply-chain operations, from distribution to point of use

Hooligan Consulting and A+ Consulting: Two of the world's largest management-consulting firms that work with national and international corporations to deliver strategy, operations, and technology solutions. General responsibilities and accomplishments included:

- Leading engagements on business-transformation activities for two large Blue Cross Blue Shield organizations. This included claims-system selection and implementation, developing process and system interfaces, and determining impacts on organization and HR
- Managing overall impact and implementation of HIPAA for several Blue Cross Blue Shield organizations in both the technology and business operational areas, as well as overall corporate strategic planning
- Implementing many additional projects for large payer organizations including imaging/workflow, producer compensation reengineering, and consolidation of HMO organizations

GPS: A national leader in technology services including infrastructure, applications, and business-process outsourcing. General responsibilities and accomplishments included:

- Leading effort on corporate strategy for two large Blue Cross Blue Shield plans to merge the existing claims and membership legacy systems that impacted many significant areas including claims, premium billing and membership, customer service, and human resources; and managing the electronic commerce department in charge of the development and implementation of a managed-care, electronic network for a major East Coast Blue Cross Blue Shield plan

- Implementing large-scale technology initiatives for many Blue Cross Blue Shield claims systems, impacting all areas of the organizations

Example 4—Showcase Resume Using a Chart

BEVERLY HOPKINS

90210 State Way ▪ Somewhere, TX 76001 ▪ cell (817) 123-4567 ▪ bhopkins@goglobal.net

Senior Vice President of Sales and Business Development
Sales Leadership ◊ Strategic ◊ Passionate

Performance Summary

Dedicated sales professional with 20+ years of success generating revenue and securing high profile clients and brokers for industry leaders, such as Fish-fil-A, Martens International, Barton, Wells Fargo, Cohans, and Yates, with excellent client retention. Experienced in every aspect of launching new startup companies. Seasoned veteran with sales experience in multiple industries.

Core Competencies

• Training	• Presentations	• Closing
• Large Account Prospecting	• Account Management	• Client Retention
• Regulatory Compliancy	• Sales Operations	• Product Dev.
• Budget Management	• Problem Solving	• Business Dev.
• Negotiations	• Relationship Building	• Push-Pull Mktg.

Revenue Growth

Maintained consistent, year-over-year pattern of increasing revenues through robust and downturn economies, from $20M to $35M as illustrated below:

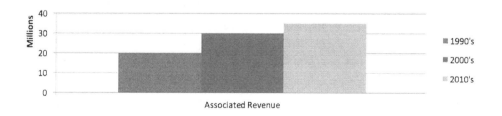

Professional Experience

RIP Consulting Group   20xx–Present
Startup company that is a distributor/wholesaler of aggregate only and spec & aggregate small group self-funded group health plans.

President, Health Division
Manage the sales and marketing for the company including direct sales and broker channel management, interface with underwriting, compliance, and investors.
- **Added 15 new accounts** through direct and broker sales in a new market.

Last Decade Healthcare   20xx–20xx
Leading company in the limited benefit medical plans industry.

Vice President of Sales and Business Development—*Promotion*   20xx-20xx
Responsible for hiring and training of five staff members (three of which were area vice presidents) and assisting them in achieving sales goals, interface with carrier underwriting to design plan and adjust rates for a competitive plan offering. Maintained and grew broker contacts and client business, negotiated major client renewals and contracts, analyzed vendors. Redeveloped the western region broker channel.
- **Maintained 100%** of all large clients negotiating multi-year contracts.
- Grew revenue from **$21M to over $30M in two years**.
- Negotiated profit sharing agreement that resulted in an additional **$200K in net profit**.
- Wrote over **$4M in new business**.

Regional Vice President—*Promotion*   20xx–20xx
Managed five AVP's and trained new staff, responsible for sales in southwestern, south central, and western regions. Controlled regional budget and those of direct staff.
- Generated over $8.5M in gross sales while remaining under budget.
- Won Fish-fil-A account resulting in $2.8M in revenue
- Implemented "Push-Pull" marketing strategy resulting in increased market penetration.

Area Vice President   20xx–20xx
Change of industries and hired to grow revenue and open a new market in the central region.
- Grew regional revenue from zero to **$1.5M in 14 months**.

American Printing   20xx–20xx

Multi-million dollar global company, leader in the wide format printer industry.

Sales Executive, Display Division

Responsible for account development and the direct sales of printers in TX, OK, LA, and AR. Greatly improved customer satisfaction among existing client base.
- Increased top line revenue **growth by 27%**.

The Pique Company   19xx–20xx

The Pique Company is centered on disruptive technologies and breakthrough solutions for the product goods packaging, graphic communications and functional printing industries.

Account Manager, Southern Zone   20xx–20xx

Developed a channel for printers in the south central region. Responsible for working in tandem with distribution partners to grow the market share. Prospected for large direct accounts and supported nine account executives.

Account Executive   20xx–20xx

Trained dealers on new digital products and worked with system integrators to generate digital portrait studio sales.
- Reached **143% of YTD goal** in seven state territory.
- Built photography business from zero to **$20M in three years**.

Specialist, Systems and Solutions   19xx–20xx

Acted as racing segment manager, worked with Pensky Racing to evaluate profitability targets of event photography of NASCAR and other venues.
- Ranked as **top producer** for three year tenure.
- Exceeded revenue goals every year while remaining under budget, **165% of quota**.

Education and Licensing

Northern Minnesota University—Somewhere, MN
Bachelor of Science in Marketing, concentration Sales and Management

"I consistently strive for what is innovative and productive in maintaining the company's competitive edge."

—Bev Hopkins

Appendix C

Sample Letters

Letter of Application

Letter of Inquiry

Response to a Job Posting

Job Match Cover Letter

Marketing Email

Thank You Letter/Response

Thank You Letter When Not Selected for the Job/Email

Introductory Email to a Search Firm

Letter of Application

Street Address
City, State ZIP Code
Phone Number
Date

George Heisler
XYZ Company
444 Anywhere State Road
Anytown, CA 00000

RE: Senior Systems Engineer

Dear Mr. Heisler,

I am a senior-level systems engineer, and in the last four years I have designed and implemented one of the first large-scale, virtual-desktop deployments used in education. I am writing to apply for the senior-level systems engineer position advertised in the *Times Union*.

The opportunity presented in this listing is very interesting, and I believe that my strong technical experience and certifications will make me a very competitive candidate for this position. The key certifications that I possess for success in this position include:

- VMware Certified Professional, Data Center Virtualization
- VMware Certified Professional, Desktop Technologies
- EMC Information Storage Associate
- EMC Implementation Engineer, VNX Solutions Specialist
- Cisco Certified Entry Networking Technician

In 20XX, I accepted the Computerworld Honors Program Laureate Award in Washington, DC, for designing and implementing virtual desktops. I believe my above certifications and past experiences qualify me to orchestrate your virtual-desktop software.

As requested, I am enclosing a completed job application, my certifications, my resume, and three references. I will contact you by next week to discuss this opportunity with you further. I can be reached anytime via email at john.donaldson@emailexample.com or my cell phone (909) 555-5555.

Thank you for your time and consideration. I look forward to speaking with you.

Sincerely,

(Signature in blue or black ink)

John Donaldson

Letter of Inquiry

Street Address
City, State ZIP Code
Phone Number
Date
George Gilhooley

XYZ Company
444 Anywhere State Road
Anytown, CA 00000

RE: Information Technology Department

Dear Mr. Gilhooley,

For the past two years, I have been working as an engineer on a cloud-based system that developed systems to support over 450 virtual desktops in ten states. I am a senior-level, cloud-based systems engineer, and I am inquiring about job opportunities in your IT department.

I am certified in:

- VMware Certified Professional 4 and vSphere 5
- IBM Certified Advanced System Administrator—Domino 7.x
- Cisco UCS
- Windows Servers

In addition to the above certifications, I am proficient in Cisco switches, EMC and Equallogic SANs, and Commvault. I have worked in varied environments from small businesses to international corporations, and this has prepared me to excel with your company's cloud-based systems software. Because of my past experience and accomplishments, I believe I am qualified for your IT department as a systems engineer.

I've included my resume for you to review. XYZ Company is an innovative and forward-thinking organization, and I want to assist you with your success and that of your company with my skills in software engineering. I will call you to discuss the value I bring. I can be reached in the evenings at (111) 222-3333 if you prefer.

Your consideration is appreciated. I look forward to connecting.

Sincerely,

(Signature in blue or black ink)

John Donaldson

Enclosure: resume

Response to a Job Posting

Director, Operations (Mail Order)

Job Description

Based on the extensive growth of our corporation, we are looking to add an accomplished professional to join our growing team, as we are expanding our mail-order pharmacy services and scope. We are a financially stable and fundamentally sound corporation experiencing tremendous success, based on our corporate model as well as our delivery methods for the patient populations we service.

Position Purpose:

Oversee pharmacy mail-order operations (inventory, shipping, fulfillment, and customer service), ensuring timely and accurate processing of related activities.

Position Responsibilities:

- Develop operational plans and implement new programs related to the processing of pharmacy mail orders

- Oversee the supporting functions for mail-service fulfillment, including customer service, product fulfillment, inventory management, shipping, and general facility management

- Oversee new-client implementation and transition of new business, including managing the IT infrastructure and web strategy

- Design and implement new processes for automation and streamline operations by incorporating cost-saving programs

- Evaluate and implement mail-service pharmacy procedures to ensure compliance with all related laws, regulations, and executive orders

Send your resume to: Bjohnson@emailaddress.biz

Date

Dear Brenda Johnson,

Would you like to increase the efficiency and revenue of your pharmacy mail orders by 20 percent? If so, I am the **director of mail-order pharmacy** you need.

With nine years of experience managing the $3.5 million mail-order division of Drugs for You, I have had the following successes:

- Led creative team to define strategic goals and design company's first pharmacy mail-order services.

- Set up software team to develop home page on the Internet for online ordering. This distribution channel increased sales by 20 percent.

- Supervised twenty-five employees in all departments, including finance, design, and purchasing to realize 100 percent of deadlines.

- Reorganized order-processing procedures, which increased customer satisfaction by 25 percent.

I am passionate about process improvement. When I look at departments, internal processes, and protocols, my mind immediately asks whether there exists a better, more efficient, or profitable way. This way of thinking has both saved money and generated new revenue sources in the past.

I believe you will find my skills beneficial to XYZ. I will follow up with you in a few days to discuss further.

Sincerely,

Joe Jones

Contact Information

Job-Match Cover Letter

Street Address
City, State ZIP Code
Phone Number
Date

George Gilhooley
XYZ Company
444 Anywhere State Road
Anytown, CA 00000

RE: Chief Sales Officer position

Dear Mr. Gilhooley,

I am an **executive vice president of sales.** For the past fifteen years, I have been leading the sales division and have served over one thousand existing clients nationwide. I am a qualified candidate for your chief sales officer position, as I have illustrated below:

Position Requirements	**Qualifications of (Your Name)**
Team Building	Transformed the sales team to Insight Selling. Achieved 103 percent of sales plan 20XX.
Product Development	Created Beyond-Check. Introduced to existing clients. Currently 122 percent of goal.
Budgeting/Forecasting	Due to company-wide budgetary realignment, implemented a variable workforce and reduced spending by $1 million.
Mentoring/Development	Led a business-development team that achieved 162 percent of plan.

In addition to the above qualifications, I led a sales team of six market managers and forty-two account executives to successfully retain and gain new business and managed $200 million in sales for this year.

I've included my resume for you to review. XYZ Company is an innovative and forward-thinking organization, and I want to assist you with your success and that of your company with my skills in sales leadership and product development. I will call you to discuss the value I bring. I can be reached in the evenings at (111) 222-3333 if you prefer.

Your consideration is appreciated. I look forward to connecting.

Sincerely,
(Your Name)

Marketing Email

Subject Line: #1 Work Comp Sales Professional

Mr. Johnson,

I am a **top-producing workers' compensation cost-containment sales professional** who ranked as the #1 sales representative amongst my peers for 20XX and 20XX. I played an instrumental role in the growth of my former employer. I am exploring a career move.

My sales achievements include:

1. Consistently **exceeded sales quota** for the last four years.
2. **Ranked #1** in sales in 20XX and 20XX. **Sales Representative of the Year.**
3. **20XX—Account Coordinator of the Year Award.**

Click here to watch a one-minute bio video.

I sold pharmacy, transportation, translation, home health, physical therapy, durable medical equipment, and other services in the workers' compensation and auto insurance industries. Territory includes the Great Lakes area, calling on nurse case managers, claims managers, and adjusters, among others. I have no travel restrictions.

If you have an interest in or a need for a sales professional with a consistent track record of new business sales, please reply or call me.

Best Regards,

Your Name

Phone Number

Thank-You Letter/Response

Issues brought up in conversation

- *Company has just restructured its accounting department*
- *Department is in the midst of automating various accounting procedures*
- *Got the feeling that the place is in chaos*
- *Indicated employee morale was down, which has adversely affected efficiency of office*

January 15, 20XX

Mr. Randy Jones, Vice President of Accounting

XYZ Corporation

123345 Main Street

Baltimore, MD 23654

RE: Our recent conversation

Dear Mr. Jones,

I appreciate you spending time on the phone with me yesterday. I understand your department is undergoing some major transitions. I am confident that my accounting-systems-conversion experience and skills would help get your department up and running in your stated goal of six months.

As we discussed, I spent seven years at ABC Company, managing its accounting and finance department. During this period, I accomplished the following:

- *Converted manual reporting systems to computerized operations, which led to a cost savings of $60,000 per year and increased efficiency by 40 percent.*

- *Participated in the downsizing process, which cut my staff from thirty to twelve.*

- *Implemented motivational programs to increase employee morale and keep productivity constant throughout this six-month period.*

- *Created a financial-operating plan to fully fund banking services of $250,000.*

- *Execution of this plan resulted in generating earnings in short-term reserves, while contributing 7 percent of revenue to long-term reserves.*

In the transitional time you are experiencing there is nothing more important than communicating effectively with your personnel and organizing the group to reach common goals. While with ABC, I completely reorganized accounting procedures following the downsizing. As you can imagine, there was a lot of resistance from the staff. I accepted that fact and reversed it. Within two weeks, I had each team member up and running on the new system with smiles on their faces! I attribute this to my team-oriented focus, clear communication style, and organizational skills.

I believe you will find my management, organizational, and systems skills are what you need during this transitional period. I will call you next week, as you suggested, to speak with you further about future opportunities.

Sincerely,

Peter Fabin

Phone Number

Thank-You Letter When Not Selected for the Job/Email

Subject Line: Thank you!—from (Your Name)

Mr. Jefferies,

I received a communication today informing me that I was not selected for the senior account management position. I want to express my appreciation for your consideration. (Company Name) is a dynamic company with strong products and services. I'm sure it will continue to succeed in the future!

I remain interested in (Company Name). Should another opportunity become available, please reach out to me.

Best Regards,

Your Name

Introductory Email to a Search Firm

Subject Line: #1 Work Comp Services Sales Professional

Mr. Johnson,

I am a **top-producing workers' compensation services sales professional** who ranked as the number one sales representative amongst my peers for 20XX and 20XX. I played an instrumental role in the growth of my former employer.

My sales achievements include:

1. Consistently **exceeded sales quota** for the last four years.
2. **Ranked #1** in sales in 20XX and 20XX. **Sales Representative of the Year.**
3. **20XX—Account Coordinator of the Year Award.**

Click to watch a brief <u>one-minute bio video.</u>

I sold pharmacy, transportation, translation, home health, physical therapy, durable medical equipment, and other services within the workers' compensation and auto insurance industries. Territory includes the Great Lakes area calling on nurse case managers, claims managers, and adjusters, among others. I have no restrictions on travel.

If there is a possible fit with one of your clients, I would like to speak with you about that opportunity. Alternatively, if I am a candidate who fits your specialty, please keep me in mind for future opportunities.

I have attached a resume for review.

Best Regards,

Your Name

Contact Information

Bibliography

Abraham Lincoln Online. "Lincoln's Advice to Lawyers." Abraham Lincoln's letter to Isham Reavis. November 5, 1855. http://www.abrahamlincolnonline.org/lincoln/speeches/law.htm (accessed February 19, 2016).

Accountemps. "Farewell to the Handwritten Thank-You Note? Survey Reveals Email, Phone Call Are Preferred Methods for Post-Interview Follow-Up." News release. June 14, 2012. http://accountemps.rhi.mediaroom.com/thank-you (accessed February 19, 2016).

Adams, Susan. "4 Ways to Use Twitter to Find a Job." Forbes. November 30, 2012. http://www.forbes.com/sites/susanadams/2012/11/30/4-ways-to-use-twitter-to-find-a-job/(accessed February 19, 2016).

Adams, Susan. "How to Ace Your Job Interview." Forbes. March 1, 2013. http://www.forbes.com/sites/susanadams/2013/03/01/how-to-ace-your-job-interview-2/ (accessed February 15, 2016).

Adams, Susan. "How to Ace a Job Interview on the Phone." Forbes. February 7, 2012. www.forbes.com/sites/susanadams/2012/02/07/how-to-ace-a-job-interview-on-the-phone/ (accessed February 19, 2016).

Adams, Susan. "Older Workers, There's Hope: Study Finds Employers Like You Better Than Millennials." Forbes. September 24, 2012. http://www.forbes.com/sites/susanadams/2012/09/24/older-workers-theres-hope-study-finds-employers-like-you-better-than-millennials/#658b87014aa6 (accessed February 4, 2016).

Aequus Wealth Management Resources. "Proactive Career Planning at Any Age." http://www.aequuswealth.com/newsletter/article/proactive_career_planning_at_any_age (accessed February 19, 2016).

Andrew, Victoria. "The Power of a Positive Attitude." Kavaliro Blog. Kavaliro Employment Agency. May 23, 2013. http://www.kavaliro.com/the-power-of-a-positive-attitude (accessed February 19, 2016).

Arline, Katherine. "What is EBITDA?" Business News Daily. February 25, 2015. http://www.businessnewsdaily.com/4461-ebitda-formula-definition.html (accessed February 19, 2016).

Arruda, William. "Is LinkedIn Poised To Be The Next Media Giant?" Forbes. March 8, 2015. http://www.forbes.com/sites/williamarruda/2015/03/08/is-linkedin-poised-to-be-the-next-media-giant/ (accessed February 19, 2016).

Asher, Donald. Cracking the Hidden Job Market: How to Find Opportunity in Any Economy. New York: Ten Speed Press, 2011.

Ayele, Daniel. "Land Your Dream Job in 2015 with These Data-Proven LinkedIn Tips." LinkedIn Blog. January 29, 2015. http://blog.linkedin.com/2015/01/29/jobseeking-tips/ (accessed February 19, 2016).

Ayres, Leslie. "Why You Need a Resume Business Card." Notes from the Job Search Guru: A Career Advice Blog. March 16, 2009. http://www.thejobsearchguru.com/notesfrom/why-you-need-a-resume-business-card/ (accessed February 19, 2016).

Badal, Sangeeta, PhD. Interview by Jennifer Robison. "Why So Many New Companies Fail During Their First Five Years." Gallup Business Journal. October 23, 2014. http://www.gallup.com/businessjournal/178787/why-new-companies-fail-during-first-five-years.aspx (accessed February 17, 2016).

Baseball Almanac. "Yogi Berra Quotes." http://www.baseball-almanac.com/quotes/quoberra.shtml (accessed February 19, 2016).

Beatty, Kimberly. "The Math Behind the Networking Claim." Jobfully Blog. July 1, 2010. http://blog.jobfully.com/2010/07/the-math-behind-the-networking-claim/ (accessed February 19, 2016).

Bergdahl, Michael. What I Learned From Sam Walton: How to Compete and Thrive in a Wal-Mart World. Hoboken, New Jersey: John Wiley & Sons, 2004.

Beshara, Tony. The Job Search Solution: The Ultimate System for Finding a Great Job Now! Second edition. New York: AMACOM, 2012.

Bible, The. New International Version. Grand Rapids, MI: Zondervan Corporation, 1978.

BrandLove, LLC. "How to Jazz Up Your LinkedIn Profile with Bullets and Symbols." February 19, 2014. http://brandlovellc.com/2014/02/19/how-to-jazz-up-your-linkedin-profile-with-bullets-and-symbols/ (accessed February 11, 2016).

Brenoff, Ann. "Older Workers Stay Unemployed Much Longer Than Younger Ones, Study Says." Huffington Post. June 17, 2015. http://www.huffingtonpost.com/2015/06/17/finding-a-job-after-50-study_n_7603590.html (accessed February 4, 2016).

Bricker, Eric. "How to Ace Your Video Interview." On Careers Blog. U.S. News & World Report. July 11, 2013. http://money.usnews.com/money/careers/articles/2013/07/11/how-to-ace-your-video-interview (accessed February 19, 2016).

Broadcasting and the Law, Inc. "Employment contracts—'blue line' rule." Abstract. Broadcasting and the Law (1997). http://www.readabstracts.com/Mass-communications/Employment-contracts-blue-line-rule-Noncommercial-stations-underwriting-announcements.html (accessed February 19, 2016).

Bucknell University. "Creating an Effective Resume." Bucknell Career Development Center. http://www.bucknell.edu/documents/CDC/Creating_An_Effective_Resume.pdf (accessed February 19, 2016).

Bureau of Labor Statistics. "Number of Jobs Held, Labor Market Activity, and Earnings Growth Among the Youngest Baby Boomers: Results from a Longitudinal Survey." News release. March 31, 2015. http://www.bls.gov/news.release/pdf/nlsoy.pdf (accessed February 15, 2016).

Byrne, Donn Erwin. The Attraction Paradigm. New York: Academic Press, 1971.

CareerBuilder. "Employers Share Encouraging Perspectives and Tips for the Unemployed in New CareerBuilder Survey." News release. March 21, 2012. http://www.careerbuilder.com/share/aboutus/pressreleasesdetail.aspx?id=pr684&sd=3/21/2012&ed=12/31/2012&siteid=cbpr&sc_cmp1=cb_pr684_ (accessed February 19, 2016).

CareerBuilder. "Forty-Nine Percent of Workers Do Not Negotiate Job Offers, Finds CareerBuilder Compensation Survey." News release. August 21, 2013. http://www.careerbuilder.com/share/aboutus/pressreleasesdetail.aspx?sd=8/21/2013&id=pr777&ed=12/31/2013 (accessed February 19, 2016).

CareerBuilder. "Get Help With Hiring . . . And More: Working With Staffing Firms: What's in It for Me?" http://www.careerbuildercommunications.com/staffing-firms/ (accessed February 19, 2016).

CareerBuilder. "Nothing Says 'Hire Me' Like 'Thank You': Thank-You Note Etiquette." http://www.careerbuilder.com/JobPoster/Resources/page.aspx?pagever=ThankYouNoteEtiquette (accessed February 19, 2016).

CareerBuilder. "35 Percent of Employers Less Likely to Interview Applicants They Can't Find Online, According to Annual CareerBuilder Social Media Recruitment Survey." News release. May 14, 2015. http://www.careerbuilder.com/share/aboutus/pressreleasesdetail.aspx?sd=5%2F14% 2F2015&id=pr893&ed=12% 2F31%2F2015 (accessed February 19, 2016).

CareerBuilder. "2015 Candidate Behavior Study." http://careerbuildercommunications.com/candidatebehavior/ (accessed February 15, 2016).

Career-Intelligence.com. "Think Over 50 Is Over the Hill? Think Again: Job Search Tips for People Over 50." http://career-intelligence.com/job-seekers-over-fifty/ (accessed February 8, 2016).

Carnegie, Dale. How to Win Friends and Influence People. New York: Simon and Schuster, 2010.

Centers for Medicare & Medicaid Services. "Durable Medical Equipment (DME) Center." http://www.cms.gov/Center/Provider-Type/Durable-Medical-Equipment-DME-Center.html (accessed February 19, 2016).

Cherry, Kendra. "What Is Flow? Understanding the Psychology of Flow." Verywell.com. Last updated May 6, 2016. https://www.verywell.com/what-is-flow-2794768 (accessed May 10, 2016).

Cialdini, Robert B. Influence: Science and Practice. Fourth edition. Needham Heights, MA: Allyn & Bacon, 2001.

Clark, Biron. "How to Explain Employment Gaps in a Job Interview." Career Sidekick (blog). December 9, 2013. http://careersidekick.com/how-to-explain-employment-gaps-in-a-job-interview/ (accessed February 16, 2016).

Claycomb, Heather, and Karl Dinse. Career Pathways—Interactive Workbook. (1995).

Cockburn, Sue. "Create Your Custom LinkedIn Web Address in 5 Easy Steps." Growing Social Biz (blog). September 30, 2015. http://growingsocialbiz.com/simple-steps-creating-your-customized-linkedin-url/ (accessed February 19, 2016).

Cohen, Elizabeth. "Blaming Others Can Ruin Your Health." CNN.com. August 18, 2011. http://www.cnn.com/2011/HEALTH/08/17/bitter.resentful.ep/ (accessed February 5, 2016).

Collamer, Nancy. "The Perfect Elevator Pitch To Land A Job." Forbes. February 4, 2013. http://www.forbes.com/sites/nextavenue/2013/02/04/the-perfect-elevator-pitch-to-land-a-job/ (accessed February 19, 2016).

Cornerstone Coaching LLC. "What Winston Churchill Can Teach Us About Inevitable

Success." Blog. February 26, 2014. http://www.cornerstoneadvisoryservices.com/blog/what-winston-churchill-can-teach-us-about-inevitable-success (accessed February 19, 2016).

CVTips. "Do Employers Expect a Job Interview Thank You Card?" http://www.cvtips.com/interview/do-employers-expect-a-job-interview-thank-you-card.html (accessed February 19, 2016).

Cybercoders. "Counter Offers." http://www.cybercoders.com/home/counter offer/ (February 19, 2016).

Design Aglow contributor Jamie VanEaton. "10 Ways You're Building a Fantastic Brand." Design Aglow (blog). February 3, 2015. http://designaglow.com/blogs/design-aglow/16728432-10-ways-youre-building-a-fantastic-brand (accessed April 14, 2016).

Dickler, Jessica. "Get Your Holiday Job—on Twitter!" CNNMoney. October 21, 2010. http://money.cnn.com/2010/10/21/pf/job_openings_on_twitter/ (accessed February 19, 2016).

DiResta, Diane. Interview by Christina Canters. "Episode 29—How to Blitz Your Job

Interview—Secrets of Executive Speech Coach Diane DiResta." DesignDrawSpeak. Podcast audio. June 12, 2014. http://designdrawspeak.com/029/ (accessed February 19, 2016).

DISYS. "Top 5 Reasons to Use Staffing Firms as Your Primary Hiring Strategy." http://www.disys.com/top-5-reasons-to-use-staffing-firms-as-your-primary-hiring-strategy/ (accessed February 19, 2016).

Dougherty, Lisa. "16 Tips to Optimize Your LinkedIn Profile and Your Personal Brand." LinkedIn Pulse. July 8, 2014. https://www.linkedin.com/pulse/20140708162049-7239647-16-tips-to-optimize-your-linkedin-profile-and-enhance-your-personal-brand (accessed February 19, 2016).

Dugan, Dawn. "10 Tips for Job Hunters Over 50: How Older Workers Can Better Overcome Obstacles to Getting Hired." Salary.com. http://www.salary.com/10-tips-for-job-hunters-over-50/ (accessed February 4, 2016).

Duggan, Maeve, Nicole B. Ellison, Cliff Lampe, Amanda Lenhart, and Mary Madden.

"Demographics of Key Social Networking Platforms." Pew Research Center. January 9, 2015. http://www.pewinternet.org/2015/01/09/demographics-of-key-social-networking-platforms-2/ (accessed February 19, 2016).

Eisenberg, Richard. "Older Job Seekers: You're Hired (For Less)." Forbes.com. March 30, 2015. http://www.forbes.com/sites/nextavenue/2015/03/30/older-job-seekers-youre-hired-for-less/#66c814595d60 (accessed February 8, 2016).

ExecuNet. "Senior-Level Business Leaders Say Positive Attitude is the Key to Getting the Job." News release. March 25, 2013. http://web02.execunet.com/m_releases_content.cfm?id=4812 (accessed February 19, 2016).

For Dummies. "Answering Interview Questions About Job History Gaps." Dummies.com. www.dummies.com/how-to/content/answering-interview-questions-about-job-history-g0.html (accessed February 16, 2016).

Franklin, Benjamin [Richard Saunders, Poor Richard, pseud.]. The Way to Wealth. July 7, 1757. American Literature Research and Analysis. http://itech.fgcu.edu/faculty/wohlpart/alra/franklin.htm (accessed February 19, 2016).

Frasco, Stephanie. "11 Tips To Help Optimize Your LinkedIn Profile For Maximum Exposure and Engagement." Convert with Content (blog). https://www.convertwithcontent.com/11-tips-optimize-linkedin-profile-maximum-exposure-engagement/ (accessed February 19, 2016).

Frasier. "Goodnight, Seattle: Part 2." First broadcast 13 May 2004 by NBC. Directed by David Lee and written by Christopher Lloyd and Joe Keenan.

Geoff. "Top LinkedIn Facts and Stats [Infographic]." We Are Social Media (blog). July 25, 2014. http://wersm.com/top-linkedin-facts-and-stats-infographic/ (accessed February 19, 2016).

Go Lean Six Sigma. "What is Lean Six Sigma?" https://goleansixsigma.com/what-is-lean-six-sigma/ (accessed February 19, 2016).

Golfswing.com. "Ball at Impact." http://www.golfswing.com.au/139 (accessed February 15, 2016).

Goodreads. "Alan Cohen Quotable Quote." http://www.goodreads.com/quotes/46591-it-takes-a-lot-of-courage-to-release-the-familiar (accessed April 12, 2016).

Goodreads. "Bill Wilson Quotable Quote." http://www.goodreads.com/quotes/805288-you-can-t-think-your-way-into-right-action-but-you (accessed February 5, 2016).

Goodreads. "David Ogilvy Quotable Quote." http://www.goodreads.com/quotes/262108-jodon-t-bunt-aim-out-of-the-ballpark-aim-for-the (accessed February 19, 2016).

Goodreads. "Jarod Kintz Quotable Quote." http://www.goodreads.com/quotes/1234580-the-only-people-who-don-t-need-elevator-pitches-are-elevator (accessed February 19, 2016).

Goodreads. "Johann Wolfgang von Goethe Quotable Quote." http://www.goodreads.com/quotes/316359-just-begin-and-the-mind-grows-heated-continue-and-the (accessed February 19, 2016).

Goodreads. "Jose N. Harris Quotable Quote." http://www.goodreads.com/quotes/415120-to-get-something-you-never-had-you-have-to-do (accessed February 15, 2016).

Goodreads. "Malachy McCourt Quotes." http://www.goodreads.com/author/quotes/3373.Malachy_McCourt (accessed February 5, 2016).

Goodreads. "Napoleon Hill Quotable Quote." http://www.goodreads.com/quotes/244859-a-goal-is-a-dream-with-a-deadline (accessed February 19, 2016).

Goodreads. "Paulo Coelho Quotable Quote." https://www.goodreads.com/quotes/599176-if-you-re-brave-enough-to-say-goodbye-life-will-reward (accessed April 12, 2016).

Goodreads. "Peter F. Drucker Quotable Quote." http://www.goodreads.com/quotes/65135-plans-are-only-good-intentions-unless-they-immediately-degenerate-into (accessed April 12, 2016).

Goodreads. "Ralph Waldo Emerson Quotable Quote." www.goodreads.com/quotes/60285-do-the-thing-you-fear-and-the-death-of-fear (accessed February 19, 2016).

Goodreads. "Rocky Balboa Quotable Quote." http://www.goodreads.com/quotes/3228059-every-champion-was-once-a-contender-that-refused-to-give (accessed April 12, 2016).

Goodreads. "Thomas Fowell Buxton Quotable Quote." http://www.goodreads.com/quotes/891186-the-longer-i-live-the-more-i-am-certain-that (accessed February 19, 2016).

Graham, Brian. Get Hired Fast! Tap the Hidden Job Market in 15 Days. Avon, MA: Adams Media, 2005.

Green, Alison. "How to Resign Your Job Gracefully." On Careers Blog. U.S. News & World Report. July 28, 2008. money.usnews.com/money/blogs/outside-voices-careers/2008/07/28/how-to-resign-your-job-gracefully (accessed February 17, 2016).

Green, Alison. "Why You Shouldn't Take a Counter offer." On Careers Blog. U.S. News & World Report. March 26, 2012. http://money.usnews.com/money/blogs/outside-voices-careers/2012/03/26/why-you-shouldnt-take-a-counter offer (accessed February 19, 2016).

Guest Author (Bob Bozorgi). "Qualifications Will Get You an Interview, but They Won't Get You Hired." The Undercover Recruiter (blog). http://theundercoverrecruiter.com/qualifications-will-get-interview-wont-get-hired/ (accessed February 19, 2016).

Hallowell, Kirk. The Million Dollar Race: An Insider's Guide to Winning Your Dream Job. Austin, TX: Greenleaf Book Group Press, 2013.

Hamodia. "Why the Texting Generation Can't Get a Job." February 2, 2014. http://hamodia.com/2014/02/02/texting-generation-cant-get-job/ (accessed February 9, 2016).

Hansen, Katharine, PhD. "Do's and Don'ts for Second (and Subsequent) Job Interviews." Quintessential Careers. http://www.quintcareers.com/second-interviewing-dos-donts/ (accessed February 16, 2016).

Hansen, Randall S., PhD. "Networking Business Cards: An Essential Job-Search Tool for Job-Seekers, Career Changers, and College Students When a Resume Just Won't Do." Quintessential Careers. http://www.quintcareers.com/networking-business-cards/ (accessed February 19, 2016).

Hansen, Randall S., PhD, and Katharine Hansen, PhD. "What Do Employers Really Want? Top Skills and Values Employers Seek from Job-Seekers." Quintessential Careers. http://www.quintcareers.com/job_skills_values.html (accessed February 19, 2016).

Hanson, Arik. "Should You Put MBA Behind Your Name on Your LinkedIn Profile?" LinkedIn Pulse. May 29, 2014. https://www.linkedin.com/pulse/20140529131058-18098999-should-you-put-mba-behind-your-name-on-your-linkedin-profile (accessed February 19, 2016).

Helmrich, Brittney. "Thanks! 22 Job Interview Thank You Note Tips." Business News Daily. March 11, 2016. http://www.businessnewsdaily.com/7134-thank-you-note-tips.html (accessed April 19, 2016).

HelpGuide.org. "Job Networking Tips." http://www.helpguide.org/articles/work-career/job-networking-tips.htm (accessed February 19, 2016).

HelpGuide.org. "Volunteering and Its Surprising Benefits." http://www.helpguide.org/articles/work-career/volunteering-and-its-surprising-benefits.htm (accessed February 17, 2016).

Hering, Beth Braccio. "How to Choose Good Job References." Newsday. July 11, 2012. http://www.newsday.com/classifieds/cars/how-to-choose-good-job-references-1.3430287 (accessed February 17, 2016).

Hill, Paul. The Panic Free Job Search: Unleash the Power of the Web and Social Networking to Get Hired. Pompton Plains, NJ: Career Press, 2012.

Honck, Alan, with Gordon Orians. "Are We Born With a Sense of Fairness?" Pacific Standard. December 26, 2012. https://psmag.com/are-we-born-with-a-sense-of-fairness-edd2d2680c10#.ce304fxbb (accessed April 18, 2016).

IBISWorld. "Employment and Recruiting Agencies in the US: Market Research Report." March 2015. http://www.ibisworld.com/industry/default.aspx?indid=1463 (accessed February 19, 2016).

International Foundation of Employee Benefit Plans, Inc. "About the CEBS Program." https://www.ifebp.org/CEBSDesignation/overview/Pages/default.aspx (accessed February 19, 2016).

Internships.com. "Understanding the Employer's Perspective." http://www.internships.com/student/resources/interview/prep/getting-ready/understand-employer (accessed February 16, 2016).

Isaacson, Nate. "Professional Designations Are Great But They Are Not A Part of Your Name." LinkedIn Pulse. April 14, 2014. https://www.linkedin.com/pulse/20140414223601-23236063-professional-designations-are-great-but-they-are-not-a-part-of-your-name (accessed February 19, 2016).

Izzi, Matthew. "California Ban on Covenants Not to Compete." LegalMatch. http://www.legalmatch.com/law-library/article/california-ban-on-covenants-not-to-compete.html (accessed February 19, 2016).

Jamal, Nina, and Judith Lindenberger. "How to Make a Great First Impression." Business Know-How. http://www.businessknowhow.com/growth/dress-impression.htm (accessed February 19, 2016).

Jobvite. "Jobvite Social Recruiting Survey Finds Over 90% of Employers Will Use Social Recruiting in 2012." News release. July 9, 2012. http://www.jobvite.com/press-releases/2012/jobvite-social-recruiting-survey-finds-90-employers-will-use-social-recruiting-2012/ (accessed February 19, 2016).

Jobvite. "2014 Social Recruiting Survey." https://www.jobvite.com/wp-content/uploads/2014/10/Jobvite_SocialRecruiting_Survey2014.pdf (accessed February 19, 2016).

Joyce, Susan P. "After the Interview, What is Taking Them SO Long?" Work Coach Café (blog). September 17, 2012. http://www.workcoachcafe.com/2012/09/17/after-the-interview-what-is-taking-them-so-long/ (accessed February 15, 2016).

Joyce, Susan P. "Job Search Success Strategy: PROactive vs. REactive Job Search." Job-Hunt.org. http://www.job-hunt.org/article_proactive_job_search.shtml (accessed February 19, 2016).

Kanfer, Ruth, and Charles L. Hulin. "Individual Differences in Successful Job Searches Following Layoff." Abstract. Personnel Psychology 38, no. 4 (December 1985): 835–847. http://www.researchgate.net/publication/227749499_INDIVIDUAL_DIFFERENCES_IN_SUCCESSFUL_JOB_SEARCHES_FOLLOWING_LAYOFF (accessed February 19, 2016).

Kaufman, Wendy. "A Successful Job Search: It's All About Networking." National Public Radio. February

3, 2011. http://www.npr.org/2011/02/08/133474431/a-successful-job-search-its-all-about-networking (accessed February 19, 2016).-

Kempka, Jill. "Resume FAQ: How Do I Handle Employment Gaps?" Career Coach (blog). Manpower. January 25, 2013. manpowergroupblogs.us/manpower/career-coach/2013/01/25/resume-faq-how-do-i-handle-employment-gaps/ (accessed February 16, 2016).

Knyszweski, Jerome. "How to Use LinkedIn as a Student—And Nail That Dream Job."

LinkedIn Pulse. April 28, 2015. https://www.linkedin.com/pulse/how-use-linkedin-student-nail-dream-job-jerome-knyszewski (accessed February 19, 2016).

Konnikova, Maria. "The Limits of Friendship." The New Yorker. October 7, 2014. http://www.newyorker.com/science/maria-konnikova/social-media-affect-math-dunbar-number-friendships (accessed February 19, 2016).

Kurtzberg, Terri R., and Charles E. Naquin. The Essentials of Job Negotiations: Proven Strategies for Getting What You Want. Santa Barbara, CA: Praeger, 2011.

Lankford, Kim. "Should You Take That Counter offer?" Monster. http://career-advice.monster.com/in-the-office/leaving-a-job/should-you-take-that-counter offer/article.aspx (accessed February 19, 2016).

Leadership Now. "Quotes on Initiative." http://www.leadershipnow.com/initiativequotes.html (accessed February 19, 2016).

Leanne, Shelly. How to Interview Like a Top MBA: Job-Winning Strategies from Headhunters, Fortune 100 Recruiters, and Career Counselors. New York: McGraw-Hill, 2004.

Leibman, Pete. "9 Keys on How to Email a New Networking Contact During a Job Search (written by Career Expert, Pete Leibman)." CareerMuscles (blog). January 6, 2011. https://careermuscles.wordpress.com/2011/01/06/9-keys-on-how-to-email-a-new-networking-contact-during-a-job-search-written-by-career-expert-pete-leibman/ (accessed February 19, 2016).

LinkedIn. "Profile Completeness." https://www.linkedin.com/static?key=pop%2Fpop_more_profile_completeness (accessed February 19, 2016).

LinkedIn. "Using LinkedIn to Find a Job or Internship." https://university.linkedin.com/content/dam/university/global/en_US/site/pdf/TipSheet_FindingaJoborInternship.pdf (accessed February 19, 2016).

LinkedIn Help Center. "InMail—Overview." https://help.linkedin.com/app/answers/detail/a_id/1584/~/InMail---overview (accessed February 19, 2016).

LinkedIn Help Center. "Showing or Hiding Activity Updates About You." https://help.linkedin.com/app/answers/detail/a_id/78/~/showing-or-hiding-activity-updates-about-you (accessed February 19, 2016).

LinkedIn Newsroom. "About LinkedIn." https://press.linkedin.com/about-linkedin (accessed February 19, 2016).

LinkedIn Talent Solutions. "2015 Talent Trends: Insights for Search and Staffing Recruiters on What Talent Wants Around the World." https://business.linkedin.com/content/dam/business/talent-solutions/global/en_us/c/pdfs/global-talent-trends-staff-report.pdf (accessed February 19, 2016).

LinkHumans. "10 Tips for the Perfect LinkedIn Profile." Slideshare. Published July 1, 2014. http://www.slideshare.net/linkedin/10-tips-for-the-perfect-linkedin-profile (accessed February 19, 2016).

Llarena, Melissa. "What to Expect During an HR Interview?—Five Questions You'll Be Asked During a Screening Interview." Forbes. October 18, 2013. http://www.forbes.com/sites/85broads/2013/10/18/what-to-expect-during-an-hr-interview-five-questions-youll-be-asked-during-a-screening-interview/ (accessed

February 16, 2016).

Love, Scott. "Counter offer—Should I Entertain a Counter offer?" The Vet Recruiter. http://thevetrecruiter.com/important-information-about-recruiters-for-job-seekers/counter   offer-should-i-entertain-a-counter offer/ (accessed February 19, 2016).

Maderer, Jason. "Here Are 5 Tips for Job-Seekers Over 50." Futurity.org. June 18, 2015. http://www.futurity.org/older-adults-employment-jobs-944902/ (accessed February 12, 2016).

Matt. "How to Use a Brag Book to Differentiate Yourself From the Competition." Career Enlightenment. April 19, 2013. https://careerenlightenment.com/how-to-use-a-brag-book-to-differentiate-yourself-from-the-competition (accessed February 16, 2016).

Maxwell, John C. The Maxwell Daily Reader: 365 Days of Insight to Develop the Leader Within You and Influence Those Around You. Nashville, TN: Thomas Nelson, 2011.

McGregor, Jena. "Interviewing for a Job is Taking Longer Than Ever." On Leadership (blog). Washington Post. June 18, 2015. http://www.washingtonpost.com/blogs/on-leadership/wp/2015/06/18/interviewing-for-a-job-is-taking-longer-than-ever/ (accessed February 15, 2016).

McLeod, Lisa Earle. "The Big Mistake People Make When They Negotiate." Life on Purpose (blog). McLeod & More, Inc. March 26, 2014. http://www.mcleodandmore.com/2014/03/26/the-big-mistake-people-make-when-they-negotiate-2/ (accessed February 19, 2016).

Mitchell, Josh. "Just How Many Jobs Are There in America? We'll Know Better Friday." Real Time Economics (blog). Wall Street Journal. February 5, 2015. http://blogs.wsj.com/economics/2015/02/05/just-how-many-jobs-are-there-in-america-well-know-better-friday/ (accessed February 19, 2016).

Moynihan, Lisa M., Mark V. Roehling, Marcie A. LePine, and Wendy R. Boswell. "A Longitudinal Study of the Relationships Among Job Search Self-Efficacy, Job Interviews, and Employment Outcomes." Abstract. Journal of Business and Psychology 18, no. 2 (2003): 201–233. http://link.springer.com/article/10.1023%2FA%3A1027349115277#/page-1 (accessed February 19, 2016).

Murphy, Mark. Interview by Dan Schawbel. "Hire for Attitude." Forbes. January 23, 2012. http://www.forbes.com/sites/danschawbel/2012/01/23/89-of-new-hires-fail-because-of-their-attitude/#425a5f366742 (accessed February 4, 2016).

Muse, The. "Let's Do Lunch: How to Prepare for a Job Interview Over a Meal." Forbes. November 12, 2012. http://www.forbes.com/sites/dailymuse/2012/11/20/lets-do-lunch-how-to-prepare-for-a-job-interview-over-a-meal/ (accessed February 19, 2016).

Neely. "How to Develop a 'Brag Book' for Job Interviews." Splash Resumes. July 25, 2013. http://www.splashresumes.com/2013/07/25/how-to-develop-a-brag-book-for-job-interviews/ (accessed February 16, 2016).

Non-Compete Agreement—Art Technology Group Inc. and Joseph Chung. http://contracts.onecle.com/art/chung.noncomp.1998.08.18.shtml (accessed March 16, 2016).

Nsehe, Mfonobong. "19 Inspirational Quotes From Nelson Mandela." Forbes.com. December 6, 2013. http://www.forbes.com/sites/mfonobongnsehe/2013/12/06/20-inspirational-quotes-from-nelson-mandela/ (accessed February 19, 2016).

O'Brien, Matthew. "The Terrifying Reality of Long-Term Unemployment." The Atlantic. April 13, 2013. http://www.theatlantic.com/business/archive/2013/04/the-terrifying-reality-of-long-term-unemployment/274957/ (accessed February 19, 2016).

OfficeTeam. "Survey: Six in 10 Companies Conduct Video Job Interviews." News release. August 30, 2012. http://officeteam.rhi.mediaroom.com/videointerviews (accessed February 19, 2016).

Oswal, Shreya. "7 Smart Habits of Successful Job Seekers [INFOGRAPHIC]." LinkedIn Blog. March 19, 2014. http://blog.linkedin.com/2014/03/19/7-smart-habits-of-successful-job-seekers-infographic/ (accessed February 19, 2016).

Over 50 Job Seekers. LinkedIn group. https://www.linkedin.com/groups/8368426/profile (accessed March 31, 2016).

Patel, Neil. "90% of Startups Fail: Here's What You Need to Know About the 10%." Forbes. January 16, 2015. http://www.forbes.com/sites/neilpatel/2015/01/16/90-of-startups-will-fail-heres-what-you-need-to-know-about-the-10/#157870a455e1 (accessed February 17, 2016).

Peterson, Marshalita Sims. "Personnel Interviewers' Perceptions of the Importance and Adequacy of Applicants' Communication Skills." Communication Education 46, no. 4 (1997): 287–291.

Peterson, Thad. "100 Top Job Interview Questions—Be Prepared for the Interview." Monster. http://career-advice.monster.com/job-interview/interview-questions/100-potential-interview-questions/article.aspx (accessed February 19, 2016).

Phillips, Simon. The Complete Guide to Professional Networking: The Secrets of Online and Offline Success. London: Kogan Page Limited, 2014.

Pine, Joslyn. Editor. Book of African-American Quotations. New York: Dover Publications, 2011.

Pollak, Lindsey. "How to Attract Employers' Attention on LinkedIn." LinkedIn Blog.

December 2, 2010. http://blog.linkedin.com/2010/12/02/find-jobs-on-linkedin/ (accessed February 19, 2016).

Pongo. "How to Explain Work History Gaps in the Interview." The Pongo Blog. https://www.pongoresume.com/blogPosts/372/how-to-explain-work-history-gaps-in-the-interview.cfm (accessed February 16, 2016).

Quotes from the Masters. "Self-Limiting Beliefs." http://finsecurity.com/finsecurity/quotes/qm103.html (accessed February 19, 2016).

Quotes from the Masters. "Unleashing Your Genius." http://finsecurity.com/finsecurity/quotes/qm121.html (accessed February 19, 2016).

Rampton, John. "50 Inspirational Entrepreneurial Quotes." Entrepreneur.com. December 9, 2014. https://www.entrepreneur.com/article/240047 (accessed April 12, 2016).

Recovery Ranch, The. "Doing What's Necessary, What's Possible, and What Seems to be Impossible." October 29, 2011. http://www.recoveryranch.com/articles/necessary-possible-impossible/ (accessed February 19, 2016).

Regis University Career Services. "Interviewing Strategies for Non-Traditional Students and Alumni." http://www.regis.edu/About-Regis-University/University-Offices-and-Services/Career-Services/Student-and-Alumni/Interviewing-Strategies.aspx (accessed February 19, 2016).

Reynolds, Marci. "How to Be Found More Easily in LinkedIn (LinkedIn SEO)." Job-Hunt.org. http://www.job-hunt.org/social-networking/be-found-on-linkedin.shtml (accessed February 19, 2016).

Roosevelt, Theodore. "The Strenuous Life." Speech. The Hamilton Club, Chicago, IL, April 10, 1899. http://www.bartleby.com/58/1.html (accessed February 19, 2016).

Rossheim, John. "Social Networking: The Art of Social Media Recruiting." Monster. February 11, 2015. http://

hiring.monster.com/hr/hr-best-practices/recruiting-hiring-advice/job-screening-techniques/recruiting-using-social-media.aspx (accessed February 19, 2016).

Rothberg, Steven. "80% of Job Openings are Unadvertised." College Recruiter (blog). March 28, 2013. https://www.collegerecruiter.com/blog/2013/03/28/80-of-job-openings-are-unadvertised/ (accessed February 19, 2016).

Sachdeva, Gyanda. "Unlocking Your Competitive Edge with the Power of LinkedIn Premium." LinkedIn Blog. December 18, 2014. http://blog.linkedin.com/2014/12/18/unlocking-your-competitive-edge-with-the-power-of-linkedin-premium/ (accessed February 19, 2016).

Safani, Barbara. "Tell a Story Interviewers Can't Forget." TheLadders. http://www.theladders.com/career-advice/tell-story-interviewers-cant-forget (accessed February 19, 2016).

Sales Performance International. "What is Solution Selling?" http://solutionselling.learn.com/learncenter.asp?id=178455 (accessed February 19, 2016).

Samuel Johnson Sound Bite Page, The. "Quotes on Perseverance." http://www.samueljohnson.com/persever.html (accessed February 19, 2016).

Samuel Johnson Sound Bite Page, The. "Rasselas: A Word of Caution." http://www.samueljohnson.com/rasselas.html (accessed February 19, 2016).

Serdula, Donna. "LinkedIn's New Requirements for a 100% Complete Profile." LinkedIn Makeover (blog). February 20, 2012. http://www.linkedin-makeover.com/2012/02/20/linkedins-new-requirements-for-a-100-complete-profile/ (accessed February 19, 2016).

Shakespeare, William. Measure for Measure. Act I, Scene IV. "William Shakespeare Quotes Measure for Measure." http://www.william-shakespeare.info/quotes-quotations-play-measure-for-measure.htm (accessed February 19, 2016).

Sibley, Lisa. "Survey of HR Managers: How Many Job Changes is Too Many?" Blog. Robert Half. January 17, 2014. http://www.roberthalf.com/finance/blog/survey-of-hr-managers-how-many-job-changes-is-too-many?hsFormKey=06a77aee09a564eca4467cf5525e3c15 (accessed February 19, 2016).

Skillings, Pamela. "The Ultimate Infographic Resume Guide." Big Interview (blog). June 18, 2013. http://biginterview.com/blog/2013/06/infographic-resumes.html (accessed February 17, 2016).

Smiles, Samuel. Character. New edition. London: John Murray, 1876.

Smith, Craig. "By the Numbers: 125+ Amazing LinkedIn Statistics." Last updated May 1, 2016. http://expandedramblings.com/index.php/by-the-numbers-a-few-important-linkedin-stats/ (accessed May 10, 2016).

Smith, Jacquelyn. "Here's What To Say In Your LinkedIn 'Summary' Statement." Business Insider. December 19, 2014. http://www.businessinsider.com/what-to-say-in-your-linkedin-summary-statement-2014-12 (accessed February 19, 2016).

Smith, Jacquelyn. "How to Ace the 50 Most Common Interview Questions." Forbes. January 11, 2013. http://www.forbes.com/sites/jacquelynsmith/2013/01/11/how-to-ace-the-50-most-common-interview-questions/ (accessed February 19, 2016).

Smith, Jacquelyn. "7 Things You Probably Didn't Know About Your Job Search." Forbes. April 17, 2013. http://www.forbes.com/sites/jacquelynsmith/2013/04/17/7-things-you-probably-didnt-know-about-your-job-search/#71fe2c6e64e6 (accessed February 12, 2016).

Smith, Jacquelyn. "The Complete Guide To Crafting A Perfect LinkedIn Profile." Business Insider. January

21, 2015. http://www.businessinsider.com/guide-to-perfect-linkedin-profile-2015-1 (accessed February 19, 2016).

Smith, Jacquelyn. "Why Every Job Seeker Should Have a Personal Website, and What It Should Include." Forbes. April 26, 2013. http://www.forbes.com/sites/jacquelynsmith/2013/04/26/why-every-job-seeker-should-have-a-personal-website-and-what-it-should-include/#73ae8b8a902e (accessed February 17, 2016).

Society for Human Resource Management. "Executive Summary: Preparing for an Aging Workforce." https://www.shrm.org/Research/SurveyFindings/Documents/14-0765%20Executive%20Briefing%20Aging%20Workforce%20v4.pdf (accessed February 4, 2016).

Strankowski, Donald J. "Your License to Brag: The Brag Book." Ascend Career and Life Strategies, LLC. April 2005. http://www.ascendcareers.net/newsletters/April2005.html (accessed February 17, 2016).

Sun, Calvin. "10+ Things You Should Do When You Resign." 10 Things

(blog). TechRepublic. March 17, 2008. www.techrepublic.com/blog/10-things/10-plus-things-you-should-do-when-you-resign/ (accessed February 17, 2016).

Sutton, Robert I., PhD. The No Asshole Rule: Building a Civilized Workplace and Surviving One That Isn't. New York: Warner Business Books, 2007.

TheLadders. "Give Thanks or Your Chance For That Job Could be Cooked." http://cdn.theladders.net/static/images/basicSite/PR/pdfs/TheLaddersGiveThanks.pdf (accessed February 19, 2016).

Thompson, Stacey A. "6 Virtues to Practice for Job Search Success." Virtues for Life. http://www.virtuesforlife.com/6-virtues-to-practice-for-job-search-success/ (accessed February 19, 2016).

Top10WebsiteBuilders. "The Best Website Builders 2016." http://www.top10webbuilders.com/?s1-google/s2-us-search/s3-website-builder-p (accessed February 17, 2016).

Townsend, Maya. "The Introvert's Survival Guide to Networking." Inc.com. http://www.inc.com/maya-townsend/introvert-networking-guide.html (accessed February 19, 2016).

Tracy, Brian. Eat That Frog! 21 Great Ways to Stop Procrastinating and Get More Done in Less Time. Second edition. Buchanan, NY: ReadHowYouWant, 2008.

True Source (blog). "Don't Do That!—Mistakes To Avoid When Working With Recruiters." November 2012. http://www.true-source.com/2012/11/dont-do-that-mistakes-to-avoid-when-working-with-recruiters/ (accessed February 19, 2016).

United States Army. "Operational Unit Diagrams." http://www.army.mil/info/organization/unitsandcommands/oud/ (accessed February 19, 2016).

University of Wisconsin. "Developing Job Search Strategies." https://www.uwgb.edu/careers/PDF-Files/Job-Search-Strategies.pdf (accessed February 19, 2016).

U.S. Constitution Online. "Constitutional Topic: The Cabinet." http://www.usconstitution.net/consttop_cabi.html (accessed February 19, 2016).

US Department of Labor, Bureau of Labor Statistics. "Displaced Workers Summary." News release. August 26, 2014. http://www.bls.gov/news.release/disp.nr0.htm (accessed February 4, 2016).

US Department of Labor. "Frequently Asked Questions About Retirement Plans and ERISA." http://www.dol.gov/ebsa/faqs/faq_consumer_pension.html (accessed February 19, 2016).

US Department of Labor. "Soft Skill #2: Enthusiasm and Attitude." Skills to Pay the Bills. http://www.dol.gov/odep/topics/youth/softskills/Enthusiasm.pdf (accessed February 15, 2016).

US Equal Employment Opportunity Commission. "The Age Discrimination in Employment Act of 1967." 29 U.S.C. § 621. http://www.eeoc.gov/laws/statutes/adea.cfm (accessed February 8, 2016).

US Supreme Court. Gross v. FBL Financial Services, Inc. 557 U.S. 167 (2009). http://www.supremecourt.gov/opinions/08pdf/08-441.pdf (accessed February 8, 2016).

Varelas, Elaine. "How Long Will My Job Search Take?" The Job Doc (blog). The Boston Globe. June 12, 2013. http://www.boston.com/jobs/news/jobdoc/2013/06/how_long_will_my_job_search_ta.html (accessed February 19, 2016).

Vaughan, Pamela. "81% of LinkedIn Users Belong to a LinkedIn Group [Data]." Hubspot Blogs. August 11, 2011. http://blog.hubspot.com/blog/tabid/6307/bid/22364/81-of-LinkedIn-Users-Belong-to-a-LinkedIn-Group-Data.aspx (accessed February 19, 2016).

Vlooten, Dick van. "The Seven Laws of Networking: Those Who Give, Get." Career

Magazine. May 7, 2004. http://www.sciencemag.org/careers/2004/05/seven-laws-networking-those-who-give-get (accessed April 14, 2016).

Walters, Lillet. Secrets of Successful Speakers: How You Can Motivate, Captivate, and Persuade. New York: McGraw-Hill, 1993.

Weber, Lauren, and Rachel Feintzeig. "Why Companies Are Taking Longer to Hire." Wall Street Journal. September 1, 2014. http://www.wsj.com/article_email/companies-are-taking-longer-to-hire-1409612937-lMyQjAxMTA1MDIwMjEyNDIyWj (accessed February 16, 2016).

Weiss, Tara. "Find Your Job by Going to a Conference." Forbes. March 24, 2009. http://www.forbes.com/2009/03/24/conference-job-seeking-leadership-careers-networking.html (accessed February 19, 2016).

Whitcomb, Susan Britton. Job Search Magic: Insider Secrets from America's

Career and Life Coach. Indianapolis, IN: JIST Works, 2006.

Williams, Armstrong. "A Few Simple Steps to Building Wealth." Townhall. June 13, 2005. http://townhall.com/columnists/armstrongwilliams/2005/06/13/a_few_simple_steps_to_building_wealth/page/full (accessed February 19, 2016).

Wilson, CJ. "Why Millennials Are Often Poor Writers." LinkedIn Pulse. December 29, 2014. https://www.linkedin.com/pulse/millennials-cant-write-because-texting-writing-cj-wilson (accessed February 9, 2016).

Woods, Jennifer. "Working Longer—Whether You Want to or Not." CNBC.com. December 23, 2014. http://cached.newslookup.com/cached.php?ref_id=105&siteid=2098&id=10359558&t=1419339600 (accessed February 19, 2016).

WorldatWork. "Bonus Programs and Practices." June 2014. http://www.worldatwork.org/adimLink?id=75444 (accessed February 19, 2016).

World of Quotes. "Carl Frederick Quotes." http://www.worldofquotes.com/author/Carl+Frederick/1/index.html (accessed February 19, 2016).

Yate, Martin John. Knock 'em Dead Social Networking for Job Search and Professional Success. Avon, MA: Adams Media, 2014.

Yate, Martin John. Knock 'em Dead—The Ultimate Job Search Guide. Avon, MA: Adams Media, 2014.

Zack, Devora. "10 Tips for People Who Hate Networking." Careerealism. May 4, 2015. http://www.careerealism.com/hate-networking-tips/ (accessed February 19, 2016).

Zolfagharifard, Ellie. "First Impressions Really DO Count: Employers Make Decisions About Job Applicants in

Under Seven Minutes." Daily Mail. June 18, 2014. http://www.dailymail.co.uk/sciencetech/article-2661474/First-impressions-really-DO-count-Employers-make-decisions-job-applicants-seven-minutes.html (accessed February 19, 2016).